"An important book I will be sharing with everyone on my team. As a woman in Silicon Valley and an ardent believer in breaking stereotypes, I found *Girl Geek Rising* to be a new manifesto for bridging the gender gap. Cabot and Walravens have conducted intensive research and bring—for the first time ever—a comprehensive and large-scale picture of what it is to be a woman in tech. Riveting for men and women alike."

—Zainab Ghadiyali,
Cofounder and CEO of Wogrammer;
former tech lead at Facebook

"*Geek Girl Rising* is an inspiring 'who's who' in tech that is a must-read for anyone wondering how women are using the power of business, sheer grit, and a lot of heart to start, build, and fund companies—companies that are driving innovation and changing the landscape of the tech industry."

—Kristy Wallace,
President, Ellevate Network

"There is nothing more powerful than role models, and *Geek Girl Rising* provides the stories and the inspiration from the women who are creating our future. Technology is changing our world, and the women in this book are front and center of today's technology revolution. Heather Cabot and Samantha Walravens take us into this world as seen from the eyes of many extraordinary women."

—Telle Whitney,
CEO and President of the Anita Borg Institute
and Cofounder of the Grace Hopper Celebration
of Women in Computing

GEEK GIRL RISING

GEEK GIRL RISING

Inside the Sisterhood Shaking Up Tech

Heather Cabot and
Samantha Walravens

St. Martin's Press
New York

GEEK GIRL RISING. Copyright © 2017 by Heather Cabot and Samantha Walravens. All rights reserved. Printed in the United States of America. For information, address St. Martin's Press, 175 Fifth Avenue, New York, N.Y. 10010.

www.stmartins.com

Design by Meryl Sussman Levavi

The Library of Congress Cataloging-in-Publication Data is available upon request.

ISBN 9781250112262 (hardcover)
ISBN 9781250112279 (e-book)

Our books may be purchased in bulk for promotional, educational, or busi-
ness use. Please contact your local bookseller or the Macmillan Corporate and
Premium Sales Department at 1-800-221-7945, extension 5442, or by e-mail at
MacmillanSpecialMarkets@macmillan.com.

First Edition: May 2017

10 9 8 7 6 5 4 3 2 1

To our children and Geek Girls everywhere,
who are building the future

CONTENTS

AUTHORS' NOTE

As mothers to young daughters obsessed with musical.ly, *Minecraft,* and messaging their friends, we embarked on this project to better understand why the number of women working in technology has been on a steady decline since the 1980s and what can be done to reverse the trend. While the media focused on sexism and the exclusive boys' club in Silicon Valley as the culprits keeping women out, we uncovered a different story: a powerful grassroots movement of women entrepreneurs and technologists who were not asking for permission from Silicon Valley—or anyone—to take part in the digital revolution. These are the stories we decided to share in this book.

It was not hard to find amazing women innovators. They were everywhere! We interviewed more than two hundred fifty people for this book. As we started to draft the manuscript, we had to make difficult decisions about which stories

to include. This led us to create a digital platform, www
.geekgirlrising.com, to highlight the many accomplished women
we interviewed but whose stories we could not fit within the
confines of a printed book. Thank you to the fearless entrepreneurs, technologists, investors, and advocates in Silicon
Valley, Silicon Alley, and tech hubs around the country who
allowed us to tell their stories. Thank you for trusting us, for
sharing your journeys, for allowing us into your homes and
workplaces—and for blazing a trail for other women and
girls to follow in the digital revolution. This book is our gift
to you.

Finally, covering startups is inherently tricky. Early stage
ventures endure captivating highs and lows, and as reporters
we experienced a healthy dose of suspense as we followed
many stories over many years (in some cases since 2011). Given
the lightning speed with which the tech startup world changes,
we hope readers will appreciate that this book is a snapshot
of a moment in time. We decided to focus on the years the
"women in tech" conversation emerged as part of the national
dialogue—2014 to the present day. We know that things will
have changed by the time you are reading the book but hope
you will appreciate our efforts to report the stories as they unfolded (especially against the dramatic backdrop of the polar-
izing 2016 presidential race and Donald Trump's win). We look
forward to chronicling these women's incredible journeys in
the future.

GEEK GIRL

RISING

CHAPTER 1

JOIN THE REVOLUTION
Champions for Change

Women have been trained to speak softly
and carry a lipstick.
Those days are over.

—BELLA ABZUG

Who would have guessed that on Super Bowl Sunday, America's manliest night of the year, the issue of women in tech would get some much-needed airtime? As 111.5 million people watched the Seattle Seahawks trounce the Denver Broncos (and revisited the pleasures of Bud Light and Doritos) on February 2, 2014, a young woman's heart raced with anticipation as she trained her eyes on the giant TV at the center of a swanky screening party in New York City.[1]

Debbie Sterling's stomach flip-flopped as she waited for the commercial that would change the trajectory of her nascent toy company. It felt like a lifetime ago, but she had set out only two years earlier to upend the world's image of engineers as a lonely bunch of boy geniuses and introduce a new kind of role model—a spunky, tool belt–wearing action figure with long, blonde, curly hair named Goldie.

It wasn't an easy sell. Big toy companies quickly dismissed

GoldieBlox, a product designed to teach girls engineering, complete with a tool kit of pulleys and shafts, as "too niche." But that didn't deter Debbie, who fondly remembers challenging boys to arm-wrestling contests in the second grade. She set out to prove the naysayers wrong by taking her story to Kickstarter, where she planned to raise $150,000 so she could manufacture the first run of *Goldie's Spinning Machine*, a storybook and building set.

In an endearing video Debbie made her simple Kickstarter pitch while wearing jeans and a sleeveless violet top as she sat cross-legged on the floor of her apartment. Scenes showed little faces lighting up as pigtailed tots played with the one and only prototype. In the video, shot by Debbie's husband, Beau, she told viewers they could inspire their daughters to be "more than just a princess" by helping Debbie fund the first production run. The play sets would mesh girls' love of stories— players follow the adventures of main character Goldie and her friends—with fun design challenges featuring wheels, axles, catapults, and gears. Girls would build simple machines alongside Goldie. The message went viral. In thirty days Debbie raised more than $285,000 and was able to produce her first order of five thousand units, which quickly ballooned to forty thousand to keep up with demand. Suddenly the toy stores were calling her.

Now, fast-forward to Super Bowl Sunday. Debbie, the real-life Goldie, the curly-haired inventor with the infectious smile, was about to go prime time. She hoped the thirty-second commercial would fuel her mission to inspire girls to break into the boys' club and start seeing themselves as tomorrow's builders and problem solvers.

GoldieBlox had won the big-time ad—worth an estimated $4 million—in a small business contest run by Intuit, parent company of QuickBooks and TurboTax. Debbie flew her entire family and twelve team members from San Francisco to Intuit's tricked-out fete on the top floor of Manhattan's Gramercy Park Hotel, which featured glitzy cocktails, hors d'oeuvres passed by servers, and even a photo booth. Just being in the room was a thrill, but the waiting was killing her.

Finally, the familiar drumbeat of the 1980s rock anthem "Cum on Feel the Noize" poured out of the screen over a raucous scene of adorable little girls in princess outfits who were tearing off their glittery tiaras and running through the streets to a park, where they constructed a giant rocket out of their dolls, pink ponies, and sparkly playthings. They sang triumphantly:

> Come on, ditch your toys
> Girls make some noise
> More than pink, pink, pink
> We want to think![2]

As the rocket launched toward the sun, the room exploded in cheers and applause. It was a game changer, and Debbie could feel it as the music faded away.

"We specifically did not want the commercial to be about the product. It 100 percent needed to be about the social mission that we're on and educating parents about shining a light on the pink [toy] aisle and how limiting it can be in terms of what girls think they are capable of and getting them interested in science, engineering, and math," she reflected when we spent the afternoon with her at Toy Fair in New York City two years later.

Mission accomplished. The commercial, and its unapologetically feminist message, touched off the first of many triumphs in 2014, a year that would galvanize disparate groups of people around the country who had long been agitating about the tiny number of women and people of color in key technical and leadership roles in Silicon Valley. That was the year the issue of women in tech started to matter to the masses. The timing was right. Facebook COO Sheryl Sandberg's *Lean In*, published just eleven months earlier, was sparking urgent conversations about women, leadership, parental leave, and the pay gap. It was inevitable that the dialogue would turn to inequities in technology itself. Smartphones and digital media had become central to most American lives, and women were the primary consumers, yet they were largely absent from the teams building new technologies. As a piece in the *New York Times*'s *Motherlode* blog in March 2014 aptly pointed out, "If men could breastfeed, surely the breast pump would be as elegant as an iPhone and as quiet as a Prius by now."[3]

Yet a quiet revolution was already in progress: a frenzy of entrepreneurial activity across the country was uniting female founders and technologists. By 2014 they were working under the radar to launch their own startups, build their own networks, crush male-hacker stereotypes, and inspire their younger sisters and daughters. Like Debbie, these inventors, builders, advocates, and connectors, uniting at the grassroots level, would become the foot soldiers of the front lines, disrupting the business-as-usual landscape of white guys in hoodies and V-neck sweaters and proving that a female point of view matters in tech—and can rock big returns in business and innovation. They are the geek girls *rising*, and you will meet them in this book.

Where Are the Women in Tech?

But first, it is important to understand why more women weren't already making their fortunes in the digital revolution by the time GoldieBlox shined a light on the problem. And for that we have to look back at the years that preceded the Internet gold rush of the late 1990s—when the world was still on the brink of breakthroughs like personal e-mail, search, and online shopping, which would ultimately disrupt life as we knew it. By the post-recession early 1990s, when we two English majors graduated from college, Wall Street was deemed the place for young feminists fresh from undergrad or B-school to make money. Finance and management consulting were where the action was. And that's where many women with hard-core math and analytical skills and Ivy League degrees went to prove they could go toe to toe with men. As one Wharton alum told us, "Feminism, with a capital *F*, stood for finance," when she graduated in 1997. A *New York Times* report about Stanford's class of 1994 described the opportunities in banking and law as "opening up to women as never before" and juxtaposed those more certain paths with the "Wild West" of the Internet, where a bright future was not necessarily a slam dunk.[4]

At the same time the number of women graduating with computer science degrees in the United States was declining from its peak in the 1985–86 academic year, when 37 percent of CS diplomas went to female grads.[5] This, as video games and personal computers continued to be heavily marketed to guys. Movies like 1984's *Revenge of the Nerds*, whose pocket protector–wearing Gilbert and Lewis decide to form their own fraternity for social outcasts and use their computer savvy to foil the jocks, immortalized the stereotype.[6] The film typifies tech's image problem, which simply turned many women off, according to Jocelyn Goldfein, who became Facebook's first female director of engineering in 2010. Jocelyn had always stood out, the rare girl who had embraced the so-called nerd path as she devoured science fiction and spent hours playing *Dungeons & Dragons* with her sister while growing up in Austin, Texas. She said it was almost subversive for a woman to major in computer science when she left for college in 1993, so she wasn't surprised when she arrived at Stanford to find few women in her CS courses, although one of her classmates was future Yahoo CEO and president Marissa Mayer. The year they graduated, 1997, 83 percent of CS degrees were awarded to men, according to the university's School of Engineering.

"In the nineties the only people in computer science were the fat, nerdy people, the four-eyes. For men too. But to be a male geek was a different kind of path than to be a female one. It was an alternative path for them versus the jock or frat path, but it was still a path. The women, however, were almost breaking our own bounds to do that," Jocelyn told us.

Jocelyn would go on to work for Diane Greene, senior vice president of Google's enterprise business and the serial entrepreneur who co-founded VMware, the company that revolutionized how operating systems run on computers. VMware was acquired by the EMC Corporation for $635 million in 2004.[7] But most people outside the Valley don't know the story of the female computer scientist who built it. The contributions of Diane Greene, like those of many of her colleagues, had been glossed over.

"Any history that holds up seven white men as the founders of the computer revolution obscures the true collective nature of innovation," writes Jessi Hempel in her *Backchannel* story, "A Women's History of Silicon Valley," penned in response to a 2016 *Newsweek* special edition issue about the "founding fathers" that highlighted only the well-known white male CEOs most people associate with tech innovation.[8]

Her point was that for decades, the tech world has suffered from the invisibility of its female leaders. This, too, contributed to the declining numbers of women who were going into computing and engineering when "the World Wide Web hit orbital velocity in 1993," as Walter Isaacson describes the dawn of the web in his 2014 book, *The Innovators: How a Group of Hackers, Geniuses and Geeks Created the Digital Revolution*. He writes that a key "impetus" was the launch of Mosaic, later known as Netscape Navigator, the first Internet browser for amateurs. It came on the scene in 1994 and changed everything.[9] It marked the tipping point for the personal computer's lightning-speed migration into our kitchens and living rooms—and eventually our purses and pockets.[10] The following year, 1995, was the pivotal one that saw the launch of Amazon, Craigslist, Match .com, and eBay.

Only a decade later, when Facebook was just a year old, nearly 85 percent of men and women would be accessing the Internet at home for banking, shopping, keeping up with the news, and downloading music.[11] The tech-centric culture for everyday people only grew with the advent of smartphones and tablets that were sleek and easy to use, thanks to Apple visionary Steve Jobs and his obsession with making computers friendly.[12]

When the iPhone app store went online in 2008, Silicon Valley was still a hot spot for smart, enterprising young people, even after the burst of the dot-com bubble in 2000. Yet even though women quickly adapted to e-mail and social media, they had not flocked to the Valley in droves during the initial boom.[13] And those who did didn't stay long. Women's representation in computing dropped from more than a third of workers in 1990 to just over a quarter of workers in 2013—the same number as in 1960, according to a report by the American Association of University Women.[14] Citing hostile work environments, a lack of flexibility, lower pay than their male counterparts, and few opportunities to advance, by 2009, 56 percent of women in tech had dropped out of the industry mid-career— leaving at twice the rate of men.[15] And they were not necessarily opting out to stay home and raise kids. Most engineers who left high tech did not leave the workforce but instead migrated to jobs in health care, education, and administration, according to research led by Jennifer L. Glass of the University of Texas–Austin.[16] So you had a perfect storm for underrepresentation—fewer women majoring in CS and engineering, combined with high numbers of women leaving the industry, especially those who had been in key technical roles.[17] The result? Few visible women in leadership during a time of incredible—and important—innovation.

Pressuring the Valley to Come Clean

In 2014, the age of Netflix, Fitbit, and Snapchat, it was downright disconcerting that so few women and people of color had a seat at the tech industry's table, especially when women were earning more college and graduate degrees than their male counterparts. It's not that no one was talking about it until 2014. There was some media coverage inside Silicon Valley, notably "The Men and (No) Women Facebook of Facebook Management," a 2007 piece by veteran tech journalist Kara Swisher that appeared on the website *All Things D* and playfully displayed head shots of Mark Zuckerberg and his six male deputies at that time—five white and two Asian guys.[18] By 2010 women increasingly were speaking up about the lack of diversity at conferences and blogging about it. In 2011 Girls Who Code and its media-savvy founder, Reshma Saujani, unleashed a national effort to encourage girls to learn computer programming. In 2012 Marissa Mayer was named CEO of Yahoo and made headlines with the announcement that she was pregnant and planning to take hardly any maternity leave. But until 2014 one critical thing was missing: actual data from some of the biggest tech companies to document the extent of the disparity. Until then, Google, Facebook, and Microsoft had resisted calls to disclose the number of women and people of color working in leadership and in technical jobs. That would change in the months ahead.

"Women in tech didn't matter to people until tech started mattering to people," explained Rachel Sklar, an activist and the originator of the rallying cry "Change the Ratio," when we interviewed her in the winter of 2016. "Tech started mattering to people when, all of a sudden, tech millionaires turned into tech billionaires, and our lives really became transformed."

When the GoldieBlox TV ad aired, the discussion of tech's gender gap was already bubbling up at insider conferences, on college campuses, and across social media. But the mainstream movement to correct it had not yet taken off, and the women who would lead it were just beginning to mobilize.

Right across San Francisco Bay from the GoldieBlox workshop in Oakland, California, one of Debbie's good friends was already working hard to spark a revolution of her own. Software engineer Tracy Chou had been putting together a public database of female engineers that, by springtime, would help force big tech companies like Google to acknowledge that their technical and leadership teams had few women—and even fewer minorities. Tracy says she was spurred to write a pivotal call to action, her October 2013 essay "Where Are the Numbers?," when one day she looked around her San Francisco office at Pinterest, the digital scrapbooking site adored by crafters, home chefs, decorators, and fashionistas, and realized that only eleven of the eighty-nine engineers on her team were women—and they were building a product *used mostly by women.*

In the spirit of the open-source programming world, in which people all over the globe collaborate on public projects, Tracy, then twenty-seven, set up a basic Google form on GitHub and made a simple request to her peers for some on-the-ground reporting: Share the numbers of women you see around you on your team.

"As an engineer, and someone who's had 'data-driven design' browbeaten into me by Silicon Valley, I can't imagine trying to solve a problem where the real metrics, the ones we're setting our goals against, are obfuscated," Tracy wrote as she called for transparency from companies and entreated other female engineers to help.

The response was swift and damning: At Yelp someone posted that only 17 of 206 engineers were women; at Mozilla, 43 out of 500; at Dropbox, 42 out of 384, and on and on. The numbers showed that, on average, only about 18.9 percent of the people building the technology for an increasingly female audience—more than half the population—were women.[19]

As the data poured in during the next few months, the big guys couldn't keep stonewalling. They were already under fire to release diversity data because Mike Swift, a tenacious former reporter for the *San Jose Mercury News*, kept filing Freedom of Information Act requests. The *Mercury News* had set out in 2008 to push fifteen of Silicon Valley's largest tech companies to disclose the race and gender makeup of their workforces, and five of them, including Google, had waged an eighteen-month battle to prevent the numbers from getting out—successfully convincing federal regulators that its workforce is a trade secret.[20]

But in May 2014, under pressure from the media and civil rights organizations, including the Reverend Jesse Jackson's Rainbow PUSH Coalition, Google finally reversed course. After the iconic civil rights leader showed up at Google's shareholder meeting, the company revealed that only 17 percent of its technical team and only 21 percent of its leadership team were female. Google vowed to do better.[21] Facebook, Pinterest, Twitter, and others quickly followed suit, announcing fresh multi-million-dollar diversity initiatives: Intel, which was one of the first companies to comply with the *Mercury News*'s inquiry, rolled out a $300 million program to invest in entrepreneurs with diverse backgrounds, to support women in gaming, and to underwrite efforts to recruit young women into the field.[22] Google committed $50 million to Made w/ Code, a video channel showcasing coding tutorials aimed at girls (the channel is best known for the dress embellished with LED lights, a collaboration of designer Zac Posen and technologist Maddy Maxey and programmed by Girls Who Code participants). And the CEO of Salesforce, Marc Benioff, publicly committed to a goal of employing an equal number of men and women within five years.[23]

We first met Tracy in January 2015 at Pinterest's headquarters in San Francisco's SOMA—South of Market Street—the hip San Francisco neighborhood that's also home to Dropbox, Trulia, and Yelp. Pinterest, a startup begun in 2010, had just moved from Palo Alto, in the heart of Silicon Valley, to the city, in part so its growing troops of young engineers could enjoy shorter commutes as well as San Francisco's nightlife, restaurants, and culture. But at 7 p.m. at least twenty-five people were still in the office, some eating dinner in the airy cafeteria in the shadow of a two-story floor-to-ceiling "pin board," a totem showing the interests of the hundred million people using the photo-tagging tool to collect, share, and organize their favorite pictures of food, fashion, and home decor from across the web. It's a towering collage of colorful magazine clippings featuring trendy shoes, purses, throw pillows, and beautiful people, including a cute male model showing off a pair of bright red shorts on a beach. Small red-and-white-striped hot air balloons dangled high above, adding to the ambiance of whimsy and charm. We took a seat, and over sparkling water Tracy opened up about what she loved about her day job and coding.

"A lot of the gratification for me is in seeing the things I can build," she explained, referring to the combination of analytical skills and creativity that coding requires.

The daughter of two computer science PhD's never expected to become the David to Silicon Valley's Goliaths. Although her parents were programmers, and she grew up in the heart of Startupland, she didn't really consider computer science as a vocation until late in her time at Stanford, where she chose to major in electrical engineering, having been intimidated in the computer science classroom. Despite her initial insecurities, Tracy would go on to become a teaching assistant for CS 107, known as the "weeder class" on campus, and she said that experience contributed to the confidence she needed to earn a master's in computer science.

She was a painfully shy kid whose teachers commented on her report cards that she never raised her hand in class. Her parents, who had emigrated from Taiwan and ran their own startup, which they sold to Oracle when their daughter was in middle school, pushed her to be more outgoing. She was a "nerdy bookworm" who would rather read on the playground than run around at recess. At one point her mom limited her voracious appetite for books to two a day, and she got around that restriction by picking out the longest books at the library. During her freshman year of high school, she signed up for the debate team at her mother's behest. That was a turning point.

"You're up in front of a podium, and you're the person who's speaking, and you have to get good at presenting your arguments. I got used to the idea of being in front of a room," she said of the tournaments that taught her to argue either side of a case before a panel of judges at a moment's notice. The experience would prove seminal less than a decade later, when she became a de facto spokeswoman for diversifying the tech industry, including a high-profile appearance during 2016's SXSW (South by Southwest), the influential music and tech festival in Austin, Texas, where President Obama was a headliner. Crucially, she could speak the language of data and metrics, which held weight with some of Silicon Valley's inner circle.

"I'm lucky to be on the inside versus on the outside trying to beat down the doors . . . I know the right people to talk to. I have rapport with the people internally. I can take the position: 'I'm right here, an engineer, one of you.' It gives me more credibility with people who are in the positions to effect change," she said.

That is why she has been tapped to discuss her thoughts on diversity with leaders of some of the fastest-growing startups like Slack, which produces a messaging app for teams. These new companies have to hire so quickly as they grow that they struggle to find enough programmers, period, never mind candidates from underrepresented groups. She is also a sought-after speaker for women's groups all over the Valley. As a result we found ourselves tagging along to the San Francisco offices of Uber at lunchtime on a Friday afternoon. It was Indian food day at the company, which is known as a unicorn—in Silicon Valley lingo, one of the elite, privately held startups valued at more than a billion dollars. Twenty engineers (sixteen women, four men) were sitting around the table and picking at curry, lentils, and rice when Tracy arrived. Knowing she had just been featured in *Vogue*, we noted her fashion-forward look: casual but pulled together in a black polka-dot sweater, red skirt, and gold flats.[24] Free meals are one of the well-known perks many tech companies provide to employees. (One person turned to us and whispered that the food is better at Facebook.) #Lady ENG, the organization of women engineers at Uber, had invited Tracy to share her story and offer advice. Staffers from two other Uber locations participated by videoconference so they could ask questions too. One woman put Tracy on the spot by asking what Uber should do to improve its image so it can recruit more women. Tracy didn't hesitate to tackle the sensitive question. "Is this a brand thing or is there actually stuff that really needs to be addressed internally?" she asked, then went on to say that Uber couldn't fix its bad reputation in regard to diversity if it didn't address concerns on the inside. The dialogue proved prophetic: in February 2017, Uber CEO Travis Kalanick and the company would come under fire after a female software engineer went public with appalling allegations of sexual harassment and an unresponsive HR department. Measurement, she said, is the key to change. And the way to convince the hacker culture that having more people with different skill sets is an advantage is to speak their language.

"I think oftentimes the people most resistant to a lot of diversity arguments are engineers who believe in meritocracy. One thing that works real well with engineers is talking with them about things they do normally, which is build products, instrument them, collect metrics. Maybe we should apply that same methodology to our workplace and how we function as teams," she said as the Uber group nodded politely.

Even as Tracy was making her case on a national stage and inside some of the biggest companies, she acknowledged she had not quite shed the old feelings of being an outsider. She still acutely recalled her Facebook internship: from her desk she looked out into an office filled with fifty people and could see only one other woman. Or when she worked at Quora, where she had the awkward experience of pointing out to the (mostly male) team that some users might not appreciate seeing content around penis size showing up in their feeds, and that they might want to consider building filters. It did not go well.

"I was put in a position of having to speak on behalf of all women and how women engage with porn and R-rated content. I think the conversation unfolded poorly because there were people that were taking the 'devil's advocate' angle, even if it was just obnoxious. We did end up building a safe filter, though," she told us.

The bottom line is that being an activist isn't easy. And it can be downright lonely. Despite her efforts, change across the industry remains slow.

"It feels [like it is] harder for me as a woman to move up in an industry whose leaders are mostly male and not people I really identify with," she told us. "And especially when so much happens in casual or semi-professional settings, like people grabbing beers after work or playing poker. Being disconnected from that network has career consequences, like missing out on critical bonding or important information about projects coming up. And I just feel like I just don't belong in that network." In June 2016 Tracy left Pinterest after four and a half years and packed her bags for a new adventure in New York City, where she plunged into work on a startup of her own.

■   ■   ■

Sex and the City Meets Silicon Valley

Building a new kind of network in which women are the insiders who pass along choice professional leads and make strategic introductions while sipping skinny cappuccinos in their own comfortable clubhouse is exactly what Shelley Zalis envisioned when she came up with the idea for the Girls' Lounge. If Carrie Bradshaw came to life as a globe-trotting, fifty-five-year-old market research guru from Beverly Hills, she would be the Birkin bag–toting, SoulCycling Zalis. The skillful connector believes deeply in the power of girlfriends and was off and running by 2014, creating her signature retreats inside male-dominated conferences like the International Consumer Electronics Show (CES). Her pop-up gathering spaces offer oases featuring white leather couches with pink throw pillows, a sparkly chandelier, and ample opportunities to trade business cards and ideas. But don't let the pink fool you.

"There is more business done in the Girls' Lounge than at the actual conference because it is an authentic unplugged space," emphasized Shelley, who is passionate about transforming the legacy rules of the workplace that she says have traditionally spurred competition among ambitious women. With sponsors that include Facebook, AOL, Twitter, IBM, and NBC Universal, the Lounge has become a must-stop for female power brokers at events like SXSW and the World Economic Forum in Davos, Switzerland. It's not unusual to find Arianna Huffington chatting about wellness with the women passing through the Lounge as she did in Davos, where in 2016, one in five attendees was female, or at CES that year where the chief technology officer of the United States, Megan Smith, narrated a private Girls' Lounge tour of the exhibit floor as dozens of women donned audio headsets to follow along.

The ah-ha moment for the glossy entrepreneur, whose mantra is "a woman trying to be a man is a waste of a woman," occurred after she invited four gal pals to her hotel room for a "slumber party" at CES in 2013. CES is a massive gadget fest that features scantily clothed "booth babes" who beckon attendees to try out new tech toys, and it was—needless to say—not the most comfortable place to be female. And Shelley, then the chief executive of Ipsos/OTX, the third-largest global market research firm in the world (which had acquired her company, OTX, for $80 million), dreaded being there alone.[25] The day after the hangout in her hotel room, she and her influential friends gathered as many women as they could find at the conference and walked the massive convention hall together in solidarity and sisterhood.

"A woman alone can be powerful, but collectively we have impact," Shelley said of the surprised reaction the fifty corporate women received from male attendees as they moved through the hall.

We first got to know her when she invited us to hang out in her hotel room in Cologne, Germany, the night before dmexco, a sort of mini-CES for Europe. As she sat cross-legged on her bed and contemplated what to wear to a VIP party that evening, we also learned that in the four years since she came up with the Girls' Lounge, fifty-five of them had sprung up around the globe and reached more than seventy-five hundred corporate women. After she decided to forgo her leather jacket and slipped on studded, pointy-toed red slingbacks (she's a shoe aficionado), she grabbed a chocolate protein bar and whisked us away in a black chauffeured Mercedes to the opening evening of dmexco. There, digital marketers from all over Europe and the United States sipped wine spritzers with mint leaves and lavender sprigs, greeting each other with air kisses under pink and blue fluorescent lights as a thumping bass played beneath the din. The next day, as we tried to keep pace with her sky-high Louboutins and her bubbly entourage of blonde assistants clad in black tees and eyelash extensions, we witnessed the Lounge in action. In one corner a chief marketing officer from a tech giant tried on vegan leather jackets in the Confidence Closet provided by the apparel line Project Gravitas. As Beyoncé's feminist anthem "Who Run the World? (Girls)" played in the background, a mid-level web designer got her makeup touched up in preparation for new head shots snapped by the Lounge's photographer. And on the shiny white "stoop" outside the Lounge, under a sign proclaiming CONFIDENCE IS THE NEW BEAUTIFUL, a clutch of high-level execs, including Meredith Kopit Levien, chief revenue officer for the *New York Times*; Laura Ipsen, Oracle's senior vice president and general manager of cloud marketing; and Allie Kline, chief marketing officer for AOL, dropped by to join Shelley in a panel discussion about the

"Shine Theory," a philosophy *New York* magazine columnist Ann Friedman (and her best friend, Aminatou Sow, founder of TechLady Mafia) introduced in May 2013. It promotes the idea that when women surround themselves with successful, confident women, we are all better for it.[26]

"Change the game and collaborate," Shelley told the mostly female audience listening intently to the discussion about how powerful women make the best girlfriends. "Show that collaboration is the new black."

It's a sentiment that binds the online network Rachel Sklar curated when she first shot off an e-mail to nineteen girlfriends in the spring of 2010. She was pissed off. *New York* magazine had run an April cover story about the social media startups that were making their home in Manhattan's Silicon Alley, and of the fifty-three people pictured in the layout, only six were women. In one photo a man's foot obscured a woman's face. Rachel, a corporate-lawyer-turned-journalist and now a frequent guest on TV shows, had been covering the media for the *Huffington Post* and later, *Mediaite,* and she was fed up with seeing that women were not getting the attention they deserved, especially in the booming tech world.

"It was the straw that broke the camel's back," she explained. And it was the spark that would unite a loosely connected group of acquaintances in New York's new startup scene into a sort of secret handshake society dedicated to elevating the profiles of female founders, software engineers, and other smart, ambitious women in their circles. April 2014 presented a prime opportunity to flex their muscle.

The *Wall Street Journal* had just announced an all-male, mostly white lineup of speakers for its marquee tech and new media conference, WSJDLive, when it suddenly faced swift and angry pushback. The editors were caught off guard as #changetheratio exploded on Twitter:

Good GOD @newscorp @WSJ @WSJD 17 male speakers,
0 women 'Where The Digital World Connects'?! In this
day & age? ow.ly/vRqMP

Seriously, how did @newscorp @WSJ @WSJD look at this
& not go, 'What's wrong with this picture?' ow.ly/vRsBI

Leading the charge was the group, now known as TheLi.st,
that had been handpicked by Rachel. Its members broadcast
across social media the battle cry "Change the Ratio," the
phrase she coined when she sent that fateful e-mail and began
a new career as an advocate for women in technology. In response to the torrent of negative feedback, the *Journal*'s public
relations team quickly backpedaled, saying it would announce
more speakers.

Rachel gave us the reasons for TheLi.st's immediate reaction
when all-male lineups or male-dominated events come to the
group's attention: "Visibility begets access. There is visibility
[from] being highlighted as an expert, as a person of value, as a
person who is a contributor, as someone who is special and is
accomplished. Then access is being in the room where it happens, being able to connect with people who are able to give
you an opportunity." As she spoke, she casually nursed her
eleven-month-old daughter, Ruby. On that windy March day
we'd caught her with an hour to kill before little Ruby's visit
to the pediatrician for a case of the sniffles. So we ducked into
CitiBabes, a hip play space with an indoor jungle gym in SoHo.

"Visibility begets access begets opportunity," Rachel continued without missing a beat as a tired toddler across the room
dissolved into a tantrum. "When you see it that way, you see
how, very clearly, a system defaulted to highlighting and
rewarding white men is a self-perpetuating nightmare for
women."

In its bid to break up the system TheLi.st remains exclusive. To become a member of its underground e-mail chain, you have to be nominated by someone in the group or know Rachel or someone who knows Rachel and can vouch for you. TheLi.st has become a sorority of several hundred women and evolved into a for-profit venture after Rachel teamed up with her longtime writing colleague, Glynnis MacNicol. Members pay annual dues of $750, and they are increasingly getting together offline for fun meet-ups like whiskey tastings, baby showers, and outings to Broadway. As in the beginning, Rachel plays matchmaker, finessing for hard-core technologists and startup founders important introductions to a mix of Hollywood producers, CEOs, fashion magazine editors, *New York Times* writers, venture capitalists, TV personalities, and philanthropists.

"It's all about shortening the distance from A to B," she explained—in other words, opening doors that might not have opened without a connection, like Listers helping one another score an invite to after-parties for the White House Correspondents' Dinner or SXSW or to attend the right dinner at the right time to gain a warm introduction to the right investor.

What TheLi.st is all about is plain and simple, according to British-born Cindy Gallop, a longtime member, irreverent champion of gender equality, and founder of two tech startups, including her #sextech venture, MakeLoveNotPorn.tv. "TheLi.st," she said, "makes shit happen for women."

It is not your typical professional networking group. Sure, job opportunities are posted daily, with an offer to pitch a "Sister Lister" for prestigious positions, and the women discuss how to negotiate consulting fees, how to respond to an off-color remark by a male colleague, how to deliver a kick-ass TED talk, and which investors might be good prospects. But at the same time, Listers take comfort in confiding in each other (in long, detailed e-mails) about troubles with their kids or deciding not to have kids or coping with breast cancer or the death of a parent. Everything is strictly off the record. It's a "place" where you can both find a solid referral for a new gynecologist and solicit front-end software developer candidates for your new startup in a single day—sometimes within minutes, given the number of members who respond with lightning speed to the flurry of conversations all day long.

"When you're a stakeholder in the success of your friend, it's good for you, so if you're two junior people and you really help each other rise, then, suddenly you're two mid-level people and you're rising together," Rachel said. "You're pulling each other up. You're pushing each other from behind. It's useful. If you can do it alone, fine, [more] power to you, but it's a lot easier to do it with help."

■　■　■

Tech Feminism Takes Off

As 2014 wore on, TheLi.st and its strategic use of social media to call out sexism, along with the growing media coverage of the women in tech meme, continued to air topics typically reserved for discussion by tech insiders. Terms like *brogrammer* (frat boy meets computer geek), *booth babe*, and *Gamergate* (the scandal that came to light in summer 2014 about the harassment and physical threatening of female game designers by misogynistic gamers) seeped into the national consciousness. In May 2014 President Obama hosted the first White House Science Fair highlighting women and girls in STEM, and in his opening remarks he called out the depressing statistics.

"Fewer than three in ten workers in science and engineering are women. That means we've got half the field—or half our team—we're not even putting on the field. We've got to change those numbers," he declared after recognizing the all-girl team of middle school students in the audience that day from Los Fresnos, Texas; they had designed an app to help a visually impaired classmate.[27]

A few months later the president would go on to make history by naming the nation's first female chief technology officer. Megan Smith, a former vice president of Google X, the company's secret research-and-development arm, would eventually help steward the president's $4 billion initiative, 2016's Computer Science for All, to make CS education a priority for all public school children. By late 2013 Smith had already spent two years working from within Google to attract more women to its huge annual software developers' conference, Google I/O. Before she left for Washington, Smith handed those reins to her colleague Natalie Villalobos, who would take the initiative, known as Women Techmakers, to the next level: increasing the female presence at I/O from 8 percent to 23 percent by 2016 and evolving the program into an open, outward-facing year-round effort to rally not just technical women but women working in all areas of tech through summits from Sao Paulo to Tokyo to Lagos to Chicago. By 2014 Natalie, a free-spirited fairy godmother of sorts who stands out in white vintage cat's-eye glasses and likes to brainstorm over Japanese green tea, was going full force to connect software developers to startup founders, and startup founders to corporate and civic leaders, online and off.

When we caught up with her in June 2016, Natalie was en route to the White House's United State of Women Summit where she met with Smith, whom she still refers to as her mentor, and then she was off to New York and Boston. She described her dream job by saying, "Women are fire starters, especially women in the technology industry, and [my job is,] 'How can I add fuel to that fire?' That's how I'm approaching my work: identifying and supporting and empowering these women to do whatever it is that they love, whatever it is that they want to do, and [asking,] 'How can I help them?'

"As women start to understand about this opportunity, how can we help them? How can we catapult them to achieve whatever it is that they would like to achieve in this industry by lowering the barriers to entry, by granting greater access? Because it's going to take this combined multi-level, global effort to really see a change."

Like Women Techmakers, other key groups, including Girl Develop It and Women Who Code, emerged to support women in tech by the fall of 2014. That September, Disrupt, the premier tech conference and startup competition sponsored by Tech-Crunch, finally acknowledged tech has a sexism problem and unveiled new anti-harassment policies.[28] (This was a year after the "Titstare" debacle, in which an app for the explicit purpose of ogling women was presented during its hackathon.) Later in the fall, Apple and Facebook rolled out egg-freezing coverage as part of their benefits packages for female employees, igniting new discussions about where motherhood fits into the hack-'til-you-drop culture.[29]

And then, just before Thanksgiving, came the furor about "computer scientist Barbie," a new character in a picture book published by Mattel. The pink pages featured blonde bombshell Barbie as a web designer who doesn't know how to fix a bug in her code without the help of her male colleagues. It incensed computer programmers and non-programmers alike. Casey Fiesler, then a Georgia Tech doctoral candidate who was writing her human-centered-computing dissertation on memes, was so fired up that she decided to rewrite the story so that Barbie is helping the men on her team and posted it on her little-known blog. The next morning she learned *Barbie, Remixed!* had gone viral, along with another digital parody of the book, *Feminist Hacker Barbie*.[30] Casey's website, which she said probably had all of eight hundred hits when she put it up, suddenly had 800,000 hits, and the remix was being shared tens of thousands of times on Facebook and Twitter. She had tapped into women's anger and frustration at sexist stereotyping and found herself featured in *Cosmo* and invited to read her reimagined Barbie book to schoolchildren around the country. Mattel would go on to win over its critics when it released Game Developer Barbie two years later with much fanfare for her realistic outfit and her ability to write kickass code on her own.

Tech's Toxic Culture on Trial

The momentum of the tech feminism movement surged into 2015 and reached a fever pitch as a plaintiff named Ellen Pao took the stand to accuse her former employer, the venture capital firm Kleiner Perkins Caufield & Byers (KPCB), of passing her over for promotions and ultimately firing her because she was a woman who had made complaints to her bosses about sexual harassment. With millions of dollars and the reputation of Silicon Valley's oldest and most venerable firm hanging in the balance, the case had all the makings of an Emmy Award–winning TV legal drama à la *The Good Wife*.

As the case played out over five weeks, tech reporters and journalists from national newspapers breathlessly covered the juicy trial. Within minutes of the jury's finding for the firm, the hashtag #thankyouEllenPao zoomed up Twitter's trending list at lightning speed. Google searches for "Ellen Pao" spiked. The blogosphere rippled with commentary on the case and predictions of its long-term impact on the insular world of startups and how they raise cash. Even Anita Hill called the Pao suit a watershed moment. For the first time the people at the epicenter of the innovation economy were forced to publicly reckon with a system that had evolved into one dominated by white men. It exposed the rarified world of the access, money, and machismo that fuel an exclusive club of entrepreneurs peddling their big ideas to potential kingmakers, who in many cases look just like themselves and share the same networks and pedigrees. Pao was a junior partner and had argued she was an outsider, excluded from ski trips, a dinner at Al Gore's condo in San Francisco's St. Regis Hotel, and other all-male outings, where her colleagues got advance information about deals and plum assignments. Although the jury rejected her claims, she had touched a nerve and put a face on a movement that had been simmering all along. In 2016 Ellen Pao teamed up with Tracy Chou and other high-profile diversity advocates to start Project Include, an initiative to support startups and venture capital firms in changing their culture and helping them measure their progress.

Trae Vassallo, who was Pao's colleague at Kleiner during the years targeted in the suit, was the first person to testify against the firm. As soon as the verdict was handed up, Trae felt its impact.

"I got this overwhelming response from all my friends, from tons of women I've never met before, who reached out and said, 'Thank you for talking, and, by the way, here's my story,'" said Trae, one of the few women to become a general partner at KPCB, when only 8.5 percent of all venture capitalists in the United States at the time were women.[31] Trae testified during the trial that she had been propositioned by the same married male partner with whom Pao had had an affair and who, Pao claimed, had retaliated against her after the romance ended. On the stand Trae also recounted the humiliation of being asked to take notes in meetings and being given a seat at the back of the room when she and Pao were the only women of their rank sitting among male junior associates.[32]

About a year after the case ended and a few months after her friend Pao decided to drop her appeal, Trae told us: "What floored me was, here I had gone through this very lonely, very horrible experience and then had to talk publicly about it. Then, to realize that I wasn't alone. There were actually tons of people who had gone through things similar, even way worse. It was an interesting catharsis in knowing that. Then I proceeded to get really angry once I was, like, 'Wait a second. From my ballpark figure here, more than half of women have had similar experiences.'"

A few months later, while on a power hike with her friend Hillary Mickell, a tech executive and entrepreneur, Trae realized what she wanted to do. They were doing their usual loop up a winding trail through the grasslands and forest overlooking the Portola Valley, not far from Stanford's Palo Alto campus, where she had once been a shy eighteen-year-old mechanical engineering student far from her home in a tiny farming town called Fairmont, Minnesota. Although she had been shy, Trae had always gone her own way. She credits her fierce independence to her mother and to growing up in a rural community where being intellectual was not particularly cool. Because of her early interests in computer programming and machines, she never felt like she fit in. Her mother told her not to care about what anyone else thought.

"She really helped give me that backbone and the confidence to go, 'Okay, well, I'm just going to be true to myself, I'm going to do what I love, and I'm not going to worry what other people think,'" said Trae, who has three children and finds herself having similar conversations with her fifteen-year-old math-whiz daughter, an aspiring entrepreneur.

As Trae and Hillary climbed the path, hearts pumping, Trae

said she wanted to do a survey, and they started talking about what it would show. Soon after, Trae teamed up with another friend, Ellen Levy, and some Stanford students to conduct the research. Then they approached Michele Madanksy, a former Yahoo executive, about joining the team to analyze the survey results from more than two hundred Silicon Valley women with ten or more years of professional experience.

Their survey, "Elephant in the Valley," was released in January 2016 and recounts anecdotes that friends and strangers in the tech world had been sharing with Trae. Sixty percent of the women queried said that they had experienced unwanted sexual advances; 88 percent faced unconscious bias, such as male colleagues who posed questions only to their male peers, men who would not make eye contact with female colleagues, or men who asked women to do lower-level tasks that the men did not ask male colleagues to do. Seventy-five percent of the women reported that job interviewers had asked them about family life, marital status, and children.[33] We first connected with Trae shortly after the survey came out, and she told us in a telephone conversation she thought that, despite the negative picture the survey painted, women might actually be empowered by knowing that if they had suffered a professional setback, it wasn't necessarily because of a personal failing but a much larger, seemingly intransigent, societal problem. One of the biggest barriers to discussing the problems faced by women in the Valley is that women who suffer discrimination fear retaliation and are concerned that speaking out will be detrimental to their careers. Furthermore, many cannot talk about it because they are legally bound to silence by non-disparagement clauses in their employment contracts. In many other cases, she said, complaints are arbitrated and therefore never make it to court and remain hidden.

She said that after twenty years in the industry, she knew

that not everyone would applaud the stand she was taking: "I think the data helped to provide people with the information that we are not where we want to be as a society. I think a lot of people didn't realize how backward we maybe were on some of these fronts. Part of it is if you are going to improve something, you have to measure it. The data alone doesn't solve any problems, but our hope in getting it out there was to educate more folks and inspire more people to do something about it or to pay attention.

"There are going to be people who look at that and go, 'Why is she doing that?' I'm doing it because I care about it. I think it's valuable, and I don't care what other people think."

The Sisterhood Stands Up

The Pao case, the sensational coverage of it, and an explosive *Newsweek* exposé that ran before the trial, "What Silicon Valley Thinks of Women," were what spurred another Valley veteran to end her silence on the issue of sexism in tech. The *Newsweek* cover story featured a saucy illustration of a woman in red heels with a cursor lifting up her skirt.[34] For years Sukhinder Singh Cassidy had felt more comfortable keeping her opinions about gender to herself. Her laser focus was on building her businesses. In her fast-paced, no-nonsense style, the Tanzanian-born executive confided to us that even as her long-time friend Sheryl Sandberg exhorted women to lean in, and after Anne-Marie Slaughter countered in the *Atlantic* that women can't have it all at the same time, Sukhinder had no desire to add to the noise. An accomplished corporate insider and founder of two startups, she felt she could have more impact on the discussion of women in tech if she just kept her head down, worked hard, and delivered.

"If I deliver, if I build a unicorn, that will do more for women in tech than anything I could possibly say," she said.

But when the airing of Silicon Valley's dirty laundry started leading the evening news, Sukhinder, then forty-four, decided it was time to take a stand and tell another side of the story. After all, she'd had a ringside seat: she is a serial entrepreneur and investor who once ran global divisions at Amazon and Google and serves on the boards of TripAdvisor and Ericsson and formerly advised Twitter and J.Crew. The story she would tell was about empowerment, about the new generation of badass female tech entrepreneurs who were rising to the top in San Francisco and New York. She was mentoring some of them, including Katrina Lake, founder and CEO of the personal styling subscription service Stitch Fix. Sukhinder's story was about the sisterhood among women in tech.

"There's so much more good about it [being a woman in tech] than bad. Of course, I've had my own incidents, but over the course of my career, is that the defining characteristic? No way," she said. That personal history was her impetus to start #ChoosePossiblity in May 2015, a company and campaign to demonstrate that women, while small in numbers, are innovating, starting and running important new companies.

Her efforts started with publishing an open letter. She got the idea to write it after she talked to Keval Desai, a former colleague of hers at Google. Keval, a partner specializing in information technology at InterWest Partners, a venture capital firm, had invested in Sukhinder's latest startup, Joyus, an online video shopping hub where you can buy everything from trendy moto jackets to three-day smoothie cleanses to age-defying hand cream and get beauty and lifestyle tips in one shot. At the time half of Keval's portfolio at InterWest was made up of women-led companies, and Sukhinder said he was downright angry that

the coverage of sexism in the Valley seemed to be overshadow-
ing the success of these businesses. He sent a note to all the
female CEOs of companies in his portfolio at InterWest and
entreated them to talk publicly about their triumphs. "Without your voice, women won't come to Silicon Valley," he said he
told them. Sukhinder responded right away.

"I told him, 'You are right. No one is telling this story. Nobody ever speaks up. I'll do it,'" Sukhinder said and promptly
started working her Rolodex. She reached out to almost one
hundred female CEOs and founders, including Care.com's
Sheila Marcelo, Gilt's Alexandra Wilkis Wilson, and Alison
Pincus of One Kings Lane, to ask them to sign a public letter
pronouncing that the story of women in tech is more than tales
of unwanted sexual advances and males' micro-aggressions.
And, of course, since this was Silicon Valley, the land of ana-
lytics, she wanted the message to be backed up by data about
female founders, so Sukhinder commissioned a survey to go
along with the text. It was published on *Recode*, the well-read
tech news site, under the headline "Tech Women #Choose
Possibility," along with stats that made the case: even in the face
of gender bias, female entrepreneurs were succeeding.

It proclaimed:

> The women on this list founded heavyweights such as
> Lynda.com, Nextdoor, Houzz, VMware, ASK Group and
> Mozilla; growth stage stars like Stitch Fix, Slideshare, Indie-
> gogo, LearnVest and StyleSeat; and earlier-stage startups
> like Lumoid, Heartwork, Other Machine Company and
> Trendalytics. On this list alone, we were able to identify 13
> IPOs and another 54 exits through M&A [mergers and
> acquisitions]. The average amount of capital raised per
> company is approximately $34 million (for a subset of 167
> companies on which data was available).[35]

Boom. Sukhinder suddenly found herself in a swirl of media attention, an in-demand speaker, and, for the first time ever, responding to a barrage of tweets and personal messages on social media—something that, as a busy mother of three, she admits she had never really made time for. She relayed the story when we met for an hour at Joyus's San Francisco headquarters, where she greeted us dressed in electric blue–dyed denim, suede peep-toed booties, and a fitted khaki blazer.

With the letter out and conversations buzzing, she craved more impact than simply expressing a point of view. The woman whose first boss in tech said that her hard-charging style "scared the secretaries" wanted to do something that would force change from the top down. And, not surprisingly, she already had an idea about how to do it.

She'd been thinking about a follow-up project since the summer of 2014, when she had a private conversation with a friend, a respected leader in venture funding and former colleague who was picking her brain about how to get more women into technology. Sukhinder said she proposed a big idea on the spot. She told her friend point-blank that it's not enough to focus on the pipeline—the code word for getting more women to earn computer science and engineering degrees and to take entry-level jobs in the industry. She wanted to force a culture shift in the boardroom that could influence the way companies were run. So she asked him: What if he, and all the venture capital partners across the Valley, decided collectively to put at least one woman on the board of every private company in their portfolio? He thought it was a good idea, but after a year it hadn't gone anywhere. So Sukhinder decided to do it on her own by creating a new private network that would introduce qualified, outstanding female candidates endorsed by their peers to venture capitalists and CEOs as prospective members of their boards of directors. Venture capitalism firms would pay to use the service to search for candidates. Members of the network could nominate new women to be listed. By May 2016 more than 1,200 women with endorsements from 650 executives had profiles in the database, and theBoardlist had placed three women as directors.

"I want to make what feels hard easy. I don't want there to be an excuse that there weren't enough qualified women. We need to make sure that the hurdle is taken away. The way boards get built is, I know you, you know me," she explained.

And because Sukhinder was one of the few women who had been a fixture in the Valley since the early days of consumer Internet, she was intimately aware of the tendency for insiders to recruit from the same well. She knew the network inside and out. She was part of it. They had all grown up together. She arrived in the Bay Area in 1997 after formative stints in media at BSkyB in London and in banking at Merrill Lynch in New York. Then she went to work for a tech startup and unexpectedly fell into what evolved, over almost two decades, into an exclusive sorority.

"You know, we all sort of lived together, even Sheryl [Sandberg] and I. The first time she came into Yodlee [the first company Sukhinder co-founded], she was looking for a role, and then the next time I saw her, I was going to Google to interview and she was there," Sukhinder said. "We grew up together in a generation. The universe of companies in which to get trained was small. There was Google and there was Amazon. Think about it: Were there even a hundred companies valued at over a billion dollars? No way." She smiled at the enormity of how much had changed.

This tiny cohort of women she met during that time emerged as a tight-knit group of corporate leaders, startup founders, and investors who socialized together, dishing about each other's romantic interests and hiking through the hills around the exclusive enclaves north and south of San Francisco, where they eventually settled with their young families. She says it was like going to college with the same people you'd gone to grade school with. There's history. And, as they married, had their kids at the same time (in many cases later in life), and dealt with sticky issues, such as negotiating child care and finances with their spouses, they looked to each other for advice and support.

"You've had your children together. You've seen people at their best and their worst. You've come into power together. It's just an in-bred network," said Sukhinder, who often spends weekends baking with her children to recharge and reconnect with them.

Now she sees a new generation of young women getting ready to make their mark as tomorrow's tech leaders, and she feels the sisterhood she relied on is paying it forward. One way her cohort can help boost the up-and-comers is with the Boardlist.

"What I see happening is a whole new level of sisterhood. Now I feel like I sit between these two groups of sister-hood, which is awesome—the women I grew up with and all these founders who are much younger than me." She noted the flurry of invitations she receives for women-focused dinners, panels, and pitches, adding, "There are so many these days, it's hard to keep up."

Nor is the momentum limited to the west coast. You can feel the solidarity in New York City, where a vibrant startup scene has been under way since 2010. Tech companies founded by women in the city grew tenfold between 2003 and 2014 and raised $3 billion in capital, according to a study by Endeavor.[36]

"I think the changes we've seen in the last two to five years around women in tech have been profound," said Deborah Jackson, a Goldman Sachs veteran and co-founder of Plum Alley Investments, a firm that invests in women-led tech startups.

"Women are supporting other women. Women are connecting through social media. Women are beginning to be outspoken [about the movement to recruit and retain more women in tech]."

Just like the pink-clad kindergarteners raging through the streets in the GoldieBlox commercial, today women are rising up and unapologetically claiming a seat at the tech industry's table in a way they never had before. The enthusiasm to break into the boys' club coincides with a new generation of enterprising women who, like the founder of GoldieBlox, are going for it on their own—building companies from the ground up, transforming society with their ideas and inventions, leaning on and lifting each other up along the way. And as we were writing this book in the summer of 2016, the historic presidential nomination of the nation's first female candidate loomed large. When Hillary Clinton told little girls who stayed up late to watch the Democratic National Convention on television that "they could be next," this sisterhood seemed unstoppable. If the last women's movement was about equality, this one is about equity.

CHAPTER 2

KICKSTART YOUR DREAM
Female Founders

The question isn't who is going to let me;
it's who is going to stop me.

—AYN RAND

Michelle Phan rose before the sun came up. She quickly fried an egg for her breakfast, fed her fish named Little Nemo, smoothed on an eye mask to take away the overnight puffiness, and assembled that day's outfit: fluffy fur vest, white blouse, cut-off denim shorts, and stiletto-heeled black leather ankle booties. At 7 a.m. "Mish" raced out the door, green juice in hand, and drove herself to LAX for a short flight to San Francisco to visit the Silicon Valley headquarters of ipsy, her e-commerce cosmetics company, valued by investors at more than half a billion dollars in the fall of 2015.[1] ipsy delivers Glam Bags filled with Michelle's favorite mascaras, lip colors, and skin creams to more than 1.5 million paid subscribers in the United States and Canada each month. With a massive customer base of young women, most of whom first discovered Michelle through her incredibly popular YouTube channel, ipsy has been profitable since Michelle started it in 2011, happily competing with Birchbox.

On the flight to SFO the youthful mogul gazed at her MacBook, fingers tapping away as she expertly edited her latest beauty how-to video—the bread and butter of her channel, which has garnered more than a billion views. And of course, in true You-Tuber fashion, she captured the entire business trip on video, giving her teen devotees what they crave: a peek at what it's like to be Michelle Phan.[2]

At thirty the dreamer once famously rejected for a job at a department store makeup counter has rocketed to CEO of her own digital beauty and lifestyle empire. And she did it by leveraging the more than eight million YouTube subscribers (the largest audience in the history of the platform) into a global brand. Crowned by *Glamour* magazine as the "next Oprah," Michelle is truly a geek girl rising—a lifelong gamer and self-described "techie nerd."[3]

When we first spoke with her in early 2015, Michelle had just returned from a whirlwind trip to Asia that included schmoozing with Victor Koo, founder and CEO of Youku Tudou, China's version of YouTube. "At a very young age, I loved machines, I loved technology, I just 'got' the Internet," Michelle told us.

In other words, she saw the future. Even before she became a YouTube sensation, she was deftly building an audience on the early blogging platform Xanga, sharing her paintings and ideas about beauty and life with a growing group of teens who ate it up. Although she felt like a nerdy outsider at her Tampa high school and her protective mother didn't allow her to go out much, Michelle enjoyed instant popularity online. She ultimately became the "most subscribed female" with ten thousand followers as she took on the bubbly persona of "Rice Bunny," named for her birth in the Year of the Rabbit and one of her favorite foods.[4] When she switched from blogging to creating videos in 2007 and posted her first seven-minute beauty tutorial on YouTube, it was no accident. She was seeking a larger canvas. Within one week, more than forty thousand people had devoured it, and she knew she had found a powerful medium.

Her most popular video is the legendary "Barbie Transformation Tutorial," in which she starts off bare-faced in her sparse new apartment and notes to viewers that she has no furniture because she just moved in. With a conversational voiceover that makes her seem like our BFF, she takes her audience through the steps of "how to look like the perfect plastic Barbie doll," including applying foundation with a special brush instead of your fingers or an applicator. Eight minutes and thirty-nine seconds in, she's wearing a blonde wig with bangs and a hot pink headband, and her face has a flawlessly synthetic cast as she playfully admits she bears a creepy resemblance to a real Barbie doll.[5] Perfect for Halloween. As of this writing, more than 65 million people have watched that video since she uploaded it in October 2009—that's more than the 52.5 million Americans who tuned into the final episode of *Friends* in May 2004, the most popular telecast of the 2000s.[6]

But when Michelle first started making her videos, no one could have predicted that YouTube would unleash a new creator-driven economy worth billions and that it would eventually disrupt Hollywood. It was a completely new frontier. But Bing Chen, Michelle's longtime confidant, who started working with her when he ran marketing at YouTube, said that Michelle saw the business potential long before most people did because of her experience: as a teen she related deeply to her audience and listened to their feedback. She understood what they wanted because it was the kind of stuff she wanted too.

"I knew that the younger generation would see YouTube as the new TV. They [would] come across my channel and . . . see a library of hundreds of videos. They're going to want to watch it," Michelle explained when we spoke a year later at ipsy's spacious Santa Monica office and studios. We asked her to explain how she knew at such a young age that it was really going to happen. "If you want to be a great creator, you have to be your own number-one fan first. You have to love what you're doing. Ten years ago I saw a glimpse of what *I* wanted to be the future of digital content. If I wanted that to come true, I had to manifest it myself by also making it myself."

She always had to make things happen herself. The hustle that led to her gig as a spokesperson for Lancôme, and the branded videos that made her a millionaire, is in her DNA. She didn't come from money. The dutiful daughter of Vietnamese refugees spent her childhood helping her mother and brother scrape together the money for food and shelter in suburban Florida after her father walked away from the family.

"When you asked Michelle at the age of eighteen what she wanted, her only goal in life was to help her mother," her friend Bing told us.

Michelle had learned about hard work and how to run a business early, as a kid answering telephones at her mother's nail salon. Michelle also sold her classmates leftover Easter candy she bought at a discount from Walgreens until she had enough cash to buy herself an iMac. Later she put herself through art school while working as a waitress, continuing to help at the salon, and sleeping on the floor of her mother's apartment. Michelle taught herself HTML so she could design her own website. Same with video production. All self-taught. In fact, until 2016 she was still editing all her videos.

The night before we met, Michelle had been up late sketching again. She often doesn't crawl into bed until two or three in the morning, since the wee hours are the only chance she has these days to work on the art for her free digital comic book series, *Helios: Femina*, a vibrant scrolling web-toon about a futuristic world in which technology has devastated society and given rise to a corrupt government. Her staff of laid-back twenty-somethings told us it's rare that she isn't drawing or doodling, whether on paper or her iPad. She always has a pencil in hand during meetings and around the office. When inspiration strikes, she's ready to get it down.

Michelle greeted us with a warm hug instead of a handshake, and as we took a seat in the wide-open white workspace, the first thing we noticed was that the fresh-faced YouTube star was still wearing her black sketching glove. She was not shooting videos that day, so she had dressed down, sporting wavy magenta locks, a knee-length slouchy khaki sweater, black leggings, and a navy corduroy baseball cap with a giant hamburger on a sesame seed bun embroidered on the front. She easily could have been mistaken for one of the skaters hanging out at the Third Street Promenade, Santa Monica's outdoor mall, which is just a few blocks from her studio. She'd recently returned from a respite in Switzerland and several weeks in Asia, where she had shot videos about her family's roots in Vietnam and met with digital media executives interested in cultivating the vlogger (video blogger) ecosystem in China and Japan. She was splitting her time between ipsy's San Mateo and Santa Monica offices, maintaining a crazy travel schedule of new video shoots and speaking gigs while also going through a phase of reinvention and personal exploration. The self-reflection was prompted in part by one of her biggest failures: losing creative control of Em, the makeup line she developed with L'Oréal USA. She met with us about nine months after the makeup giant sold Em to Michelle and ipsy in October 2015.

She told us that Em, which means "sister" in Vietnamese, had been her biggest misstep because she had not overseen either the marketing or the pricing of the products (a report in *Women's Wear Daily* blamed Em's pricing for the lagging sales).[7] That's changed. A cluster of young women, including two college interns and Michelle's friend and mentee, YouTuber "Jkissa," went back and forth with Michelle as she contemplated stacks and stacks of vibrant purple, blue, yellow, and green eye shadows. Together they "swatched," or brushed the colors onto their wrists, and chatted about the textures and shimmer and whether the products would appeal to Mish's fans. The discussion had the feel of a teenage sleepover. Michelle's red-headed production manager, Flannery Underwood, said that comes straight from Michelle's personality—she always tries to make others feel comfortable. The kindness and serenity she exudes in her videos—in which she shares her life and advises viewers on relationships, family, and even job searches—seem to be genuine, underscored by what her squad calls "that soothing Michelle voice."

And she is passionate about supporting the next generation of beauty bloggers, including Jkissa, the tattooed, silver-haired twenty-two-year-old who was shooting eight new videos that day alone. Next door to the ipsy offices, which feature shelves crammed with hundreds of nail colors and a shoe rack with purple platform sandals and stilettos, sits ipsy Open Studios, a ten-thousand-square-foot top-of-the-line production space that is part of Michelle's efforts to groom a new generation of digital stars. Aspiring beauty bloggers vetted by Michelle's program, which also is called Open Studios, can use the facility for free and take classes in editing, lighting, and coding. She is building a library of original music they can use in their videos to avoid the kind of licensing snags she hit early on. Ten thousand bloggers or "creators" are affiliated with the program, and they reach thirty million women through owned media channels, according to ipsy.

Jkissa told us her idol has become a good friend, guiding her and other YouTubers on the ins and outs of the business, especially how to avoid being exploited. This is Hollywood, after all, and lots of opportunists are angling to make a quick buck off the growing number of aspiring stars. Jkissa, who grew up in Eugene, Oregon, confided that when she was fifteen, she suffered merciless bullying because of her appearance. Michelle's videos became a refuge and ultimately an inspiration for Jkissa. She moved to Los Angeles to follow in Michelle's footsteps and now, instead of shooting videos for her 300,000 fans in her apartment with her husband behind the camera, she was working under professional lighting, with a willing ear just across the breezeway.

"Working with Michelle is literally like a dream come true because she's the one that started it all. When you think of the beauty blogger, you think of her. To be able to work next to her, and to learn from her, is something that I think every beauty blogger has dreamed of, so being able to literally ask her any question is really life changing," Jkissa said as she swabbed off her makeup after a long day of shooting.

Michelle, who said she was trying to slow her frenetic pace and tendency to multi-task, is constantly experimenting with storytelling. She's looking for the platform that will be the next YouTube. Her digital comic book, which she proudly showed us on one of her two mobile phones, features a continuous vertical scroll of haunting images in the Japanese animé style. As she swiped the comic up and down, she pointed out the lack of negative space or boundaries between the illustrations. She said this is the first comic ever laid out that way. She's also obsessed with virtual reality and immersive content, and she had just sent her small team to a virtual reality class to learn more about how to produce in that format.

"I really do believe that the next frontier is media you can interact with, media you can be a part of. You're not watching it, you're interacting with it," she said, predicting a time when people will shop in virtual stores with a 360-degree point of view. Imagine browsing on Amazon but being able to feel like you are walking through the aisles, able to pick up and compare products as if you are in the store. She's also passionate about the future of virtual reality in the classroom, envisioning journeys into history that allow students to fully experience an event they are studying. Those are the kinds of problems she wants to tackle next.

"If you truly want to become an entrepreneur, you have to do it with a sense of conviction, of passion, but most importantly, you [have to] want to solve the problem," she said. "It is a mission for you to solve the problem. Not to solve a problem to add more zeros after your bank account. It's really more to solve the fundamental problem that really, really, truly stems from something that's inside of you."

While we talked, her creative team of four young women was busy testing self-tanners for a future video. They challenge her to keep experimenting. That was why she finally hired a team after ipsy raised $100 million from institutional investors in the fall of 2015. Having done everything herself for so long, she wanted a team that was fearless.

"I've noticed that when I keep myself on my toes, and I remove the limitations of my creativity to the point where it's not even about me becoming the most popular person on the Internet, it's really just about me continuing to trail-blaze content, community strategy development, but most importantly just continuing this authentic sharing conversation I've been developing for so long with my audience," she said. "That's really my job. I'm happy doing that." She smiled as she settled into a comfy spot on the floor around a low coffee table for take-out veggie burgers and fries with her crew. Fresh air from the Pacific a few blocks away breezed in through the open studio doors as Michelle and her team dug into their meal and brainstormed about the next project—the next season's Halloween video. Maybe it will be in virtual reality? Stay tuned.

Fighting Fundraising Hurdles

The story of how this consummate creator leveraged technology into a big-time business is dazzling. But most women embarking on tech startups don't have celebrity on their side and find that starting a high-growth venture and gaining traction is a steep, slow climb. And raising the capital to significantly expand a company is even harder. One of the biggest problems is that women usually do not start with a network like men do, and women are not as willing to tap the connections they do have. Men are five times more likely than women to ask their personal network of family and friends for money, and men are nearly three times more likely to ask their business acquaintances for capital, according to a 2014 report by the Ewing Marion Kauffman Foundation.[8] And that's just seed money—the initial infusion of cash a founder needs to keep going once she's run out of options for funding the business herself. When it comes to raising so-called growth capital, the money she needs to build her company, chances are slim that she'll land it from venture capitalists, who manage tens or hundreds of millions of dollars in institutional money on behalf of their limited partners—corporate pension funds, insurance companies, family trusts, endowments, foundations, and superwealthy individuals. A report from the Arthur M. Blank Center for Entrepreneurship at Babson College concluded that only 2.7 percent of venture-backed companies were run by a female CEO, and those companies captured only $1.5 billion of the $50.8 billion invested from 2011 to 2013.[9] And not much has changed since then. Dr. Candida Brush, the study's lead author, told us in the summer of 2016 that of the four thousand firms then receiving venture capital, 85 percent were led by a male-only executive team.[10] And another study, by academics from MIT, Harvard, and the Wharton School, found that investors tend to favor pitches by male entrepreneurs.[11]

If a female founder is hawking a product or service with a majority-female audience, getting money from venture capitalists is even tougher, because they are overwhelmingly white and male and tend to take calculated risks only on what they know and understand.[12] The dreaded "let me see what my wife thinks" is a refrain all too familiar to these female founders. Unconscious bias can take hold as venture capitalists look for familiar patterns in both the businesses and the personal attributes of the founders, including whether they fit the geeky "two guys in a garage" stereotype that has defined so many Silicon Valley successes of the past.

"It's a mirror-ocracy, not a meritocracy . . . [It] looks at something and it likes what it sees in the mirror. It likes to see itself," proclaimed investor Adam Quinton, founder of Lucas Point Ventures and an outspoken advocate for women, when he was asked why founders who are not white guys struggle to raise capital. Social scientists call his mirror-ocracy "pattern matching." And most of the up-and-coming female tech entrepreneurs don't fit the pattern. Eighty-four percent of the three hundred top woman-led startups are headed by someone without an engineering or computer science degree, according to the 2015 survey Sukhinder Singh Cassidy commissioned and published on *Recode* (see chapter 1).[13]

"Pattern recognition and luck are the key to funding," explained Shadi Mehraein, one of the handful of female venture capitalists in the Valley; she started Rivet Ventures, a $50 million fund to invest in the female consumer market. And Shadi, who worked in some of the best-known venture capital firms, said the personal qualities that make a male entrepreneur stand out, like swagger and being pushy, often are the very same characteristics that can prevent a woman from sealing the deal—which is ironic, because those are exactly the characteristics that a founder needs if she is going to deliver on her vision.

Staring Down Sexism

It's a double standard, for sure—one that Kathryn Minshew, CEO of The Muse, faced on the long road to building the most popular online job search destination for millennials—taking on the giants LinkedIn and Monster. She is a female co-founder of a tech startup who doesn't have a technical degree, although she was a top computer science student who aced the advanced placement exam for computer science when she was in the tenth grade at Thomas Jefferson High, a prestigious math and science magnet school in northern Virginia. For fun she and her friends used to pass notes in class that they'd written in computer programming languages, but she never saw herself going into tech as a career. That was something for guys who lived in their parents' basements. She opted to study French and political science at Duke and planned to join the Foreign Service. With her wide-set green eyes and long brown hair, Kathryn could easily be mistaken for the actress Katie Holmes. You can just imagine the reaction when she first approached a roomful of investors more accustomed to being hit up for funding by guys in hoodies, especially at a time when so few women were bringing on startups. She was almost a curiosity. She had to play down her movie-star looks while coming off as assertive but not bossy, whip-smart but not arrogant. Talk about a tightrope.

"The bar for a woman's behavior to be [deemed] unpleasant

or difficult to work with is very low in Silicon Valley," she told us as we took in The Muse's eighteen thousand square feet of office space in Manhattan's Garment District just a week after the firm moved in. The light-filled space has a whimsical vibe—it features an outdoor-indoor feel with potted plants hanging from the ceiling, a cozy wellness room for nursing mothers and employees making use of the "baby-at-work" policy, which allows parents to bring babies to the office until they are either six months old or crawling, and an accent wall covered in ivy in the sleek cafeteria. But it's not fancy. And Kathryn assured us the company was still running lean and mean. The furniture was just a step up from Ikea, and the founders had to barter for some of the decor, which includes an array of standing desks and sofas and a "quiet room" to appeal to people with a wide variety of work styles. We met at 7 p.m. on a Friday night, and the youthful staff was still unpacking boxes from the move, but they seemed to already feel at home, kicking back with beers and indie music to usher in the weekend. On some Fridays, The Muse has a whiskey tasting, and for a recent epic guacamole competition, the teams got twenty bucks to buy ingredients before going head to head. But the lights were turned off promptly at eight—an effort to remind people to go home and have a life. Culture is key for The Muse, since its business is based on matching ambitious millennials with cool companies that care about their employees. The company leadership has to walk the walk.

Kathryn, who said she always was confident in the business idea and the problem she and her team wanted to solve—to create a more personalized and engaging way for young people to find jobs early in their careers and for companies to recruit them—told us that in the four years after she first started raising money, she grew more aggressive when facing prospective investors who raise sexist or uninformed questions. Instead of arguing she goes into a dead stare, looking across the table with a straight face for one second longer than necessary, and then smoothly steers the conversation to another topic.

"It's a nice boundary because, in general, the risk that somebody will react badly to a young woman telling them off is not worth it. So usually, that sort of stare, [and] silence and chang[ing] the subject, is both very authoritative and a subtly aggressive move without actually making them lose face," she said. "It was just the most natural way of balancing the fact that I needed to show them that I couldn't be pushed around but also didn't want to come off as overly unpleasant."

The technique worked. The Muse secured $16 million in its third round of financing from institutional investors in the spring of 2016, capital that will allow the company to double its workforce to two hundred people. The Muse took over the entire twentieth floor of the new building and may take the floor above in the near future. This was no small feat, given the chill in the market—venture capitalists were pulling back in the last quarter of 2015, just as The Muse founders were going out for funding again. But it helped that The Muse had fifty million people using its site per year by the summer of 2016, its revenue was multiplying fivefold year over year, and it was hitting the benchmarks that proved the business was taking off. Kathryn and her partner and COO, Alex Cavoulacos, both former consultants at McKinsey & Company, the international management consulting firm, raised $28.7 million over five years from firms that included Aspect, which was founded by two women venture capitalists, as well as boldface names like Tyra Banks and Cathie Black, the former chief of Hearst Magazines. Adam Quinton was also an early backer.

"I invested in The Muse in fall 2012," Adam told us. "It was early days for them, but there was an energy, drive, commitment, and professionalism to everything they did that was very impressive. And of course their business seemed like a great idea at a great time and potentially very *big*. So [it was] a very compelling package."

Doing Battle in Black Leather Pants

But for Kathryn, it was a long hard slog, including lots of awkward drinks with self-styled investors who really just wanted a date, and rude exchanges with venture capitalist firms about whether she was being too aggressive in following up. And then there were all the times she and Alex were patronized by investors who said the pair were just "too nice" to run a big company and wanted to know if they understood just how hard starting a business would be. They actually asked why she and her co-founder didn't just go get nice cushy jobs and call it a day.

Even after they moved to Mountain View, California, from New York in January 2012 to participate in Y Combinator, the prestigious twelve-year-old boot camp for startups that incubated Airbnb, Reddit, and Dropbox by investing $120,000 in each company in exchange for an average 7 percent equity, Kathryn and Alex faced lots of sexist comments about the product itself.[14] They initially pitched The Muse, built on the learning from their first business, PYP (Pretty Young Professionals), as the ultimate online destination for young female job seekers looking for both career advice and a peek behind the scenes of companies. Many male investors just couldn't relate to the target audience: young professional women.

"Some actually said, 'I am just worried you will lose all your users when they turn thirty—implying that all of our users would stop being users when they turned thirty because they would be having babies and not care about their careers," Kathryn said. Pitching was exasperating at times. "We got to see a lot more sexism because we were pitching a product about women and their careers."

At one point Kathryn, who had previously worked in Rwanda to implement a national strategic plan for the human papillomavirus vaccine, got so frustrated with dealing with investors who were either dismissive or flirty that she A/B tested the outfits she wore to pitch—just to get more insight into how she could tinker with her presentation and appearance to be more successful. As she tried to persuade investors that the $124 billion job-and-career-search market was a hot prospect, what she learned is that conservative sheath dresses didn't make much impact. But leather pants did. Now she dresses like a warrior for her meetings: an all-black, take-no-prisoners approach. Not only does it make her feel strong, she thinks it bolsters the belief of her audience in her ability to deliver as CEO.

"I dress like a knight to kick somebody's ass. It is mostly a joke to us—but there certainly seems to be something to it," she laughed. "I wear all black to almost every pitch meeting. I look at my calendar every single morning to see whom I'm meeting with and then decide whether I can wear my more-like-tiger outfits or my more chill outfits," she said.

Some investors really were angling for nothing but a date. Kathryn, who was single when she and Alex were first raising money, could tell within minutes if the investor had an ulterior motive for a meeting. She mostly said nothing about those experiences, until 2013, when an acquaintance from the close-knit startup scene broke down in tears as she shared a sickening story about an investor on the make: he was thirty years her senior, promised her the world, and then disappeared after confessing he was in love with her and could no longer invest in her business. The woman had wasted four precious months engaging with the man, who was championing her startup, "saying all the right things," and supposedly was rounding up big money from other investors. The company eventually went under. The woman confided to Kathryn that she thought it was her fault. That bothered Kathryn—so much that she decided to go public with her own stories of would-be investors who had come on to her, including the man who rescheduled their pitch meeting to a bar at his hotel and started asking her personal questions as he leaned into her space.

"I was sitting with my arm in a blocking position because he was so close. I was basically pushing his chest off me. So after not long, I said, 'I have to leave,' and left," she told *Wired*.[15]

She knew telling her story to the world was risky, and many people warned her it could be detrimental. Now that the business is flourishing, and the company estimates one in three millennials visits The Muse, she feels being open about the struggles can only help others.[16] All her experiences taught her a lot about finding the right investors and gave her the fortitude to hang in there for the next generation of women entrepreneurs. Kathryn and Alex even turned down an attractive acquisition offer from a big corporation, opting instead to play the long game. As this book went to press, nearly seven million people were visiting their site each month. As they forged ahead—recruiting like crazy and working late into the night—they zeroed in on their goal of creating the most trusted and beloved career resource, bar none.

"It doesn't happen overnight. I think that's why it is so important for people to share more honest stories about how you build businesses, because it is really, really hard, and there's some luck involved, but very few companies are sort of like a magic—you know: 'We came up with this brilliant idea and then immediately we had millions of users and became an overnight success,'" Kathryn said. "I think that the more companies that are founded by women that go farther, the more it will be obvious to people that don't take women founders seriously that they're missing out on money."

More women *are* jumping in. Since we first met Kathryn and Alex, when The Muse participated in Y Combinator as one of the first female-founded companies accepted by the program, the number of businesses started by women has grown tremendously. An analysis by the open data platform Crunchbase, which crowdsources information about tech startups, revealed that the number of companies with at least one female founder nearly doubled between 2009 and 2014—rising to 18 percent of all companies in its database.[17] A December 2015 report by the National Women's Business Council says women-owned businesses are growing three times faster than their male-owned counterparts.[18] The boom has coincided with an explosion of entrepreneurial activity across the United States since the real estate market crashed in 2008.

But so many more women could be starting businesses, if only they change their mind-set, according to Yunha Kim. Yunha is the co-founder of Locket, a company that transformed the way Android mobile phone users engage with the screen of their device. She told us that, despite the deeply embedded sexism of the tech industry (which she has experienced firsthand), sometimes women stand in their own way.

"I would say that the number-one obstacle to being female in startups or in the tech industry is believing that being female is a disadvantage. Instead of listening to that voice, think more about the fact that there are plenty of other women who have all succeeded," she advised. She practices what she preaches. In 2014 Yunha wrote an essay for *Medium* in which she bravely called out all the things that stink about being a female tech CEO, like being called a bitch for being aggressive and getting asked out by engineers she is recruiting (she even published an e-mail from one especially frisky candidate).[19] But at the same time she challenged female founders to embrace how being different from the average dude in a hoodie can work to their advantage.

"The lesson here is that it is all about how you frame your perspective. If you are committed to believing that it sucks to be a female CEO, you will be right, and it will suck to be you. If you are committed to believing it's awesome to be a female CEO, you will be happier and confident to be you," Yunha wrote about a year into her journey as a startup founder and CEO in the viral post. It featured a photo of her in a t-shirt given to her by one of her high-profile investors, Tyra Banks. The t-shirt says, I'M AN ENTREPRENEUR, BITCH. In other words, deal with it.

No Risk, No Reward

Scrappiness helps too. In 2012, less than a year out of college and with student loans still to pay, Yunha ditched her cushy investment banking job in Manhattan for the chance to become an entrepreneur. Gone were the $35 sushi lunches and swanky address, traded for frozen pizza dinners and bunk beds in a cramped two-bedroom that doubled as office space for a team of five people (plus three dogs and a hamster). Fully aware of the risks, Yunha, like many entrepreneurs we met, started off self-funding, or bootstrapping, the business as she tested her hypothesis. Given the challenge of fund-raising, female founders tend to be especially deliberate about experimenting with prototypes, getting user feedback and making sure a true market exists before they start to invest time and energy in looking for outside money and giving away ownership in the company. Making the leap was the toughest decision of her life, and she left a lot of money on the table. She was a mere sixty days away from her first Wall Street bonus when she decided to build Locket with her best friend from high school.

"I felt like I was letting my parents down because they really liked the job that I had. Just quitting and being unemployed just doesn't sound right," she said about breaking the news to her parents, both college professors living in South Korea. Needless to say, they were worried. But Yunha, who studied economics and Chinese at Duke University, said she knew in her gut that because the eighty million Android phone users in the United States alone were averaging more than a hundred looks at their phones every day, the potential market for advertisers was huge. She started doing research while still working as an analyst and became convinced she could make a better lock screen than what was then available. She figured that, even if she failed, she would probably build the first lock screen company, so taking on the challenge would be worthwhile.

Little did she know the struggles and hard choices were just beginning as she embarked on getting the actual business under way. In her tiny apartment the team worked non-stop for more than a year on a product that reimagined the typical boring blue lock screen on Android phones as an addictive interface for gaming and other branded content.

Once they built the screen, Locket grew quickly, from 25,000 users on its first day on the market to more than 150,000 in a matter of months. But that's when a major flaw in the business model became apparent. Yunha's plan was to reward users with a small cash incentive when they swiped their lock screens, but because the number of users had grown so fast, Locket didn't have enough money to pay users before its advertisers paid their bills. Locket was running out of money fast.

Locket would have to make a move to ensure its survival. Yunha had to quickly and nimbly change course and start over—and that meant laying off the entire team. Yes, the people with whom she had been sharing the apartment. It was one of the worst days of her life. But she didn't give up, mostly because she had accepted that "failing forward" was part of the process and the journey was really just beginning.

So she made another high-stakes bet and moved the operation out to San Francisco and started fund-raising like crazy. Within months she had raised $3.2 million from high-profile venture capital firms. Her backers included the former supermodel Tyra Banks, Great Oaks Venture Capital, and Turner Broadcasting. Yunha brought in new engineers, and the Locket screen went through multiple iterations until they finally brought to market a product that allows users to personalize their lock screen with news feeds and photos. Then they developed a second product, ScreenPop, a social tool that allows users to message with friends from the lock screen. Google named Locket a Best App in 2014.

"At the end of the day, my biggest fear is that later I [will] have regrets. We went through these pivots—I made so many mistakes here at Locket. I don't regret many of them," Yunha told us just a few months before she made headlines with a spectacular exit from the company. Wish, the number-one mobile shopping startup in the United States and Europe, acquired Locket for undisclosed terms in July 2015. When the deal became public knowledge, *TechCrunch* reported other suitors, including Yahoo and Facebook, were also possibly trying to scoop up the company. Yunha's no-risk, no-reward approach clearly paid off.

Now she is working on her second startup, Simple Habit, a "Netflix for meditation," which curates hundreds of five-minute guided meditations led by mindfulness and wellness professionals from around the world. And she has some advice for aspiring female founders who are hoping to build the next Locket or some other amazing new invention: Get out of your own way.

"If you're really passionate about it and you want to do it, just start, instead of thinking about why you shouldn't be doing it—you will have so many reasons why you shouldn't be building a new business, so just go ahead and do it," she advises.

Reality Bites

The harsh reality is that most startups fail.[21] Studies have shown that as many as 75 percent of venture-backed startups never return cash to investors. (And those are the ones that get far enough to seek outside investment.)[22]

"We've romanticized this process. [But] it's really hard work. Brutal. It ends badly for most people. Three-quarters are going to fail," Tom Eisenmann, a professor at the Harvard Business School, said. We were asking him how the B-school has adapted its courses to better prepare students for the rocky road of starting tech companies. Failure is so common that it has become part of the startup vernacular: entrepreneurs are advised to "fail fast, fail often" or "fail forward." Whether you are at a tech conference, perusing postmortems on *Medium*, or hanging out at a co-working space, failure is just part of the Silicon Valley culture.

So you don't have to look far to find cautionary tales. Bea Arthur (no relation to the *Golden Girls* actress), thirty-three, spent five years building one of the first companies to deliver psychotherapy by videochat. Her business, initially called Pretty Padded Room, grew quickly, eventually serving people in thirty states and twenty-three countries. And the telegenic woman whose friends affectionately call her the "Beyoncé of Tech" for her glamorous weave and Pepsodent smile got lots of good publicity along the way, including TV appearances and being a named an "Entrepreneur to Bet On" in 2014 by *Newsweek*. But even though the business grossed more than $600,000 during its lifetime and helped her pay off her grad school loans, it fizzled out when she couldn't keep up with expenses, including paying her staff. One of her lowest days ever came in April 2016 when she posted to her friends on Facebook that she was finally calling it quits after months of trying unsuccessfully to raise more money from investors. She crawled under the covers and spent five weeks crying, drowning her sorrows in burritos and wondering what to do next.

"The startup life is what really made me unhappy this year," she told a sympathetic room of about seventy-five women who had gathered for a day of networking and socializing for female entrepreneurs, journalists, and technologists at the TheLi.st Power Conference in Manhattan a month after Bea told the world she was shutting down her startup. The one-time domestic violence counselor had leaned on this group of professional acquaintances and friends for support throughout all the ups and downs of the previous five years. Now, dressed in strappy high-heeled sandals and a pretty black and white sleeveless dress with a full skirt, she dished onstage along with several other entrepreneurs about what happens after your startup dies. Keeping it real, she said her current focus was losing the fifteen pounds she gained while sitting shiva for her company. Even as she joked about "finding her abs" again, everyone there could sense her grief was still raw. As soon as she stepped off the stage many greeted her with hugs and offers to help.

It had been a wild ride from the very start. Bea started the company in 2011 because she was passionate about making mental health care more accessible and affordable for the average person. Clients would pay $200 per month to subscribe to the service, which would introduce them to an array of therapists specializing in everything from marriage counseling to weight loss. Customers would book monthly packages through the website and conduct their therapy sessions via Skype. In 2013 the bubbly psychotherapist with a master's from Columbia was invited to join the cast of ABC's *Shark Tank*, where she learned the hard way—and on national television—that when you're raising money from investors, you'd better know the business's finances inside and out. Shark Kevin O'Leary mercilessly shredded her after she pitched a $100,000 investment in exchange for 30 percent of the business and stumbled over her revenue projections. She blew the deal. But even as she wiped away tears after being grilled by the panel, O'Leary went a step further and embarked on a Darwinian fable about an island off the coast of South Africa where thousands of hungry seals salivate over the largest sardine population in the world. The first seal in the water will be devoured by great white sharks, he told her, but one seal has to go first so the others won't follow and get eaten. "So, do you know who you are in this story?" he asked Bea rhetorically. "Others will never come in here again without their numbers. They will learn from the blood in the waters you provided." Then he told her he was "out." She prayed the episode would never air.

But it did.

She told us what the aftermath was like: "If I was awake or alone, I was crying after *Shark Tank*. Yes. I'd cry on every subway line in New York City. Nothing can prepare you for that mentally as a person. It was like walking down a dark alley and being like, 'Oh, there's a surprise party,' and then getting jumped and everyone telling you, 'Your mom's a ho.' Think about something you love so much and people are just pooping on it to your face." It had been three years since the taping, and it still upset her to talk about it.

As awful as it was, she kept going and the publicity actually ended up boosting sales. When the rerun of her ill-fated appearance on the show ran about nine months later, she gave in to her boyfriend's offer to whisk her away to the fancy Amanyara Resort in Turks and Caicos for some pampering. There Bea decided she could get used to the pristine white sand beach, turquoise water, and tennis lessons alongside the actor Chris-topher Walken. Maybe all the aggravation was worth it if some day she could retire and soak up the sun in a place like this. She arrived home refreshed and resolved to get a better grasp on the company's finances, and in the summer of 2014 she became the first African American woman whose company was ac-cepted for Y Combinator, the same ultracompetitive startup ac-celerator that had helped her friends who started The Muse.

"They [Y Combinator] told me I got in because I'm a 'by any means necessary' kind of girl. And it's true. I've found a way. It's been all me to make it happen," Bea told us. This was about a year before she closed the company. She was kicking back in thick glasses, no makeup, hair swept up in an African printed scarf, while she worked in her apartment, prepping to speak at the Forbes Women's Conference the next day and writing a *Medium* post about police brutality pegged to the officer filmed while slamming a black teenage girl to the ground at a pool party in McKinney, Texas. The story resonated deeply with Bea, who grew up in the Lone Star State, the first generation child of immigrant parents from Ghana. From the time she was in middle school, her parents worked punishing hours to build their own small business. She inherited their grit.

So she wasn't naive about how challenging it would be to keep growing the business, which she renamed In Your Corner after her experience at Y Combinator. Even with the $120,000 investment from the prestigious program and the opportunity to meet with some of the important investors in Valley, she knew it would be tough. But it was easy to get swept up in the lofty dreams of Startupland, where businesses can be valued in the millions before turning a real profit. With the credibility she gained from participating in Y Combinator, she was able to raise some money in Silicon Valley. But then she hit some rough patches right away. She decided to outsource the engineering to a team of software developers overseas, and it turned out to be a crucial mistake. It was really difficult to train the engineers, and ultimately she lost control of the process and ended up with garbage code that cost the business tens of thousands of dollars. She felt powerless over her own product and felt like she couldn't tell anyone about it.

"Who are you going to tell? Especially as an entrepreneur. Your investors? Your employees? Your friends, who don't really want to hear about it? It's hard when you are kind of visible. This is a very lonely experience," she said, reflecting on how the difficulties actually reinforced the whole mission behind her business.

Despite the drama behind the scenes, In Your Corner continued to match therapists with clients for the next eighteen months—and was still making money, grossing more than $400,000 during 2015. But because the company's expenses were increasing, she was quickly running out of cash. In desperation she borrowed from her family and then took out a loan with a punishing interest rate to keep the payroll going. She would later reflect in a postmortem for *Women@Forbes* that her biggest mistake was that she "began to drink the startup Kool-Aid." In other words, once she had secured the "investors cushion" in the months after Y Combinator, she started burning through it by renting a fancy office she thought she needed, even though most of the small team worked at home, and by rebranding the site with new features that didn't work quite right because she didn't hire the right technical team. "I made unfocused and wasteful decisions. In an effort to mirror the startup stories I'd seen out West, I took wild, risky steps instead of smart strategic ones," she wrote. At the beginning of 2016, she started trying to raise money again. Yet the more she diverted her attention from sales and the daily running of the business, the more she encountered problems.

"The investor thing, it's just such a mind-fuck. All the things I love about my company I wasn't getting to do, not even a little bit," Bea told us over lunch one February afternoon in Manhattan, two months before she closed the company. She told us she was restarting her private practice as a therapist. She had stopped taking a salary from In Your Corner months earlier. She needed to pay her rent.

By the time she called it quits, she had hit rock bottom, blindsided by two of her longtime therapists who decided to go out on their own and compete with her. She felt heartsick that all the energy and love she had put into her startup seemed to vanish in an instant. How would she introduce herself from now on? As the founder of a failed startup?

At the depths of her funk, an invitation to see the hit Broadway show *Hamilton* snapped her out of it. One of her investors, who had become a friend, generously offered to take her to see the hottest show in town a few weeks after she'd announced the shuttering of the business. Bea got goosebumps from Lin-Manuel Miranda's modern retelling of the story of "young, scrappy, and hungry" Alexander Hamilton, an orphan who came from nothing and rose to become one of George Washington's closest advisers and the first Treasury Secretary of the United States. One song from the electrifying hip hop score really got to her: "Wait for It," the soliloquy belted out by the character Aaron Burr, Hamilton's nemesis, as Burr wills himself to keep climbing even as he watches his relentless rival pull ahead of him.

> We rise and we fall
> And we break
> And we make our mistakes
> But if there's a reason I'm still alive
> When so many around me have died
> I'm willing to wait for it[23]

Bea was hit with a wave of inspiration. During the intermission she rushed to the lobby to scribble ideas for her next chapter.

"It really ripped me on fire," she told us a few weeks later and sounded more optimistic than she had in a long time. She was expanding her private practice and parlaying her experience on camera into a new gig hosting a digital video series about women and relationships for VProud.tv (which bills itself as a "video-driven conversation platform, built for women by women"). She also was writing a regular column for *Women@Forbes* and embracing her story as a badge of honor. "This [the startup] was a really tough formula for me to figure out, and I feel like this gave me my skin. And now I'm in this elite group of people who knows what it's like to go through hell and come back from it," Bea said.

Necessity, Mother of Invention

What we found as we peered inside the high-stakes world of startups, following geek girls who are blazing the trail for a new generation of female founders, is that, like Hamilton, they seemed to share an intense drive to build something from the ground up and see it through no matter what. The passion to solve a problem, as Michelle Phan told us, has to be all consuming. You have to be unrelenting. You have to be fearless.

"You can tell the difference between a founder who has to be doing this, who literally cannot imagine doing anything else, [and someone else]. You have to have tenacity and that original sense that 'I am doing the thing I was put on this earth to do'," the secret sauce that makes a successful founder, according to Susan Lyne, founder of BBG Ventures, a fund that invests in women-led consumer tech startups.

Necessity is what drove forty-five-year-old Sheila Lirio

Marcelo to figure out a new way for families to find and hire caregivers. In 2006 she founded what would become the largest online platform to connect families seeking domestic help with nannies, elder care aides, dog walkers, and tutors looking for work. The challenge was ignited by her own struggles with balancing babies and aging parents.

Sheila, an immigrant from the Philippines, was a rising junior at Mount Holyoke, where she was majoring in economics, when she learned she was pregnant with Ryan, her first child. She became a mother and wife at twenty, living off campus with her twenty-one-year-old husband, Ron, whom she had met through a Filipino student organization one weekend at Yale. He, too, was still in school. She was lucky that Ron's first day of spring break coincided with the day she went into labor. That vacation constituted his paternity leave. With no family nearby, they tracked down a day-care center so she could return to class. But when the facility closed, her only choice was to tote her infant into lecture halls and seminars in a baby backpack.[24]

"When he would cry, I'd have to step out of class. There was not a backup option. I couldn't afford it, and there wasn't anything available," she said, recalling their stressful days and sleepless nights as new parents. After graduating from Mount Holyoke and spending a few years working as a consultant and juggling new motherhood, she enrolled at Harvard to pursue both a law degree and an MBA. By the time she started working at the startup Upromise, she and Ron had two boys, and her parents had moved in to help take care of them. But when her father suffered a heart attack as he was carrying their second son Adam up the stairs in their home, their world was turned upside down. Sheila didn't know where to start to arrange care for her children and for her father at the same time. She was working at an Internet company, yet she was literally going through the Yellow Pages in her scramble to line up help. She called a nanny agency, but its rates were way too expensive. She and Ron weren't earning much money and had student loans to repay. In the end a distant relative offered to step in while her father recovered.

"I was just shocked that there weren't marketplaces available for [caregivers]. Because I had researched real estate and started to think about marketplaces, that's when it started to dawn on me. There really should be options here for families. Not just [for] myself but [for] the millions of families that go through it," she told us when we met at the global headquarters of Care.com in Waltham, Massachusetts. She built the company from the ground up over ten years. And then, in a trailblazing step, she took the company public in 2014, ringing the New York Stock Exchange bell on January 24 with her family in tow and celebrating a market value of $554 million.[25] Care.com was the only woman-led tech startup to issue an initial public offering that year and one of a handful ever to do it. By the fall of 2016 Care.com had amassed 12.4 million families and 9.6 million caregivers in nineteen countries who were using its services, including an app to find back-up and date night childcare, tax preparation for household employees, and a new international program to train and place skilled nurses for elder care. And if that wasn't enough validation, in June 2016 Google Capital, a growth equity fund backed by Alphabet Inc. (Nasdaq: GOOGL), made a $46.35 million investment in the company, making Google Capital the largest shareholder in Care.com. It was Google Capital's first-ever investment in a publicly traded company.[26]

Looking back, Sheila had a clear idea of the problem she wanted to solve. She had lived it herself. But before she took the leap, she had to get over her hang-up about being a female executive running a business focused on women. She told us about it as we sat in her windowed office overlooking the Cambridge Reservoir; lining the sill were baby photos of Ryan, now twenty-four and living in Washington, D.C., and Adam, sixteen and a high school junior. At first, she said, she worried that she would not be taken seriously. The self-doubt was magnified when one of her female B-school classmates, by then at a top investment bank, asked her why someone with dual degrees would want to run a "babysitting service." The turning point came when she was weighing a job at a hot mobile media startup versus embarking on her own venture, and one of her mentors, the well-respected venture capitalist David Skok of Matrix Partners, where Sheila had been an entrepreneur-in-residence, told her she had to look in the mirror and decide who she wanted to be.

He asked her: "Are you starting this business because you're in the pain business that is solving consumer problems? Or are in you in the pleasure business because you want to be part of this media company? Who are you?"

The conversation forced her to dig deep. She realized all the challenges she had faced had brought her to that moment and she couldn't let her worries about others' opinions hold her back. She had to stop focusing on what everyone else might think and get to work.

She shared that wisdom with the next generation of women entrepreneurs on a glorious spring evening as we sat among four hundred female founders on the top floor of a posh event space in Tribeca with the late-day sun gleaming in through tall windows. Everyone was staring up at two large screens that displayed large illustrations and mulling a brain teaser led by Sheila, who looked the part of the badass #girlboss in a ruffled black leather cardigan, boots, and her shiny chin-length blowout. As each image flashed, she prompted the crowd: "Do we see robin's eggs in the safety of a nest or do we see a bird taking flight? Do we see a mother taking care of her chicks or the pensive face of a woman?"

It's an exercise geared to challenge women's perceptions of what they see in front of them and how society's expectations can shade those views. You cannot let those opinions hold you back, she said. Instead, you need to seize on those instances and turn them into opportunities, transforming them into what she calls Katniss (as in *The Hunger Games*), or Clark Kent, moments, unleashing your inner superhero when someone underestimates you.

She told her attentive audience that, as an immigrant and a woman of color, she knows a little something about what it is like to feel invisible or discounted. Like the time she ran to the store early in the morning—sans makeup, hair in a ponytail— to grab eggs and soy milk for her family and shocked the cashier by speaking fluent English. Another time, shortly before she took Care.com public, she was about to meet with investors and, out of habit, poured herself a coffee and offered some to everyone else in the room. They assumed she was an assistant from the bank, not the founder, chair, and CEO. She made a conscious choice not to let it ruffle her and politely moved on, concentrating on walking the walk.

"You can be in a room with a group of men who automatically judge that you're probably meek, quiet, or will not make a good point, and [wonder whether] you [are] even following the point," she continued. "I tend to really focus on acumen, staying on point on logic, advocating for myself, being strategic in the moment. I think that turns around those perceptions, and the more we can role-model those things, I think it changes those unconscious biases that I think may not be intended."

In 2007, as she began to build the platform to match caregivers with families and to eventually convince investors of the market opportunity, she held on to what she still calls her

North Star: that what she could sell was much bigger than helping parents. Given the world's aging population, increasing rates of divorce, and falling birthrates, she predicted a massive shortage of caregivers of all kinds. She wanted to tackle senior care, pet sitting, tutoring, and other informal service markets that were disorganized and ripe for professionalization. She saw the global potential very early.

After working at two different Internet startups, she was well aware of the highs and lows of startups and the risks. And as a kid growing up in the Philippines, she remembers her parents working incredibly hard to run their various businesses, which ranged from raising chickens and growing coconuts to trucking and owning restaurants. Her parents had dreamed that their inquisitive and talkative child, who was reading the newspaper at four or five, would be the lawyer in the family, but they eventually came around. And her parents were role models to her in other ways, too, that would shape her life with her husband and fuel her ideas about caregiving responsibilities in her own home. She fondly remembers how her parents evenly split the household duties.

"You're a partner, you're a spouse, you're splitting everything both at work and home. I never questioned that," she said of her parents, who still live with her and Ron today.

Now that she has become a highly visible role model for women in business, her mission has been expanding into the public debate about women, work, and leadership. She advocates for domestic workers, paid parental leave, and greater access to affordable care for children and seniors. The day we visited the office, we ran into Ai-jen Poo, the director of the National Domestic Workers Alliance, who has been collaborating with Sheila and Anne-Marie Slaughter of the New America Foundation on a new initiative to redefine care in the United States as an economic and moral imperative.

In announcing their collaboration at the White House United State of Women Conference in June 2016, Sheila said: "Care impacts everyone at multiple points in their lives and yet it's often dismissed as a 'soft' subject. The reality is that care is a fundamental building block to our economy. Without a strong care system, we won't be able to support the ever-increasing demand for care that we are facing as millennials—the largest workforce population—have children and baby boomers turn sixty-five. Our workplaces and policies do not meet the care needs of American families and without meaningful change, our economy will lose valuable workers as they care for their loved ones." Five thousand women convened at that conference to network and brainstorm about everything from paid leave to wage inequality to entrepreneurship to violence against women.[27]

The first project of the collaboration produced a "Care Index," the first-ever ranking of the availability of quality child care across the United States. Sheila came home from Washington energized. She loved seeing President Obama take the stage and declare that he is a feminist. In the summer of 2016, weeks before the nominating conventions and in the midst of one of the most misogynistic and racially charged presidential races in history, not to mention one with the first female nominee at the top of the ticket, friends started to ask Sheila if she was thinking about going into politics or maybe even a position in the next administration. But she demurred. She had not solved the problem she set out to solve ten years earlier. She predicts it will take ten or twenty more years. "I have this continued North Star vision around the kinds of things we need to keep building," she said. "We're only halfway there."

CHAPTER 3

FUEL THE FIRE
Feminist Financiers

There is a special place in hell for women who don't help each other.

—MADELEINE ALBRIGHT

On a gloomy rainy morning in Greenwich Village, the movers and shakers of New York City's burgeoning tech scene—and the reporters who cover them—had gathered at the Skirball Center at New York University. Getting there was a nightmare. Gridlock clogged the streets. It was wet and cold. Yet there was electric anticipation as the Silicon Alley crowd shook off their umbrellas and hurried to their seats in the amphitheater, awaiting a glimpse of fourteen companies that just might be the next Google or Facebook. Holding court at the back of the sleek auditorium was a stylish brunette in her fifties who was dressed in black and surrounded by a half-dozen female friends, including a commercial real estate investor, a serial entrepreneur, and a startup CFO. She had invited these women to sit with her to view Demo Day for the fall 2015 graduates of Techstars New York. Techstars is the prestigious multi-city boot camp for startups that has produced such darlings as

ClassPass, the boutique gym subscription service, and Plated, the meal delivery company.

As the lights dimmed, and anxious entrepreneurs swallowed their nerves and took the stage, Joanne Wilson smiled like a proud mama. She had been coaching two of the women-led ventures on how to talk to investors who might approach them after the morning's pitches. Her mentees included the founders of Jewelbots, which makes friendship bracelets that teach girls to code, and Flip, an online marketplace that allows people to buy and sell apartment leases. And her pupils were kicking ass on stage. Joanne whispered to us that she'd already written them checks.

No woman may have more skin in the game when it comes to female-led startups than this consummate New Yorker. In 2003 she began musing about contemporary art, restaurants, hip hop, and the importance of date nights with her husband, among other nuggets of life advice, on her well-read *Gotham Gal* blog. Joanne is what's known as an "angel investor," someone who invests her own assets in startups, as opposed to venture capitalists, who invest millions on behalf of institutional partners like pension funds. Joanne has backed more than ninety female-founded companies, and her portfolio continues to grow. They run the gamut and include littleBits, open source circuit modules that teach kids about electronics; HopSkipDrive, the "Uber for kids" founded by three mothers that employs teachers and child-care workers to ferry children to activities; Union Station, an online rental service for bridesmaid dresses; and DailyWorth, the finance education site for women. She goes with her gut. She's looking for high-growth businesses that solve problems she understands, started by women she believes will deliver.

"I'm not investing in something like a dating app, where there's 500,000 of them out there. I'm really interested in things that come across my desk and I think, 'That makes sense and why hasn't anyone built a business around this model?' I've been really lucky. I mean, I think I've had a good nose in who've I've invested in," said the alternative music buff who prides herself on being on the cutting edge of arts and culture and is generous with her opinions.

She always had a nose for business. Her younger sister, Susan Solomon, grinned as she recalled putting on plays for the kids in their Ann Arbor, Michigan, neighborhood, when she was four and Joanne was six. Through all their childhood adventures, Joanne was always front of the house, while Susan felt more comfortable behind the scenes. It was Joanne who went door to door to get all the children together to see the show and even persuaded them to pay admission.

Looking back, Joanne can see that "the dots connect." Early in her career she was the primary breadwinner, overseeing 150 women in the cosmetics department of the massive Macy's in Kings Plaza Shopping Center in Brooklyn, a job she loved. She ultimately rose through the ranks to become a buyer for the department store chain and went on to a succession of business development and executive roles until she decided to step away from retail to focus on family. She was thirty-nine and had two daughters at home. Blogging became a creative outlet as she immersed herself in motherhood and added a third child, a son. Staying home was a blessing in disguise. Those were years in which she made sitting down for dinner a family priority and served on the executive board of her children's school. In 2015 her son was finishing up at Wesleyan, and her two daughters were living in Brooklyn and starting their careers. The routine of making time to connect with each other had evolved into a ritual as important as observing the Jewish holidays. They are a close family, and she still shares all of it with her audience for *Gotham Gal*.

After she turned to featuring interesting female entrepreneurs on the blog every Monday, she unexpectedly found herself becoming a "chick magnet" for ambitious women looking for guidance in their careers and in life. When you meet Gotham Gal in person, you understand why. For all her business prowess and her reputation as a blunt, shrewd negotiator, she is incredibly warm and funny—a true mensch. We liked her as soon as we met her at her office. It's on a tree-lined block on the edge of Manhattan's West Village, in the shadow of the Whitney Museum, steps from the Hudson River to the west and, to the east, some of the trendiest shops in the city.

"She's the first person I call when something great happens, when something bad happens. I pick up the phone, any hour of the day, she answers," said Caren Maio, co-founder of Nestio, a fast-growing platform that "enables residential real estate professionals to communicate in real-time." Caren met us for coffee the morning after she secured $8 million in funding from venture capitalists. It came after a five-week sprint of pitching investors in Silicon Valley just as venture funding was beginning to slow in late 2015. In truth, she had not felt ready to start fund-raising again, but she told us that Joanne, who sits on Nestio's board of directors, gave her the push she needed. She convinced Caren the time was right for raising more cash, that Nestio had "product-market fit" and that Caren needed to occasionally take a break from running the day-to-day operations and think bigger. On the day of one of Caren's first crucial meetings, her tireless champion held her to it.

"She called me that morning and she said, 'You have an amazing company. Think about all that you've built. I've been there from the beginning. Go in there and kick some ass.' She's like my work mom. It was like hearing from your mother, giving you that boost that you needed," Caren said.

We heard the same thing from many of the women the prolific investor has backed through the years. It's clear her commitment to these companies transcends business—it's personal. Erin Newkirk, founder of the e-card app Red Stamp, told us Joanne always texts her on her birthday. Erin, Caren, and Food52's co-founder, Amanda Hesser, spoke of Joanne's welcoming them into her warm apartment to hang on her couch, and her treating them like family, while they vented about the highs and lows of running their businesses. Joanne attends their weddings. Listens to them cry. And even tells them when they need new clothes. "I'm brutally honest. Somebody has to be," she said dryly.

"She'll advise on everything, like 'fire somebody,' or 'this is who you need to bring on' or 'here's what you should say in this e-mail.' Big-picture things and also the minutiae of how to communicate," said Jessica Banks, founder of RockPaperRobot, a Brooklyn studio that produces eye-popping furniture and home accessories based on the principles of physics, like floating tables and robotic chandeliers.

"She's a total mentor in more ways than just business too. I see how she approaches her position, and I also know what challenges she faces, especially with Fred being so visible in the world," Jessica said of Joanne's husband. "There is a tendency for the public to almost [make a judgment] like, 'Oh, this is the wife of Fred.' But knowing their relationship, I'm, like, 'Other way around.'"

Fred Wilson is co-founder of the storied Union Square Ventures, named by CB Insights in 2016 as the one of the top twenty venture capitalists worldwide for his foresight in backing Twitter, Etsy, Zynga, and Tumblr, among others.[1] He also blogs. Joanne and Fred met as college students in Boston in the 1980s and have been married for more than two decades. And it was Fred who ultimately encouraged Joanne to focus on investing in women. The inspiration came after she had a fateful breakfast with Rachael Chong, the founder of CatchAFire (the online marketplace that matches volunteer-minded people with non-profits that need their professional skills), who at the time had only male investors and really wanted a woman's perspective. She hastily asked Joanne to be her mentor as they raced to catch a cab after their meal. In her no-nonsense style, Joanne brushed off the mentor idea and in the moment threw out a counteroffer to invest.

"I remember going home [after breakfast] and thinking about all of these things, and really it was my husband who said [later], 'You know, you talk to all these women. You understand their businesses. You can connect with them on a level other people can't," Joanne recalled.

The evolution of that vision was on full display on a cool morning in April 2016, when we ascended to the top of One World Trade Center in lower Manhattan. As the sleek elevator doors opened on a loft-like space with dramatic 360-degree views of the city and clusters of chic leather chairs and low tables adorned with fresh flowers, we also got a window into Joanne's next act. We had arrived at the Women's Entrepreneur Festival, or WeFest, her signature event for introducing ambitious women to each other. From the menu of motivational talks to the giant signage that commanded us to CONNECT AND BE HEARD, it felt like the sky was the limit for the crowd of founders and investors from the around the country. Care.com's Sheila Marcelo had given the inspiring keynote the night before. The idea was to put on the ultimate networking event for enterprising women with the feel of a music festival where they could easily move in and out of the panels on fund-raising, storytelling, and hiring and, most important, enjoy a comfortable place to schmooze at length. As she kicked off the day, Joanne entreated the crowd to lift each other up and, to resounding applause, proclaimed the rise of female entrepreneurship as "the new women's lib." As soon as she stepped off the stage, the line to talk to her grew long. Attendees from several generations waited patiently to introduce themselves and pitch their ideas to their urbane hostess, who was looking youthful and downtown in trademark black, silver hoops, cropped leather jacket, platform booties, and her razor-sharp bob.

As we wandered into one of the packed sessions, Joanne marveled, "I don't think we could have gotten four hundred women in a room like this six years ago. This is definitely a movement."

Yet it is a movement that cannot flourish without sustained access to cash and a strong network to open doors. Joanne's role as an angel is strategic. For more than half the founders she's backed, she's been the first investor, dictating the deal terms while bringing the coaching and contacts these new businesses need. But once the companies begin to grow and prove out their ideas, their need for cash expands exponentially—and fast.

"I'm not a VC because I'm an angel. I'm never going to be the person to write that big check," she said. "But I probably am your biggest champion and consigliere. And everyone needs one."

Those really big checks come from powerful venture capital firms in hopes of backing the next billion-dollar tech giant.

No matter who you are, male or female, trying to raise money from venture capital firms is just plain hard.

"For every 100 business plans that come to a venture capital firm for funding, usually only 10 or so get a serious look, and only one ends up being funded," according to the National Venture Capital Association.[2] But securing funding has been especially tough for women and people of color. For example, only 0.2 percent of all venture deals from 2012 to 2014 went to startups founded by black women (24 out of 10,238), according to a report by the nonprofit digitalundivided.[3] A big reason is venture capital firms still employ few female decision makers (and people of color), and they are especially scarce in the most influential offices, which are clustered in a rather boring stretch of office parks on the famous Sand Hill Road in Menlo Park, California.

And the number of women with real power—those who become general partners—is tiny. The 2014 Diana Project, the research consortium at Babson College that is investigating women's access to growth capital, found that only 8.5 percent of general partners in U.S. venture capital firms were women, a drop from 10 percent in 1999.[4] The 2016 CrunchBase Women in Venture report on the top one hundred venture capital firms put that number at 7 percent.[5] The lack of women, black, and Latino investors with influence has been a major problem for underrepresented business owners trying to pitch their ideas and themselves to the other side of the table, which is populated overwhelmingly by white male Ivy Leaguers. Historically, investors take a chance on entrepreneurs with whom they can relate most closely. Candida Brush, the Babson professor, told us by e-mail that when venture capital firms have a woman partner, they are 40 percent more likely to invest in a startup with a woman on the leadership team.[6]

"Let's face it: men weren't interested in building a better breast pump for nursing. That's not very interesting to them," said Kay Koplovitz, founder of USA Networks and later cofounder of Springboard, the first business accelerator for women in tech.

In its seventeen-year history the program, which trains female entrepreneurs to build megabusinesses, has graduated the heads of thirteen companies that went on to issue initial public offerings, including Zipcar, the company that disrupted the rental car business, and MinuteClinic, the venture that put walk-in health care inside CVS and Target.

"Not every woman starts a cookie-making business, although there's nothing wrong with cookies. The perception [among venture capitalists] was that women would only be in these sorts of domestic or consumer product categories, and we're proving every day that women are disruptors in technology and life science," said Kay, who also founded the Sci-Fi Channel (later known as SyFy). She remembers what it was like to be one of only a few women when she started out in the business world in the 1969, going on to be the first woman to helm a cable network in 1977.[7] Those were days when advancing your career was often a zero-sum game because a company could have only one token woman at the top. She's delighted to see that dynamic changing in recent years as the sisterhood has emerged in tech and entrepreneurship.

At the same time fighting stereotypes is difficult, and so is breaking into the fraternity of venture finance—yet the chummy nature of this work is exactly how deals get done. In many ways it's a lot like dating. Keval Desai told us that the dance that precedes the marriage of an investor and entrepreneur necessitates close contact, so they can really get to know each other. That can be awkward when parties are of the opposite sex.

"Investors and entrepreneurs spend a lot of time together— lunch, dinner, call at 10 p.m. There are all these interpersonal things that happen between an investor and a founder. If it's a man and a woman, you're not going to get a call for a drink or at 10 p.m. at night to discuss a hiring plan or other question. Before you make the investment, if you had a male-male relationship, it would be easier," he said. "To solve for that, you need more women VC's. That will lead to more women getting funded."

Meet the "Girls' Club" of Venture Capital

With this in mind we were curious to meet the small tribe of women who work inside some of the mostly male venture capital firms. In the first weeks of 2016 we found ourselves in the luxe hub of Silicon Valley's deal makers and dreamers, a private club in downtown San Francisco called the Battery. The posh leather couches, fancy wine list, and cast of casually dressed billionaires feels like a scene out of HBO's *Silicon Valley*. We were invited into this exclusive den by the decidedly cool Jenny Lefcourt, one of three general partners in the venture capital firm Freestyle Capital, co-founded by two men. She introduced us to some of her friends and wingwomen, like Jenny Fielding, the managing director of Techstars; Maveron's Rebecca Kaden; Steph Palmeri, a partner at SoftTech VC; Google's Aditi Maliwal; and Tania Binder, a high-profile executive recruiter for Spencer Stuart. Also dropping by to say hello were Sarah Kunst, founder of the fitness app Proday and an outspoken advocate for diversity in tech; Kristen Koh Goldstein, founder of HireAthena; Rachel Sheinbein, an angel investor and co-founder of Makeda Capital; investor Shelley Collins Kapoor; and the millennial CEO of the nascent messaging platform On Second Thought, Maci Peterson. We felt like we'd stumbled into a secret club of superwomen. Joanne Wilson had introduced us to Jenny. She and Jenny sit on the board of Nestio, Caren Maio's company, and Freestyle Capital had led Nestio's very first round of fund-raising. What we saw is that this world is all about who you know. This is an especially important point for the women navigating the fraternity of Silicon Valley.

Jenny, who always gets up at dawn to catch her barre class and answer e-mail before her three kids wake up, co-founded the first online wedding gift registry, WeddingChannel.com. It was acquired in 2006 by XO Group for $90 million and became part of the publicly traded company the Knot (XOXO). She had dropped out of Stanford Business School to start the wedding registry with her classmate Jessica Herrin (who went on to found Stella & Dot) after they landed a term sheet (commitment of funding) from the prestigious Kleiner Perkins VC firm—the one later sued by Ellen Pao. Jenny knows what it is like to be an early innovator—and to raise capital in a man's world. Back in the late 1990s, though, being a woman didn't hold her back, she said.

"The best thing was, we didn't even think about our gender for a moment when we were going through it, whereas I feel like now that would be almost impossible," she observed.

Ironically, on the January night we got together, the "Elephant in the Valley," the depressing survey on the state of women in Silicon Valley, was making news, revealing what these women already knew: that sexism and unconscious bias is commonplace in the industry (see chapter 1).[8] Many of the women nibbling on appetizers and exchanging business cards that evening run in the same small social circle as Pao, the former venture capitalist whose gender discrimination lawsuit against Kleiner Perkins ended in defeat but exposed how white and male tech finance had become (for more about the suit, see chapter 1). Even so, as we sipped red wine and chatted with this stylish group of confident, diverse women, many seemed bullish about the future in the Valley and especially about the power of their own network in an industry in which success hinges on who you know.

"There's a very, very strong group of incredibly smart women, and they gravitate to each other. They help each other. I think they are more transparent with each other than a lot of men are," said thirty-one-year-old Rebecca Kaden, the lone female general partner at Maveron, the venture firm founded by Starbucks CEO Howard Schultz that invests in consumer-technology businesses.

Rebecca estimates that three generations of women venture capitalists are now populating this exclusive world of deal makers and talent scouts. And they all seem to know each other. Rebecca, who grew up in New York City with three older brothers, told us that the younger venture capitalists like her often seek advice from the women who came before them—on everything from deal flow to marriage and kids. It can be a lonely job, with many days on the road. When they can swing it, her tight-knit group of millennial friends gets together for dinners and drinks downtown. The Battery is a popular place. But they also make efforts to trek out to the 'burbs closer to Silicon Valley for the chance to socialize with their more seasoned counterparts, who are now raising families while balancing high-powered jobs.

"I think they [women] are more willing to talk about compensation. Be an open book about career path. About how their firm is structured. About problems they are facing at the firm," the Harvard grad and Stanford MBA told us.

Almost every woman venture capitalist we interviewed, whether she worked in Silicon Valley, LA's Silicon Beach, or New York's Silicon Alley, talked up the new opportunities to replicate the kind of organic networking that has always been a mainstay for men, whether on hunting junkets or deep-sea fishing trips or on the golf course. In April 2016 Shanna Tellerman, the serial entrepreneur who was also an investing partner at Google Ventures (a division of Alphabet, Google's holding company, which invests in startups), invited more than fifty of the most influential women investors and founders to an exclusive retreat in Park City, Utah, during the city's new Thin Air Innovation Festival, a three-day ski fest for thought leaders in tech.[9] Shanna was working on her second startup, Modsy, a futuristic take on home design that marries three-dimensional imaging and e-commerce in an immersive online platform. She said it was magical to gather women from around the country, some of whom didn't know each other well, and set them up with unstructured time amid the rugged snow-capped peaks to just hang out.

Joanna McFarland, a co-founder of HopSkipDrive, the driving service for kids, took time off from her crazy schedule of running her startup to fly to Utah, and said it felt strange to ease into such a loose agenda. But that was the point, she said: "We're all here, we're in Park City, we're skiing, and we all felt kind of guilty because we were skiing on a Thursday. [We felt] like 'I should be working.' And then we realized that was the point of the whole retreat . . . to get to meet other women and share experiences. We were, like, 'Men go on golf outings all the time and nobody feels guilty about it. That's work.' We were all, like, 'We're working right now.' "

Discussions that started that weekend on ski lifts, at wine tastings, and while listening to live music continued off the slopes and long after they left the ski lodge and returned to reality. They're doing deals together. They are continuing to make introductions and meet each other, said Shanna, who plans to continue the Pinnacle Project next year.

"I felt like you cannot just leapfrog multiple steps, like what guys have—the old boys' network. We haven't had the equivalent for women. How do you build an old boys club? It has to be friendships. It has to be a foundation of actually knowing one another and then connecting to do business together," Shanna told us.

More than twenty-five years ago, that kind of bond fostered a deep friendship between Aspect Ventures co-founders Theresia Gouw and Jennifer Fonstad, who met in their twenties at the management consulting firm Bain & Company, where they worked on a four-person team that forecast beer production for Anheuser-Busch. Their closeness would only grow as they went on to navigate motherhood and high-powered careers in a man's world.

"She has four kids. I have two kids. We were always the ones [who] would have coffee or lunch, and we would talk business at lunch, but we would talk about the whole everything. What's it like to go tell all of your male partners that you're having a baby? How do you figure out the whole balancing of work-life?" Theresia said when we met her on a bone-chilling February afternoon in Manhattan.

In 2014 the two friends began Aspect Ventures, one of the first and most prominent venture capital firms founded by women, and have emerged as high-profile role models.

"We're just going out there and we're doing it. We've embraced being very visible female leaders in tech investing, and the result has been that our portfolio has 60 percent all-male founding teams, but 40 percent with [a] female founder or cofounder. That looks more like the real world, and it is about double what it is in most venture capital portfolios," Theresia said.

Running her own fund and living the storied Silicon Valley life couldn't be further from Theresia's childhood as the daughter of ethnic Chinese immigrants who had fled oppression and unrest in Jakarta for a tiny town in western New York in the 1970s. Middleport is just outside Buffalo, near the hometown of Oklahoma City bomber Timothy McVeigh, who went to a neighboring high school. The two teens worked at the same Burger King at the same time. It was a community where few kids left home for college. Theresia opted for Brown and was only the second student from her town to attend in a century. Her parents wanted her to be a doctor. But she gravitated to engineering, and after her stint at Bain, she went to Stanford for business school, then became a founding VP of Release Software, a successful business that helped software companies manage digital rights and payments. She and Jennifer Fonstad reunited when Draper Fisher Jurvetson (DFJ), the venture capital firm where Jennifer worked, invested in Theresia's company, and they unexpectedly ran into each other in the boardroom.

Theresia, forty-five, had been a partner at Accel Partners for fifteen years, earning kudos for high-stakes bets, including investing early in the publicly traded real estate giant Trulia. Jennifer, a Harvard Business School grad, spent seventeen years as a partner and managing director at DFJ, where she oversaw a range of investments in health-care tech and went on to run funds in Israel and Vietnam. She told us that what helped her thrive as one of the only women in her firm for all those years was putting gender aside and simply approaching her work as a problem that needed a solution or a question that needed an answer. That gave her the natural impetus speak up in partner or board meetings.

"I think that that enabled me not to think about what I should or shouldn't be doing or feeling self-conscious. It was neither overconfidence [n]or underconfidence. It was just focusing on the problems that needed to be solved. That, I think, carried me through that type of environment," Jennifer told us.

As she and Theresia discussed the next chapter of their careers during three lunches overlooking the peaceful Rodin sculpture garden on Stanford's campus, they hatched their plan to start Aspect. They chatted about how much they missed rolling up their sleeves and working with young companies, meaningful experiences that had faded away as their firms grew and they moved up to management roles. Jennifer encouraged Theresia to get involved with Broadway Angels, the angel group she co-founded in 2010 that brought together some of the highest-profile and most well-respected female power brokers in the Valley—top tech executives and alumnae of prestigious venture capital funds—to scout startup prospects. Theresia, who was named to *Forbes*'s Midas List of best tech investors in 2016 for the fifth time, thought it over and eventually joined

Broadway. But the idea of starting something all their own from scratch and running it had incredible appeal to both women. Of course, they knew they would be leading by example by starting a venture capital firm focused on tech. But they were really moved by the market opportunity to work with start-ups that were raising their first infusion of institutional cash. They decided to go for it. And it just so happened that when they announced their partnership in February 2014, the conversation in the national media about women in tech was just heating up.

"It was very clear to us when we started to talk to people about what we're doing, that there were a lot of things going on with women in tech. It had kind of been bubbling, as you know, for a while, but something about 2014, and then into the beginning of 2015, it went from being a sidebar conversation to being a mainstream conversation with men and women," Theresia explained.

They raised $150 million from institutional investors to start their first fund and shortly thereafter celebrated the $250 million acquisition of their investee, woman-led LearnVest, by the insurance company Northwestern Mutual.[10] They've invested in the beauty subscription company Birchbox and in The Muse, companies many male investors really did not understand at first. Now more than ever, both believe diverse teams make for smart investments.

"Think about it logically. How is it if you're not employing 50 percent of the potential brain power and talent in the world into your company, how can that not be bad for business? Then there's all the public data that shows how it actually is good for business . . . [The] return on equity [of public companies with diverse boards] is 15 to 20 percent better than those that have no diversity," Theresia noted.

Like many of the feminist financiers we met, the founders

of Aspect also believe that opportunities will not open for female innovators unless men are part of the conversation. "Women in tech is not a women's problem. It is a people's problem. It cannot be solved by women alone. It cannot be solved by men alone," said investor Adam Quinton, who often speaks at conferences about loading his portfolio with women-led companies because he wants to make money.

Back in Manhattan, circulating among the energetic crowd at Joanne Wilson's WeFest was a small contingent of southern women from Chattanooga, Tennessee, who had done just that—successfully persuaded some of the most prominent male civic and business leaders in their close-knit community that betting on women-led businesses in the region was worth their while—and that the local women could be shrewd investors.

Badass Investors beyond Silicon Valley

At first glance you might not think of Chattanooga, the gateway to the Deep South, with its pre–Civil War traditions, debutantes, and genteel way of life, as a hotbed of high-tech innovation—or feminism. But as we learned, when we got to know some of the women who make that city run, Chattanooga has always been a place for big ideas. The mid-size city, known for its entrepreneurial roots—the Coca-Cola bottling empire was started there in 1899—has been going through a rebirth. In 2010 the city once known as the "Dynamo of Dixie," for the myriad big businesses begun along the banks of the Tennessee River, was attracting tech entrepreneurs with its superfast broadband, which has been hailed as the fastest Internet connection in the country.[11] But all the startups were run by men.

"We kept getting together and talking with groups of women about, you know, 'There's a lot of cool things happening in Chattanooga around entrepreneurship,' but we were really worried we just weren't seeing women. We weren't seeing women on the stages, definitely not in the audiences or as investors," recalled Kristina Montague, managing partner of the JumpFund, the female-run firm she co-founded in 2014 that invests in cutting-edge businesses founded by women across the Southeast. The innovations the fund has infused with cash range from Feetz, a company that makes custom 3-D–printed shoes for hard-to-fit feet, to Dynepic, which "focuses on building the Internet of Toys®," according to its website, to Partpic, which provides an image search technology for replacement parts for industrial machines. We heard the story of how the JumpFund came about, and how Kristina and her partners eventually began to collaborate with their male counterparts, as the fortysomething mother of two showed us around the city's new Innovation District in her SUV one spring afternoon.

At every turn, new and old collide in this city in transition. Chattanooga has a CrossFit, a Lululemon, an artisanal cheese shop, and lots of brightly colored murals and contemporary sculptures in the shadow of boarded-up and abandoned warehouses and factories, relics of the city's industrial past. Kristina, whose husband's great-great-great-grandfather was John Thomas "JT" Lupton, one of the original Coca-Cola bottlers, was working as an assistant dean of the business school at the University of Tennessee when the city made its initial attempts to attract tech startups. She and a few friends, including Shelley Prevost, a psychotherapist who was vetting companies for one of the city's first venture capital firms, Lamp Post Group, decided Chattanooga needed to bring in more women. They were convinced the only way to do it was to personally bankroll a fund they could use to back female entrepreneurs.

But in 2013, when they first approached some of the local male investors with their idea, they weren't exactly encouraged. The guys at the Chattanooga Renaissance Fund (CRF) told them female tech entrepreneurs were hard to find, and, frankly, the men didn't think Chattanooga women, many of whom were extremely active in local charities, would be interested in investing. "I think we all, or at least I did, just underestimated how many potential woman investors really were out there," reflected David Belitz, a CRF general partner when we spoke with him. As Kristina tells it, she and her friends took up the challenge and teamed up with women they knew through local banks, the PTA, country clubs, and charitable boards and set out to raise the cash and find companies for their portfolio on their own. In a matter of months their social connections and business contacts were talking up the JumpFund at book clubs, on the way to yoga class, and while picking up their children at Chattanooga's exclusive private schools.

"When we were able to raise a $2.5 million fund within six months from 98 percent Chattanooga women, that opened some eyes," Kristina boasted with a smile. The really delicious part is that the male investors in town now look to Kristina and her group to find potential deals, and they've even co-invested and share office space. And in the fall of 2016, the JumpFund announced it would be raising a second $5 million to $7 million fund to deploy even more capital to women-led ventures.

"There are badass women in Chattanooga and they own it. They don't apologize for it, they don't hide from it, they own it. And it's not in an arrogant or snotty way, it's just they are who they are, and I love that," said Cathy Boettner, the fifty-year-old former president of the local plastics manufacturer Cleveland Tubing and one of the original fifty-four limited partners in the JumpFund.

"As I tell my children, 'Never dim your light for anyone. God gave it to you to shine it on whoever you can shine it on, and you should do that.' And that's what I love about Chattanooga women," she said as we sought to learn more about the new and growing class of active investors across the United States that is helping to finance women-led businesses and encouraging geek girls everywhere.

Their numbers are still tiny. But, according to the Center for Venture Research at the University of New Hampshire, the number of women angel investors, about eighty thousand in the United States, jumped from just 5 percent of all angels in 2004 to 25 percent by 2015.[12] Not everyone can pay to play. To participate, one must be accredited, which under federal law means they must earn an individual income of $200,000 per year or $300,000 jointly with a spouse or have a net worth exceeding $1 million either individually or jointly with a spouse.[13]

The women of the JumpFund insisted on showing us some southern hospitality while we were in town. At a leisurely get-together that started with deviled eggs, the local delicacy; fried pickles(!); and lots of white wine and laughter at one of the new farm-to-table restaurants, we chatted with Kristina and Shelley and a dozen other women who had decided to invest at least $30,000 each in the first fund. We immediately understood why the well-dressed women at the long table, who ranged in age from their early forties to their eighties, have been described as real-life steel magnolias.

Among them were Mary Kilbride, a CPA by training who has spent thirty years as a volunteer and serves on six nonprofit boards, including the Chattanooga Women's Fund, which successfully lobbied Tennessee lawmakers to strengthen sex trafficking laws; Molly Hussey, the curly-haired mother of two who is a talented painter and advocate for the arts; Ashlee Patten, fourth-generation Chattanoogan and successful wealth manager who specializes in working with women; M. J. Levine, a Wellesley alum and outspoken community leader; Andrea Crouch, a former top marketing executive and investor in a

chain of blow-dry bars; and JoAnn Yates, a generous philan-
thropist who grew up in the city during the Depression and
now supports many foundations, including the city's first
STEM charter school for girls. As they talked up the eighteen
investments in their portfolio, they clearly were moved by the
ingenuity behind the businesses. And while the idea of helping other women is attractive, their involvement is not charity.
They expect a serious financial return.

"I guess it isn't always polite to say, but I enjoy making
money," said JoAnn, one of the more seasoned women in the
group, settling into a comfortable wing chair in the fund's well-
appointed office. She was surrounded by old photos of the
Lupton family and a framed map of the United States pinned
with the locations of the original Coca-Cola bottling plants.
JoAnn was tastefully dressed in a cream-colored cardigan,
matching slacks, striped silk blouse, flats, and a sparkly diamond
ring.

"I just plainly enjoy seeing things grow. I don't live frugally,
but I don't live frivolously. I like to see these things compound-
ing," she told us in her gentle Tennessee drawl. JoAnn said she
had always enjoyed talking business with her late husband, a
successful textile manufacturer, and reading business magazines. When Chattanooga got its first brokerage firm back in
the day, she often wandered in to watch the stock ticker.

"Sometimes, when the market is low, I make a joke about, 'I
go shopping.' I'm thinking, 'I'll get this and hold it, and then I
can give it away some time later at this big profit,'" she said,
describing how she became more assertive with her finances
through the years.

The JumpFund's seven managing partners sought a crash
course in investing from one of most active angel networks focused on women in the country, Golden Seeds. It coached them

on how to find deals, aka "deal flow," how to assess business models and markets, how to research the company's founders and clients (due diligence), and how to negotiate deal terms and agree on the value of a company, among other essential lessons. Golden Seeds, a group of three hundred women and men, invests in high-growth woman-led businesses and was one of the first firms to look for early opportunities to invest in women. When Golden Seeds was first conceived in 2004, women looking to finance their businesses had trouble finding outside investors (see chapter 1), and very few were able to secure loans from banks.

As Loretta McCarthy, managing partner and an original member of the New York–based group that syndicates deals through its Boston, Silicon Valley, Southern California, and Texas chapters, explained, "It was distressing to realize that women were starting businesses in large numbers but were simply not getting funding. We really did feel that it was women who were going to have to step up and lead the way and just start writing checks." And by 2004 they finally had the means to do it. The longtime marketing executive and her baby boomer peers by then had twenty-five or more years of solid career experience in banking, law, medicine, and other high-paying professions, and they had built bank accounts that allowed them the freedom to start investing.

"There really was such a powerful recognition that this is something that we are in a position to do, because we have this capital and the skills and the networks to do it, and that, it seemed to us, . . . the earliest members at Golden Seeds, . . . it was really a mandate [to] do this. We had operating experience, we know how to run businesses, we knew how to attract teams. We had done all of this in our prior careers. It was not unfamiliar to think of mounting a large organization to tackle an issue that we cared about," noted Loretta, whose résumé includes stints as executive vice president and chief marketing officer for OppenheimerFunds and vice president of marketing for American Express.

Since Golden Seeds began investing more than a decade ago, more than a dozen other angel groups focused on women have bubbled up across the nation, from San Diego to Kansas City to Madison, Wisconsin. Some, including Astia Angels, 37 Angels, Broadway Angels, and Plum Alley Investments, offer formal in-person showcases for investors. Others, like Portfolia, curate investing opportunities online. According to the Angel Capital Association (ACA), a national organization of accredited angel investors, more women are joining angel groups and increasingly are investing alongside their male counterparts. And that bodes well for female entrepreneurs. At the ACA's 2016 national conference, 30 percent of the attendees were women, and they were truly fueling the earliest stages of innovation.

"Angels are funding 90 percent of the outside equity for startups. So it's not coming from venture capital, it's not coming from banks or anything like that. It's coming from angels," stressed Marianne Hudson, executive director of the ACA.

Changing the Face of Angel Investing

One person who has made it her mission to cultivate all these new female angels and ensure they are not all straight white women is Natalia Oberti Noguera. The outgoing self-described "cis" (not trans) queer Latina is the Brooklyn-based founder of Pipeline Angels. Thirty-three-year-old Natalia is "changing the face of angel investing" by offering boot camps for diverse people who identify as women and non-binary femme (neither female or male/third gender) to learn how to invest in for-profit social enterprises led by equally diverse founders. Since

Pipeline opened in 2011, it has graduated more than two hundred angels and deployed more than $2 million to startups, including PhilanTech, which writes grant management software for non-profits; DogPatch Technology, which created the Flower app, a mobile platform for caregivers to use to manage doctor appointments, nursing, and therapy for loved ones; and Blendoor, maker of software that helps companies remove bias from the process of screening résumés.

Both of us went through the Pipeline program, Heather in 2013 in New York and Sam in San Francisco in 2015, and our experiences were, in part, what inspired us to write this book. Along with the other women in our classes, we spent about six months being schooled on deal making (often by Golden Seeds mentors), screening dozens of companies in what Heather described to her children as *"Shark Tank* for women," and ultimately investing $5,000 each in a startup. And, like many women in our classes, we never really thought of ourselves as investors. At first it was intimidating on many levels—the risk and also the knowledge gap for those of us who had no experience in finance or entrepreneurship or tech. Natalia seeks out women with a wide range of backgrounds: from attorneys to doctors to journalists, even a baker and a jewelry designer, who want to learn together and invest as a group. Some women have taken time off to raise families and are looking to rejoin the working world. Others are entrepreneurs. And there are those who are retired and eager for a new chapter and a way to apply their professional skills.

Natalia, who often punctuates her points with her favorite Twitter hashtags, such as #languagematters, is known for her passion for social justice, pushing the boundaries of society's entrenched gender norms and advocating tirelessly for female entrepreneurs. During her childhood the Yale alumna, whose father worked for the United Nations, moved every couple of years throughout Central and South America, including stints in Ecuador, Honduras, Colombia, and the Dominican Republic. She was entrepreneurial from a young age but didn't realize it until she was much older. She and her mother and sister once started making pizzas in their apartment kitchen in Bogotá and sold them to their neighbors. Natalia remembers being eight or nine years old and designing the flyers and sliding them under doors around their complex, her version of selling Girl Scout cookies. But Natalia did not connect that experience to the idea of one day owning a business herself until she got to Yale, where she started a college magazine. After college she got involved in social entrepreneurship and started a network for women who were starting for-profit ventures focused on changing the world. She learned that women had a hard time raising capital to build their businesses. People expected them to be doing charitable work and offered to make donations but backed away when they realized the women wanted to make money. This was happening even as male-run companies with a social mission, such as TOMS shoes and Warby Parker eyeglasses, were making headlines with successful rounds of fund-raising. She realized that by recruiting wealthy women as investors, she might be able to help.

"I saw how there were so many high-net-worth women out there making a positive impact with their money through philanthropy, through charity, through donations, and so I decided that I wanted to create a bridge between philanthropy into angel investing and share with these same high-net-worth women that they could make a positive impact with their money," she told us. As Natalia started her boot camps for women in 2011, she realized that the female investors, too, needed to shift their mind-sets. As we experienced when we participated in the program, some of our cohorts were more accustomed to giving time and money to charitable causes and sometimes undervalued the other assets they could bring to helping to grow businesses.

"One of my favorite definitions of angel investing is that it's smart money. Meaning that it's not just the financial capital, it's the human capital and it's the social capital. So, you know, what sort of connections and net worth can an angel provide to an entrepreneur? What sort of skills can an entrepreneur leverage from an angel?" Natalia said. "I often say that a lot of women are already doing two of those three. It's called volunteering. It's called community service. It's about that third, the financial capital, being, 'Hey, actually have some skin in the game.'"

Shining a Spotlight on Diverse Founders

As advocates like Natalia work to diversify the rarified investment world, another outlier is also making waves. Arlan Hamilton didn't start out in tech or finance. Her journey to becoming a feminist financier was sprinkled with more than a little stardust. She came up through the music industry, touring and working on shows with stars like CeeLo Green, Pharrell, Justin Timberlake, Toni Braxton, and Jason Derulo as she wrangled lighting technicians, backup dancers, and costume designers behind the scenes. Now the former tour manager is trying to draw attention to female, black, Latino, and LGBTQ entrepreneurs by showcasing them to Silicon Valley royalty with her new "micro-VC" fund, aptly named Backstage Capital. The tall earnest young woman with the eyes of an old soul emerged as an evangelist for underrepresented CEOs in late 2015. And establishment investors have been taking notice.

"What I believe in and love about her is that she is getting up and saying something that insiders are not willing to say," said Jocelyn Goldfein, one of the first investors in Backstage and a former director of engineering at Facebook.

Arlan, who is both African American and gay, aims to raise up to $10 million to fund one hundred companies founded by underrepresented CEOs in the next few years. By November 2016, she had secured enough capital to make twenty investments and to pay herself and a small staff. Several well-known investors have put money in the fund, including Marc Andreessen, co-creator of Mosaic and co-founder of Netscape, the first Internet browsers for consumers; Leslie Miley, Slack's director of engineering; and Lars Rasmussen, the co-creator of Google Maps.

Arlan's unexpected foray into the world of venture started in 2012 when she started reading that stars like Ashton Kutcher and Ellen DeGeneres were investing in Silicon Valley startups along with people in their Hollywood orbit, including Troy Carter, Lady Gaga's former manager; Scooter Braun, Justin Bieber's manager; and Guy Oseary, Madonna's manager. Arlan, who had run a small indie magazine that folded in 2008, started devouring books and blogs about Silicon Valley and became obsessed with the startup culture and its emphasis on failure as a teacher. She was inspired by the idea that failing is an innate part of the journey and that it can actually be regarded as a badge of honor. Just as she made her way into showbiz by cold-calling and networking until she got a break, she set out over three years to absorb everything she could about startups and especially how they are financed. She even e-mailed prominent tech industry kingmakers like Chris Sacca (an early investor in Twitter, Uber, and Kickstarter, among others) and Brad Feld (whose early investments include Fitbit and Zynga) for guidance and tips. All wrote back and she began to quietly pull together a network of mentors made up of some of the insiders with the highest profiles.

"I could choose anything I wanted to do because I was going to try to make it happen from scratch," Arlan said.

At the same time she started volunteering to advise up-and-coming entrepreneurs, including Jewel Burks, CEO and co-founder of Partpic, the visual recognition software company (who would go on to count the JumpFund and Joanne Wilson among her investors in her first attempt at fund-raising). Arlan drew on her expertise in managing celebrity personalities and their entourages and technical teams to help scrappy entrepreneurs who needed assistance with just about everything from hiring to marketing to production. She soon found she had an instinct for picking winners.

"I had an eye for companies really early or companies that were going to end up at least getting to the next stage they need to get to. For some reason I was just naturally good at identifying that in a very Simon Cowell kind of way. Where he has no talent, I have no talent, but we can sniff it out, right?" she said with a laugh.

Ultimately, she decamped from Austin for San Francisco and eventually took part in a selective two-week investor-training boot camp at Stanford University, which was partnering with 500 Startups, the well-known accelerator committed to backing diverse CEOs. The program, eventually called Venture Capital Unlocked, sought out people of color, especially women.

Arlan found it a surreal experience. She was training to become a venture capitalist while living paycheck to paycheck between touring jobs and crashing with friends. At one point she found herself temporarily homeless. She never let on to her colleagues that she had hit financial straits. But then something amazing happened. In the summer of 2015 she posted an essay on *Medium* about her dream of helping to raise the profile of the founders she had met along the way. "Dear White Venture Capitalists, if you are reading this, it's (almost!) too late" went viral. In it she ominously prophesied, "If you *haven't* hired a team of people who are of color, female, and/or LGBT to actively turn over every stone, to scope out every nook and cranny, to pop out of every bush, to find every qualified underrepresented founder in this country, you're going to miss out on a LOT OF MONEY when the rest of the investment world gets it."[14]

Built by Girls

One of the highest-profile investors who "gets it"—and got it very early on—is Susan Lyne, the charismatic veteran media executive who was the visionary behind ABC's *Desperate Housewives*, *Lost*, and *Grey's Anatomy* when she ran the network's entertainment division. And that was just one of her fascinating posts in a storied career. Her path zigged and zagged to some of the most intriguing heights of media, entertainment, and e-commerce and often in the glaring lights of the public eye. She gracefully stepped in as CEO of Martha Stewart Living Omnimedia while Stewart served her five-month sentence in a West Virginia federal penitentiary. In a prescient move Susan then served from 2008 to 2013 as CEO and later chair of Gilt Groupe, the luxury flash sale site once valued at $1 billion that was sold to retail conglomerate Hudson's Bay, owner of Saks Fifth Avenue, for $250 million in January 2016.[15] She went on to step into the role of CEO of AOL Brand Group.

Now the mother of four grown daughters is hunting down the best and brightest business opportunities for BBG Ventures, the $10 million AOL-backed fund she founded to invest in early-stage digital businesses led by women. A second, larger fund was set to launch in 2017. On the day she announced she was stepping down as CEO of AOL Brand Group to run BBG, her first call was from none other than Joanne Wilson. The two have gone on to invest in multiple deals together.

"Anyone who says they can't find good women entrepreneurs to invest in is not looking," Susan famously declared in 2015, a few months after launching BBG.[16]

"BBG" is a tip of the hat to five enterprising summer interns, grads of Girls Who Code, the coding classes for teens, who in the summer of 2014 helped to reboot AOL's celebrity gossip site, Cambio, during a prestigious summer internship program that would go on to be named #BUILTBYGIRLS.

"What really came out of it [the internship] was this idea of code as religious and the nucleus in the beginning of all of this innovation," said Nisha Dua, Susan's BBG partner and founder of #BUILTBYGIRLS, who said that the young women's passion for tech, which they regard as an extension of their lives, was a revelation for the BBG team. They had enlisted the seventeen-year-olds to dream up and build a site that would attract their friends. Susan and Nisha observed the fluidity with which the young women moved from computer programming to design to creating editorial content to their appetite for learning how to run a digital media company. The teens' enthusiasm and skills pointed to a coming revolution of female-powered innovation that most other investors had perhaps not yet recognized.

Susan, who turned sixty-five in 2016, sports a warm youthful smile, on-trend accessories, and the energy of the millennial founders she invests in. She came out of legacy media (she was once managing editor of the *Village Voice* and started *Premiere* magazine) just as it was beginning to crumble under the weight of the Internet revolution. She then spent a decade at Disney, ABC, and Martha Stewart before seamlessly transitioning into e-commerce and digital media. She clearly saw the opportunities emerging for women as the next generation of tech trailblazers when, early in 2008, the smartphone and the app store began to change everyday lives.

"When that happened, I think it consolidated and sort of accelerated a shift that was taking place anyway, which was from a geeky guy early adopter to a much more broad-based early adopter and, more specifically, a young female early adopter," Susan explained when we visited AOL's hip downtown offices in Greenwich Village. Susan had spent much of her career tuned in to the particular tastes, interests, and motivations of the "female end-user." When she took a seat on the AOL board in 2009 and agreed to run the AOL Brand Group in 2013, the company was already strongly focused on engaging women. She distinctly remembers when CEO Tim Armstrong presented a key factor to the board, he put up a slide with "80 percent" in boldface—the percentage of all consumer purchasing decisions made by women in the United States (today the figure is 85 percent). Those "chief household officers" would go on devour the array of emerging social tools for connecting them to their friends, families, images, and purchases.

"By 2014, that was eminently clear. Snapchat had launched, Pinterest had launched, Instagram had launched. You know all of these platforms that are dominated by females and [they] are a large part of the reason that social [media] is growing as fast as it is," Susan told us as we chatted under the hot pink fluorescent light spelling out #BUILTBYGIRLS.

As the female appetite for social media grew and, with it, online shopping, Susan began to observe a new wave of female entrepreneurs who were building businesses focused on consumer tech. The barriers to entry for starting those digital ventures were dropping precipitously with the advent of the iPhone in 2007, followed by the app store a year later. Suddenly it cost hundreds of thousands of dollars, not millions of dollars, to create a digital prototype and to test it on an audience, because anyone with an idea could build it using the open tools called APIs, or application programming interfaces. This is code that enables software applications to communicate with each other and computer operating systems.[17] You didn't need to be backed by venture money to get started or be working for a university "to play," she explained. It was a crucial shift from only techies in Silicon Valley holding the keys to the kingdom to a new crop of enterprising people coming out of B-school or from careers in media, fashion, health care, and real estate.

"It [the shift] is really about a move from a tech economy to a tech-enabled economy. That is what this world has become," Susan underscored to us. And it opened a whole new world for innovating women who saw problems in their lives they wanted to solve. By 2014, when Susan and Nisha unveiled BBG onstage at TechCrunch Disrupt, they had already been meeting dozens and dozens of women developing mobile apps, media/content platforms, and e-commerce. Ironically, the old guard was oblivious to the rising tide, Susan said.

"It felt like a huge opportunity. We launched the fund so that we could invest in the best of these female entrepreneurs because we think there is a great deal of money to be made and also because anytime you back a female founder, you're making the lives of millions of women better because what they are building is very specific, and it is very much to fix a problem," she said of the 1,400 companies that have pitched the fund and the forty startups BBG has backed since 2014. These include Modsy, Shanna Tellerman's home design app; Rocksbox, the jewelry rental subscription service; Ringly, the online jewelry store; and HopSkipDrive. The competition was stiff. In its first twenty months BBG looked at more than nine hundred companies founded by women—90 percent of those pitching sought out BBG. BBG didn't need to go hunting down deal flow, because it was exploding. And Susan and Nisha could have met with even more founders if their team had been larger, countering the oft-heard excuse of legacy investors that female founders are hard to find.

Susan is one of four sisters, a close-knit group who spent their childhood in Chestnut Hill, Massachusetts, a village near Boston, and she has found that empowering women has been a hallmark of her personal and professional life. She is incredibly generous with her expansive network of media elite, business executives, and celebrities, sometimes hosting intimate dinners for female mentees at her warm Upper East Side apartment where she raised her girls. The place brims with old family photos, keepsakes, and hundreds of books. On a recent evening she invited some of the promising entrepreneurs in the BBG portfolio to her gracious home for a get-together at which she made key introductions to tech journalists. "Her willingness to share her network and serve as connector is another example of her generosity towards entrepreneurs. She helped us understand [that] relationship development starts early," said Alexandra Friedman, co-founder of LOLA, an online subscription service that delivers organic tampons to your door each month.

During her long career Susan has certainly endured many instances of being one of the only women in the room. Such experiences make her highly regarded and trusted as a coach, beyond the valuable connections. She and Nisha agree that often what female founders need to hear most is that they should think bigger, that they must step back and look beyond what they have built so far and see how a good idea can become a giant idea.

When Alexandra and her partner, Jordana Kier, pitched LOLA to Susan, it was the first time they had ever presented the business to any investor. As the two young co-founders of the company recall the story, Susan nodded along, listening intently, and then, when they finished, crinkled her brow and paused for a beat.[18] Alexandra and Jordana were sweating and holding their breath. After mulling the final slide of the presentation, which listed their three-year financial projections, Susan asked, "That's it?" And then, with an enormous smile, she followed up by saying, "Don't you think you can grow it bigger than that?" It was a key moment.

"Susan taught us to sell the dream," Alexandra said.

CHAPTER 4

DREAM IT, DO IT, OWN IT

Confidence Coaches

It's not your job to like me, it's mine.

—Byron Katie

Power is not given to you. You have to take it.

—Beyoncé

Dona Sarkar was wearing leopard and owning it. It was midnight in downtown Seattle, and the Renaissance woman was in her element on a giant soundstage. She was hosting the world's first HoloHack, a forty-eight-hour brainstorming session for one hundred techies, filmmakers, 3-D artists, and sound engineers to try making the first apps for Microsoft's augmented reality device, the HoloLens.[1] It's a futuristic headset that enables 3-D images called holograms to leap from computer screens into real life, where they can be manipulated with the swipe of finger. At thirty-six Dona is a hardware geek, as well as a fashion designer and novelist, and she is leading the HoloLens outreach program, confirming her status as a rising star at Microsoft.

It's hard to believe she failed her first computer science class. But she did, and her story of resilience is one she tells often as she travels the country, inspiring young women to charge ahead in their engineering studies and hang on to their jobs in the male-dominated world of tech. As a longtime developer for Windows operating systems, Dona likes to think of tech as the "invisible fairy godmother who makes things happen," and as of June 2016, she was overseeing Microsoft's Windows Insider program, which has millions of users giving feedback about beta versions of updates.[2]

"My biggest success is being a senior woman in one of the biggest software companies in the world. Microsoft is a legendary software company, and being a principal-level woman here, a principal-level engineer, really is a huge achievement," the dark-haired polymath with a penchant for pink lipstick told us. "When I was [growing up] in Detroit, if someone [had] told me, 'Hey, Dona, you're going to be making a really, really great salary working at Microsoft as a very senior person,' I would [have] just hysterically laugh[ed]."

That's because Dona didn't know anyone like the woman she would one day become. She grew up in downtown Detroit, where her parents—immigrants from Kathmandu—worked in the auto industry, and her grandmother, a seamstress and fashion designer, ran a small dress shop for fifty years. The computer lab at Dona's inner-city high school consisted of some ancient PCs and a clique of teenage boys who laughed her out of the room when she approached them about joining the computer club. She had been fascinated by computers ever since she first laid eyes on an old Macintosh in the back of her fifth-grade classroom. Her father, who read the *Wall Street Journal* with her in high school and followed all the news of the technology titans of the 1990s, encouraged Dona to pursue computing as a practical career move. He felt this new industry wasn't as entrenched as legacy tracks like banking or law and that his studious daughter might just have a shot at a better life if she pursued it. He scraped the money together to sign her up for a coding course at a community college while she was still in high school. But it wasn't enough to prepare her for CS 100, the introductory programming class at the University of Michigan, which crammed seven complex concepts into one semester.

She felt like her male classmates, most of whom, she later realized, had taken Advanced Placement computer science in high school (something her school did not offer), were speaking a foreign language as they paired up for assignments.

"I would listen to them all the time, and they would just say, 'God, I can't believe how easy this stuff is. Why are we even doing this? Who doesn't know this?' And I'm sitting there, like, 'I don't know this. I don't know this at all. I don't even know what that word means. What are *bits*? What are *gates* [building blocks of programming]? What's N? What's X or—' And the teacher would start talking and the guys would be, like, 'We already know this, move on,' and they would yell this out," she recalled. Dona failed the course because she grew too embarrassed ask questions. She didn't want anyone to think she was an airhead and resolved to just muddle through on her own.

Immediately afterward, she thought about dropping her CS major altogether. But then she started thinking about how she had learned to ride her bike and how she would skin her knees, cry a lot, and vow never to do it again, only to get back in the saddle two days later. She took the course again, and this time earned a B.

"It's not the best score," she said, "but it was far better than what I had, and I realized how much I'd learned. I could actually do the projects. I was suddenly validated as I just needed to be exposed to it twice, just like those guys. It's not like they got it on the first try."

The message she wants to send women is that you can't give up on your goal because it didn't work out the first time. "That's like saying, 'I ran a race intending to win first place. I came in second so I quit running.' It's so funny, the concept is so weird to me, like, 'What are you people talking about?' and a lot of people don't go for things unless they're guaranteed success. And I believe if you get 50 percent of the way or 75 percent of the way, that's far better success than zero percent of the way," she said.

That was why she pushed herself to learn how to use a sewing machine as an adult—she wanted to take a fashion design class—and why she kept on penning stories in her creative writing workshop even though her first attempt at a novel fizzled. Her sheer persistence eventually led to the launch of Prima Dona Style, her new fashion line; *Fibonacci Sequins*, a style blog devoted to STEM; and a three-book deal with Penguin Random House.

Success Starts with Failure

Along the way, Dona was reminded over and over again that innovation itself is achieved only through trial and error. You have to be open to taking risks and learning from failure. That's why rapid prototyping is key—testing an idea, seeing where it goes, and tweaking it along the way. Mistakes and missteps build knowledge and confidence. That attitude is baked into the culture of Silicon Valley, yet it runs counter to the way many women are raised. The pressure for perfection among young women and girls in Westernized countries often trumps the desire to try. The best-selling book *The Confidence Code*, published in 2014, argues that encouraging girls to be people pleasers or compliant from a young age can do long-term damage.

"Research shows that when a boy fails, he takes it in stride. When a girl makes a similar mistake, she sees herself as sloppy and comes to believe that it reflects a lack of skill," write

Katty Kay and Claire Shipman as they highlight research by Peggy McIntosh of the Wellesley Centers for Women.[3]

The difference in perception can stem from what Stanford University researcher Carol Dweck calls a "growth mindset versus a fixed mindset." Her findings are often cited by advocates trying to understand and close the gender gap in high tech, but the lessons apply across fields. People with a growth mind-set are more resilient and less daunted by failure, because they believe that intelligence or talent can be honed over time, whereas people with a fixed mind-set believe that people are born with a set amount of innate intelligence or talent. When you apply this logic to industries and academic environments such as computing and engineering, where women may not feel like they "belong," their underrepresentation starts to make more sense.[4] As discussed in the 2015 AAUW report "Solving The Equation," Erin Cech, an assistant professor of sociology at Rice University, and her colleagues looked at the difference between the confidence an engineering student needs to take a math or science test and the confidence one needs to imagine him or herself applying for a job as an engineer and actually visualizing working in the field. They found that "a conception that some people's brains are hardwired to do engineering work (and that men are better at math and science than women are) contributes to low professional role confidence that some people are natural engineers while others are a poor fit for engineering."[5]

"That's one thing that I wish more girls and women knew is that you don't necessarily have to be the best engineer to take engineering classes. I wish that there was less pressure. I put so much pressure on myself to get straight A's and had I known that coding generally will be an incredible skill that you'll use for the rest of your life, I probably would have treated it differently," said Melody McCloskey, who ended up with a double

major in International Relations and French at UC Davis instead of computer science but ultimately went on to found Style-
Seat in 2011. It is the largest online U.S. marketplace for beauty
and wellness services, and the company saw 100 percent year-
over-year growth in 2015 with 23 million appointments booked
through its site that year.[6] "I wish more women knew that you
don't have to be the best engineer in the world—or an engineer
at all—to start a company or work with a [tech] company."

As we spoke with some of the most accomplished technologists, entrepreneurs, and investors in the United States, we re-
peatedly heard stories about how they, at various times in their
lives, had grappled with feelings of self-doubt or insecurity
because of the pressure to be perfect. Dr. Maria Klawe,
president of Harvey Mudd College and a world-renowned
mathematician and computer scientist, as well as a respected
champion of women in STEM, told us she has suffered her entire life from what is known as "impostor syndrome," the phe-
nomenon of highly qualified people who feel like a fraud.[7]
Now in her sixties, Maria tries to leverage her anxieties as a way
to keep herself on course.

"The way I describe it for myself is, I have one side of my
head that is constantly feeling like I'm a failure. I have another
side of my head that is saying, 'I can change the world! I can
make a big difference!' I have to listen to the failure side in
terms of analyzing how I'm approaching things and being willing to acknowledge that things could be done differently or
better, and I have to listen to the 'I can change the world' side
in terms of setting ambitious goals. It works," she told us.

She's so passionate about being open about the prevalence
of imposter syndrome that she talks about it every year at
Mudd's matriculation ceremony, letting students—male and
female—know they are not alone and that they need to learn to
ask for help: "We want them to learn to ask for help because,

when you go out into the world, you're going to be faced with problems that are really challenging all the time. So we would like you to know that it's really okay to ask your co-workers, to ask your boss, to ask the person who works in the building beside yours. 'I'm struggling with this, what advice do you have?' Or, 'Can you show me how to do this?' Our students learn that."

Coaching Women to Take Risks

During the five years we spent delving into women's lives and careers in tech, we witnessed the explosion of new opportunities for bolstering their confidence—boot camps, pitch competitions, conferences, and workshops for tech women that are promoted as a way to set them up for success in both the corporate and startup arenas.

We could feel the energy in the air the moment the elevator doors opened to the Spotify offices in Manhattan. Huddled around tables were teams of three to four women, some wearing headscarves, others sporting colorful highlights. They were engaged in deep discussions as they tapped away at keyboards and thoughtfully glanced back and forth at their MacBook screens. We had stepped into SheHacksNYC, a women-only hackathon. The intense weekend culminated with a competition in front of some well-known New York investors, including Alicia Syrett, a judge on CNBC's *Power Pitch*.

Participants told us this felt different from the mostly male hackathons that predominate in Silicon Valley. There was not an empty pizza box or keg in sight. Instead, the dinner buffet featured organic wild rice, chickpea salad, and sliced fruit. And at 5 p.m. the entire room paused for a meditation break. A bespectacled yogi led everyone in a sequence of mindfulness exercises to ease stress by focusing on empathy and compassion—essentials for teamwork and unleashing creativity, she explained. With their eyes closed, the women inhaled together and then let out an audible exhale as Miriam Bekkouche, the founder of The Brain Spa, whose day job is managing events for 37 Angels, the angel investing group focused on women-founded startups, led the room in a simple meditation practice. It was a moment of relief for the sixty enterprising women who had sacrificed the weekend to get out of their comfort zones and take a risk.

After meditation was over, we met twenty-two-year-old Christine Pha, a newly trained front-end web developer who was working with her team to build an app to help musicians track when they are in tune and rates them over time. Her husband is a serious jazz musician who practices constantly, and she thought there had to be a better way than some of the existing tuning apps to help him improve his art. She was inspired to try after a chance-of-a-lifetime encounter with none other than Sheryl Sandberg, who had hosted a gathering for a handful of Lean In Circle members at her home one summer and impressed upon Christine and the other young women who attended that if they wanted to work in tech, they should look beyond marketing and public relations. "Her call to action in that moment was, 'We need women in products. We need women in operations. We need women creating things,'" she told us. "Up to that weekend, I was focusing on my marketing and design career. I went home from that, and now I hope to build stuff." And here she was, putting her new skills to the test for the first time.

This was exactly the opportunity SheHacks co-founders Diana Murakhovskaya and Irene Ryabaya had in mind when they first dreamed up the idea of "bridging the gap between women developers and women with ideas." It all started when the two friends, who had long covered commodities on the trading desks of major banks, decided to create a mobile app called Monarq, to help professional women like themselves strike up friendships with other smart, ambitious women. Inspiration struck on a hill in Borneo, Malaysia, when the two adventurers were on a vacation trip in 2014. They gave themselves thirty days to work on Monarq when they arrived home. Diana, a mechanical engineer by training, and Irene, who has a computer science degree, decided from the start that they really wanted a female software developer to build Monarq because they thought a woman could relate to their vision. But they couldn't find one for the job, even after they went looking at a few hacker events. So they decided to throw their own hackathon just for women in the hope of finding enterprising developers and to engage them with the startup world. The first event attracted forty women and SheHacks was born. They've expanded from New York to Phoenix and Houston and have expanded their offerings to include mentor dinners, investor breakfasts, and even a conference at which SheHacks participants can keep building their networks and their confidence. What we found most interesting about the evening was that, while many of the women who attended were young, they were not just out of school. They were transitioning from one career to another in which they might apply their new digital skills, and they were looking for a safe space to practice, build their résumés, or try out their business ideas.

"I think women require just a little more of a high-touch situation. You need a lot of encouragement," said Diana of the reluctance of some women to show off their skills or tell the world about ideas that are not yet fully formed. All the projects for that day's event were prescreened, and the teams were matched up in advance. But Diana said that once the programming was under way, people kept stopping her in the ladies' room to say they had an idea but didn't think it was good enough to submit or that they didn't think their coding skills were good enough to lead the team. She and Irene say that is exactly why they wanted to make the hackathons for women only and included male and female coaches and mentors in the groups with express instructions to stress that there are no dumb questions. They wanted SheHacks to feel nurturing and safe. And it did for Christine Moy, an investment banker who had recently taken some coding classes. The mother of a toddler won the event's pitch competition with her team and their work on her idea, Babyhood, a social network for new parents. This was the first time she had described her project in public, and it felt good to see what was in her head evolve into a real prototype.

"You're around all of these invigorated, strong, smart women that are like you, and you get feedback. You each have your own little niches, like what you're good at, what you're focused on, what you're interested in. And then you share and then you come away [saying], 'Man, I learned something today and I feel like I've got a team,'" said Christine, who, as of this writing, had not yet quit her day job in banking but was still working on her idea.

The Art of Self-Promotion

Learning how to share big ideas and parlay them into promotions and plum assignments is why about a hundred female software developers were passing around M&M's on a spring afternoon. They split up into small groups, and as part of an icebreaker game, each had to answer a personal question based on the color of the candy she was handed. If you got a blue one, you had to talk about your greatest hack—the workaround, either professional or personal, that made you most proud. A red one—you had to reveal your biggest failure. Many of the women were at mid-career, and this event, Write/Speak/Code, was a rare chance to connect and speak openly among peers about their accomplishments and missteps.

The three-day conference held in New York in 2015 had a clear mission: to empower female computer programmers to develop the confidence to "own their expertise" through publishing and public speaking. The boot camp, created by Chicago-based developer Rebecca Miller-Webster, grew out of her own desire to move up in her career, which she really did not know how to do.

"One of my frustrations was that I felt like there was this big conversation about women in tech, except it mostly talked about teaching women how to code, and it didn't talk about the women who were there, and the problems that they're experiencing, and how to make change around that," said Rebecca, thirty-three, whose blue-streaked platinum blonde hair made her stand out in the crowd. She realized communication and self-promotion are essential skills that many of her colleagues were missing—and perhaps keeping them from landing bigger jobs and better pay. On a whim, she took an Op-Ed Project workshop in 2013 to learn how to write and publish opinion pieces.

On the day we attended Write/Speak/Code, we noted how the organizers did their best to lower the barriers for mothers by offering child care and a nursing room, a rarity at professional conferences, especially technology events. The attendees were serious about getting the most out of the time, and by the end each was expected to come up with at least one idea for a blog post they could publish right away. They also practiced pitching themselves for seats on panels and as speakers for groups, as well as being interviewed by reporters. Developers who have successfully raised their profiles, within their companies as well as in the public eye, offered feedback and tips for getting published. In 2016 the workshop moved to Chicago and hosted an even bigger lineup, with 150 in attendance.

"I think the first step [toward closing the gender gap] is to promote ourselves—whether we should have to or not, we do. I don't want [tech] conference organizers to come to me and say, 'I need to have more women, but I don't know any women.' I want them to know who the women are," Rebecca told us.

Poornima Vijayashanker and Karen Catlin believe one sure-fire way for women to gain that recognition and promote their expertise is by raising their hands to give talks and presentations as often as possible. The upbeat team calls public speaking the "multi-vitamin" that can ignite a woman's career. When we met them in person, they were fresh from leading a workshop at the largest gathering of women in tech in the world, the 2015 Grace Hopper Celebration of Computing in Houston. It was an audience that could relate to them. Both women have earned hard-core tech credentials, and both have overcome their own reluctance to address an audience. Poornima was the founding engineer of Mint, the online personal accounting service, and had struggled with extreme shyness as a child until she tried out for the debate team in middle school. She went on to become Mint's spokeswoman and a sought-after speaker for Fortune 500 companies after Intuit acquired Mint in 2009. Karen is a software engineer and former vice president at Adobe Systems who says she never took much pleasure in making presentations to all-hands meetings or speaking on panels—that is, until she made a pledge to herself to start speaking in public at least once a month. That turning point came in 2012, during a hike in the hills near Stanford with a trusted mentor as she was contemplating leaving Adobe and starting a consulting firm focused on helping women advance in the technology world. Her mentor asked if she did much public speaking.

"Oh, my gosh, all the stage fright I had ever felt through my whole career, every time I got on stage, kind of hit me like a wall. But I realized she was asking because that was going to be critical for me: building up a consulting business for talking in front of women and hopefully inspiring some women in tech. It was going to be the key to unlocking this new thing I wanted to do," Karen said. And it was. She forced herself to sign up to present once a month, including delivering a TEDx talk. Her business took off, and she eventually joined forces with Poornima, who had been offering online communication courses to engineers and entrepreneurs since 2007 through her blog, *Femgineer*, which she later turned into an education company of the same name.

We sat down with Karen and Poornima about a month before their new book, *Present! A Techie's Guide to Public Speaking*, was set to debut. They would soon go on a book tour during which they planned to offer practical tips for everything from overcoming stage fright to finding the right audience to handling Q&A's when you don't, in fact, have all the answers. Poornima, a Duke grad who majored in electrical engineering and computer science, filled us in on some of the advice they give their students, both in person and in the eight-week online Confident Communicator classes they run through Femgineer. She showed us one of her old debate tricks that helps with diction—putting a pen in her mouth and reading the newspaper or a book aloud for fifteen minutes a day. She said it helps open up the cheeks and helps the speaker concentrate on articulation and pacing. They encourage students to do a "meet and greet" with the audience before they give a talk, so they can warm up and connect with attendees. Poornima and Karen strongly discourage their students from memorizing entire speeches and instead advise them to work on the first fifteen to thirty seconds.

"Nail that—memorize it—because when you get on stage, that's when stage fright is the worst. That very beginning. If you can deliver the first few sentences of your talk, and just have that in the back of your head, you'll be fine," Karen said.

A few months after we saw them in Houston, we attended a lunchtime book talk they gave at Facebook's headquarters in Menlo Park, California, and participated in the confidence-building exercises that Poornima and Karen led that day.

"We want to see more women leaders," Poornima told the women at the Facebook workshop. "Part of being seen means that they are up here presenting. So our goal in giving this talk today is to really encourage you afterward to just maybe take a baby step of speak[ing] up at the next meeting or mak[ing] a more audacious leap and sign up for an event, or sign up for a TEDx talk."

They started by asking the attentive audience of fifty female engineers what they feared about public speaking. Hands shot up.

"I have horrible stage fright," one woman said.

"I'm afraid of losing confidence when I start speaking," another chimed in.

During this hourlong workshop, Poornima and Karen gave the engineers some simple techniques they could start using right away. They started with some "power posing."

They asked everyone to stand. Then they asked attendees to raise their hands high above their heads in a *V*, for victory.

"This is a power pose," Karen explained. "You see Olympic athletes do it when they cross the finish line. You see kids do it when they score a goal on the soccer field. And today you even see brides and grooms doing it after they exchange their wedding vows. It crosses cultures, and it crosses genders."

They were referring to research by social psychologist and Harvard Business School professor Amy Cuddy, who says in her viral June 2012 TEDGlobal Talk, that striking a power pose for two minutes actually raises your testosterone levels—in women and men—and makes you feel more powerful. Karen added that, at the same time, it lowers cortisol, or stress, levels.[8]

"By raising your hands up in a power pose, you can fake your body into thinking it just scored that goal, that you are on top of your game," she said. "It's a perfect way to combat stage fright. You can do it before you speak, before you go into an interview or have a difficult conversation. Poornima and I did it before our talk here today." It *does* feel good.

Both women shared with the crowd their own fears and past missteps. Karen confided that she was notorious for cramming way too much text on the slides for her presentations. Poornima talked about the time she showed up for a talk completely unprepared and how she bombed. They wanted this group of smart, ambitious engineers to leave with the message that public speaking takes practice but they can do it—and it's worth the effort.

"Public speaking changed my life," Poornima said. "I nailed my college interview, my first job interview, and then went on to do other things, like give presentations for the startups I've founded. I've helped raise capital and recruit teammates. Now public speaking is part of my career. I didn't always think about it in terms of what it could do for me. It was more me saying I didn't want to be shy anymore. I wanted people to take me seriously and to be noticed."

Fueling Female Innovation

As Poornima learned in the early days of building Mint, public speaking is part of the job of being a startup founder. After giving a polished pitch, the ability to clearly and confidently explain your vision, and especially its financial details, is essential to success. Since the mid-2000s dozens of business incubators and accelerators have cropped up around the country to help jump-start ventures that have at least one female founder.[9] These newer female-focused programs are similar to the famous Y Combinator in that they promise entrée to industry mentors, early funding, and extensive coaching. Incubators tend to help new companies ideate and get started, whereas accelerators help them mature and grow—and some offer seed money in exchange for equity. For example, the Refinery, a school for female tech founders in Westport, Connecticut, provides weekly five-hour classes that culminate after twelve weeks in Demo Night, when the women present their businesses to local investors. It costs $2,500, which goes toward the cash prizes awarded at the final pitch competition. Another company, MergeLane, established by "an investment firm with a training program" in Boulder, Colorado, is a twelve-week program that offers three weeks on site and the remaining nine weeks online to afford greater flexibility to founders with families. MergeLane invests $20,000 upon acceptance into the program, with the possibility of an additional $100,000 at the end in exchange for an equity stake of 6 percent.

Make no mistake, said Sue Heilbronner, the fifty-year-old co-founder of MergeLane: the intensive coaching of CEOs and work on "product solution fit" is not philanthropy. This is about making money and betting that diverse teams will deliver big returns to the MergeLane fund and its investment partners.

"There's this assumption that if you're doing anything that addresses a topic around women or diversity in general, you're doing it as a charitable act. We're just aggressively contradicting that perception," stressed Sue, a former federal prosecutor turned CEO and investor, as she described the first two cohorts of companies to go through the program since it started in 2014.

The common theme at MergeLane and among the growing

array of courses and classes is that they help founders hone their business plans and teams while training them to convincingly articulate their vision—especially to rooms full of male investors.

"A lot of this is, 'How do I get more comfortable in my own leadership?' Being more comfortable in your own leadership involves valuing everything about you that makes you a leader, not just your sales ability or your coding skills," Sue explained, adding that MergeLane is playing a long game and that if one day the program is obsolete, it will have done its work.

Ari Horie, too, believes those crucial leadership skills are rooted in authenticity—embracing who you are as a whole person and the feeling deep inside that what you are doing is what you were meant to do. Not far from the Facebook campus, she runs her immersive two-week Women's Startup Lab for eight female founders who dig into their feelings as well as their financials as Ari brings in industry experts to coach them on the nitty-gritty of creating a business and the art of leaning on each other. The mantra of the program is *hito*, the Japanese symbol for human, which depicts two people leaning on each other. It's a key part of how Ari hopes to build a community of women entrepreneurs who will support each other and hold each other accountable long after they go home. That's why she insists that to participate in her workshop, they have to live together for the full fourteen days. They bunk at a home, known as a hacker house, in a Foster City, California, subdivision, which Ari describes as an intimate, trusting environment where the women can let down their guard and talk about the real issues they're facing as entrepreneurs.

When we arrived at 7 p.m. on a Wednesday evening, the smell of sizzling onions and grilled steak welcomed us at the front door. A dark-haired little girl wearing a red dress and an ear-to-ear smile watched us intently from behind the kitchen table as we took off our coats in the front hall. When we smiled at her, she ran into the kitchen and wrapped her arms tightly around her mother's legs.

Kerri Couillard, a young software developer-turned-entrepreneur from Santa Fe, led us into an expansive living room where three women were sitting at a communal table and typing away at their computers. Two other women were talking quietly by a whiteboard that had terms like *key metrics* and *value proposition* scribbled at the top. We caught a glimpse of what appeared to be an espresso machine in the corner—it turned out to be a 3-D printer. Power strips, charging stations, projectors, printers, WiFi—everything an entrepreneur needs to start a company—were there, within arm's reach.

"Today is Day Ten in the hacker house," Kerri told us as she led us up a narrow stairway to the bedroom she shared with three other women. "We're working on our pitches that we'll present to the group on Friday."

The bedroom was clean but sparsely decorated, with four bunks, two sets of drawers, and a desk. The carpets and walls were white. No paintings hung on the walls.

"I wasn't sure if I was going to make it the two weeks," she confessed as she climbed into her upper bunk to show us how she could barely sit upright on her bed. "I was concerned about sleeping on bunk beds and not having any privacy. I'm an introvert. I mean, I can go days without talking to people. I'm just proud of myself for doing it, because this is definitely a stretch for me."

As we soon learned, this unassuming two-story house in a quiet residential neighborhood in pricey Silicon Valley was one of many whose owners rent out rooms (through Airbnb) to aspiring tech entrepreneurs. For just $45 a night, guests got a bunk in a shared room and a homemade meal. Luckily for the guests of this house, the hosts were a young couple from Japan—he was the founder of a tech media company, and she was trained as a gourmet chef, so meals were delicious and plentiful. Dinners were served family style, with meat, fish, fresh veggies from the farmers' market, and plenty of rice and potatoes to fuel the brain for late-night hacking sessions. Breakfast included freshly baked bread, cinnamon buns, and egg sandwiches.

Unlike the sloppy, fraternity-style hacker houses portrayed in movies like *The Social Network* and television series like HBO's *Silicon Valley*, this house felt more like a home, in part because the couple's four young children were roaming through the house and sharing meals with guests.

"The kids are so well behaved," Kerri said. "They never disrupt us when we are working. Even with four of them, it's always really quiet in the house. If you want to make a phone call, you have to go in the garage [so as not to disturb anyone]."

A typical day in the program started with a 5 a.m. wake-up and breakfast, followed by a full day of back-to-back workshops and mentoring sessions at the Startup Lab's Menlo Park offices.

"We get back to the House at 7 p.m.," Kerri said, "but dinner usually isn't until nine. I work till midnight, crash, and start again the next day. There's definitely a boot camp-ishness about it."

But for Kerri, two weeks away from the demands of her two children and family were just what she needed to take her company, Babierge, a rental service for baby equipment like strollers and cribs, to the next level.

"The experience really changed me," she told us a few weeks after she finished the program. "I have this confidence now. I'm not thinking small. I'm not struggling with fear or wondering if I am going to make it. My husband, he doesn't know what is going on. He told me I needed to take a few days and be Mom again and I am like, 'No. I really cannot go back to what it was like before.'"

This newfound confidence was what Ari had in mind when she began the Women's Startup Lab in 2013. Her goal was to help female founders grow nascent companies into full-blown businesses by having the women examine their inner fears, passions, and sense of purpose. Participants drilled down to their sense of self while learning what they need to get their business to the fund-raising stage. This is done with the help and guidance of Silicon Valley veterans—entrepreneurs, venture capitalists, and startup advisers like marketing guru Bill Joos, venture capitalist Heidi Roizen, serial entrepreneur Fran Maier, and well-known author and speaker Guy Kawasaki.

While some other accelerators focus on hitting growth targets, the Women's Startup Lab is more interested in developing women as CEOs and instilling in them the confidence they need to be effective leaders.

"Most people think, 'Women founders are not getting funding, so let's get them funding and that will solve the problem,'" Ari explained. "But often the issue is much deeper than that. I saw all these capable women, but no one was helping them get to the funding-ready stage."

That was certainly the case for Jill Richmond, co-founder and chief marketing officer of Kraver at the time, who said she and her co-founder were having a "complete leadership disconnect" when they arrived for the accelerator program. Mentoring sessions turned into relationship counseling for the pair.

"We had many 'come to Jesus' moments at the lab, where advisers stepped in and identified this was a problem," she told us. "We took on some outside executive leadership coaching, got our messaging straight, and in two weeks were literally able to shore up the positioning of the company, get three major advisers on deck, and close our first lead investor, which wouldn't have happened otherwise."

Ari played mother hen with the cohort, Jill said, telling us, "I felt comfortable enough, when things were hitting the fan with my co-founder, to call her in[to] a room and ask her, 'Ari, what you would do if you were me right now?'" Rather than exchanging expert advice for equity in a company, Women's Startup Lab charges a flat fee for the two-week program ($10,000 as of this writing). For many businesses that have yet to make a dollar, that is a lot of money to shell out.

"We had lots of concerns about spending this kind of money upfront," Jill said. "It wasn't so clear, when I applied to Women's Startup Lab, that I was going to derive any value. But we liked that we didn't have to give away equity."

Jill said calling the Women's Startup Lab (WSLab) an accelerator is misleading. "It's an executive leadership program," she explained. "Anyone who's applying to an accelerator thinks that they're going to raise money at the end. This doesn't happen at WSLab."

Unlike the projects of many students in her cohort, Babierge, Kerri's business, was already profitable when she came to the Startup Lab. But she had to use an online fund-raising campaign and take a sizable chunk out of her retirement account to foot the tuition. The trade-off for her was that she didn't have to part with ownership of any percentage of her company.

"Ten thousand dollars is a lot," she told us. "But the quality of instruction and mentorship I got—it was worth it. I saw the value in paying versus giving a piece of my baby away."

Soon after she completed the program, Kerri stepped aside as CEO so Fran Maier, the co-founder of Match.com and a WSLab coach, could lead the company to its next phase of growth. Signing Maier was a coup that could not have happened without the network the lab opened to Kerri.

The Startup Lab also differs from other accelerators in the type of founder it attracts. Rather than baby-faced programmers fresh out of Stanford, participants are mostly mothers who are juggling the nurturing of their startup with picking up children from school and getting the grocery shopping done, as well as women in their forties and fifties with previous careers in law, retail, and education.

Ari, a serial entrepreneur herself, understands the unique challenges female founders can face, juggling roles as CEO, mother, wife, and head of household. She grew emotional as we delved into her personal life and how the death of her mother and divorce from her husband had fueled Ari's ambitions. Before Women's Startup Lab, she had started B! Minds, a tool to teach bilingual children a third language.

"There is a higher chance . . . women [will] give up because they have more to juggle. They don't have the resources or network to reach out to for help," said Ari, who has two middle-schoolers. We were sitting in a pleasant conference room where SHIT HAPPENS EVERY DAY is written in red on a whiteboard over a flow chart of action items scrawled in blue.

Her own journey included a delicate dance between *hito*—leaning on others—and a rugged individualism fostered by her mother. She had divorced Ari's father when Ari was a baby and raised her daughter as a single mother—which was taboo in Japan at the time. From an early age the astute little girl knew what it was like to be an outsider. The parents of her school friends wouldn't let their kids play with her because her mother was single. Ari's mother, who was the daughter of a governor, responded by telling Ari that popularity and fitting in are not important. That attitude was quite rebellious, given that in Japan at that time, being a part of the community was seen as essential, Ari said.

To instill in Ari a sense of individuality, her mother required

Ari to wear a pink backpack to school when all the other girls in her school carried red backpacks and the boys wore black ones. She wanted her daughter to feel unique among her peers and embrace being different.

"She purposely made me different . . . She was constantly saying, 'I want you to gain the confidence. It comes from having your own opinion,'" said Ari, who looks trendy but unfussy in a black cardigan with leather sleeves and silver hoop earrings.

Ari first came to the United States as a high school exchange student who was hoping to learn English. But she quickly found herself an outsider, dropped into a tough high school in Orange County, California, with a host family that was less than friendly and even excluded her from meals. At school she endured taunts and even witnessed gang conflicts, but she was hell-bent on sticking out the year. It was a life-affirming experience. The value of standing out is something she invokes often with her Startup Lab students, reminding them that their unique perspective is the most important thing they bring to the table as women in the male-dominated tech world.

"Being an entrepreneur is all about really constantly dealing with something you don't know," explained Ari of the distinct characteristics that enable the best entrepreneurs to rise above doubts and take the next step. She says the courage stems from a true sense of purpose. "It gives you the direction. People leave this place becoming so clear, and it's not about what they have done in the past, but because they're so clear on where they want to go," she said.

Changing the Culture, Not the Women

It's important to point out that for all the excitement around female-focused accelerators like Women's Startup Lab and the tangible benefits that their graduates tout, there is disagreement about how much these efforts are actually changing the landscape for female founders who are trying to raise money. Sharon Vosmek, CEO of Astia, an angel network and fund, says there's a danger in teaching women to conform to the demands of the current system of venture capital, which tips toward making the culture of white men the norm, instead of fixing the underlying problem of bias.

"I am interested in fixing the ecosystem," Sharon said. "Every time we focus the effort on women, we try and change how women behave so it can fit within a male paradigm. That doesn't get us any closer to changing what needs to change, which is the paradigm."

Other advocates, like Allyson Kapin, founder of the networking group Women Who Tech and of the Women Startup Challenge, the competition for female entrepreneurs that she runs with backing from Craig Newmark, founder of Craigslist, said she has mixed feelings about focusing on gender. At the challenge's 2016 competition finals, held at LinkedIn's global headquarters in Mountain View, California, the contest awarded $50,000 to SIRUM, a "Match.com for unused, unexpired medicine which matches it with people in need," as described by the contest organizers.[10]

As Allyson put it, "In an ideal world, we wouldn't have to do something like this because things would be fair. Women would be getting invested in, people of color would be getting invested in, there wouldn't be these types of diversity issues at conferences and at tech companies and startups. But that's not the world that we live in, and so that's why we have to do stuff like this, and I hope that one day we're going to get to a point where Women Who Tech and the Women Startup Challenge don't need to exist because it's a fair game."

And when we met Kathryn Finney she cautioned us to be careful about extrapolating from the experience of some women and applying it to *all* women. The founder of DigitalUndivided, a group that advocates for black and Latino women in tech, and co-author of *The Real Unicorns of Tech*, a damning 2016 study about the critical funding gap for black female founders, said minority entrepreneurs are not reaping the benefits of the new attention on women in tech: "I don't think there has been an innovative approach to inclusion . . . It's interesting to me that it's an industry that prides itself on innovation. I mean, people who are creating driverless cars are doing 1980s practices for inclusion. Hiring a chief diversity officer. Having an event. I mean all those things have been done many, many, many times before and obviously they haven't worked because you still have the problem."

She was one of first fashion bloggers and one of the first African American bloggers. The style maven would go on to leverage the massive audience for her *Budget Fashionista* blog into a formidable business and sell it to a medium-sized Midwestern media company for an undisclosed sum in 2013. The daughter of one of the first African American engineers at Microsoft grew up around technology and remembers traveling with her father on business trips to the campus in Redmond, Washington, from their home in Minneapolis. She learned to code when she started her style blog in 2003, so she could self-publish the photos of the purses and shoes she coveted and share deals and discounts with her fans.

In her trademark leopard-print cat's-eye glasses, coral sneakers, and a gorgeous dove-gray Prada handbag, Kathryn looked every bit the fashion plate we had seen on the *Today* show back when she was a contributor to the show. Even though she has a master's in international epidemiology from the Yale School of Public Health, Kathryn says she was immediately dismissed by her male peers when she joined a New York tech accelerator to work on an e-commerce subscription idea around beauty products—which she described as "Birchbox for black women." She remembers vividly the day in 2006 when she finally volunteered to talk about her business idea in front of the white male cohort.

"The assumption was that I didn't know what I was talking about. That I didn't have the skill set," she said. One guy actually asked if she knew any fashion bloggers—when a quick Google search would have revealed her to be one of the most popular at that time. She was incensed that none of them had even bothered. "I wasn't even worth Googling," she said.

That experience and other instances of bias eventually led her to start multiple initiatives, including conferences and a fellowship program to engage and empower underrepresented founders. But by 2014 she was frustrated with the lack of progress and decided to spend a year digging into the thorny questions behind that bias—Who is actually getting funded? Why? Where did they go to school?—and challenging even her own assumptions about what was happening for women of color in the startup world. She found that accelerators often did not accept black women because they didn't have a technical co-founder or because the programs did not relate to the women's target market. The result of all her research was #ProjectDiane, which produced the first in-depth report on tech entrepreneurship and black women. It found that only eleven companies founded by African American women had ever raised more than $1 million from investors.[11]

The findings set the stage for Kathryn's next chapter: the BIG Innovation Center, an Atlanta-based four-month accelerator for black and Latina tech founders that opened its doors in September 2016. It also offers a paid internship program for minority students studying software development. The center partnered with nearby HBCUs—historically black colleges and universities—including Spelman, the highly regarded women's college, to recruit participants. The accelerator program will offer coaching and funding through the Harriet Fund and Harriet Angels Syndicate, in which Kathryn has invested her own money. Kathryn told us she wants to dispel myths around leadership and black women, and her mission is to set women of color up for success by opening up a new kind of network so they can meet the right people to kick-start their businesses.

Black women in tech "want it," she said. "We want to go for it. We're ready to go for it. We tell people we want it. Our problem is that we didn't have sponsors. No one would sponsor us. No one would go to bat for us and say, 'This is the person who should have it.' We didn't have sponsors, and we didn't have mentors."

The lack of any network for many women led Kay Koplovitz, a trailblazing cable TV executive, to start Springboard, the first accelerator for women, in 2000. Back in the 1990s the "irrational exuberance" about tech startups—as Alan Greenspan, then-chair of the Federal Reserve, called the tech gold rush in 1996—had enabled techie guys to raise millions before the bubble burst.[12] Kay observed that women entrepreneurs, too, were starting tech companies, but most didn't have a clear entry point for raising institutional money.

"I looked at all of this money pouring over the transom. It was like over $100 billion in venture capital going into companies to secure a piece of equity to get some ownership in the company, and women were not part of that marketplace," she recalled. In the late 1990s, during Bill Clinton's second term, she chaired the National Women's Business Council. "I realized that we had to create an on-ramp. We had to knock down the door."

Springboard did so by arranging the very first pitch competition for women with the goal of getting one hundred companies to apply. Instead Springboard received 350 applications and selected twenty-six entrepreneurs to make presentations after going through a boot camp. The boot camp gave them access to a dream team of advisers—lawyers, accountants, entrepreneurs, investors—all in preparation for the women's big moment when they would discuss their companies before four hundred venture capitalists and angels. This was the first time many of the women entrepreneurs had ever pitched to professional investors.

It was January 27, 2000, and no one really knew what to expect, Kay said. But twenty-two companies secured funding, and five, including Zipcar, went on to issue initial public offerings. Sixty days after the event the tech market collapsed. In subsequent years venture capital funds would shut down as tech startups failed. Yet for Springboard there was no turning back. The non-profit would go on to put 642 companies through its program, and they collectively have raised $7.4 billion in capital. Thirteen have gone public and in 2016, 81 percent were still in business.[13]

According to Kay, Springboard's success comes from selecting founders who have a high tolerance for ambiguity. "They have learning agility. They are not fearful being in the unknown. They are not fearful about going forward without having the answer. They're inquisitive. They seek knowledge, and they import that into what they're doing on a rapid pace into their companies. They are able to learn and iterate quickly," she said.

What they get out of the Springboard program is a huge network of influential advisers, the human capital that so many people told us is critical to success. They also get help with fine-tuning their pitch presentations and take a confidence-building course focused on "speaking financial"—the language of investors—as well as what investors expect and the mechanics of selling to them. The program also emphasizes helping the women to become comfortable with self-promotion, which continues to be a sticking point for many women.

"What we have to get [them] more confident in is talking about themselves. It's a generalization, but it's still largely true: women don't like to brag about their own accomplishments. We have to teach them that that is something they must do in order to be successful," Kay said, echoing the advice of "selling the dream" that we heard from feminist financiers Susan Lyne and Joanne Wilson.

Paying It Forward

At 9 a.m. on a sunny spring Saturday morning in New York City, 150 female entrepreneurs from around the country listened intently as the glamorous Jenn Hyman, CEO of the fashion tech startup that democratizes luxury fashion, recounted the story of how she and her partner, Jenny Fleiss, sold their dream for Rent the Runway: as "Netflix for your wardrobe."

"In one of our first investor decks [presentation to investors], I used the phrase that I want to 'put the closet into the cloud,' just like music subscription has been put into the cloud via Spotify, [and] entertainment subscriptions [are] put in the cloud just like Netflix," Jenn said as she and Jenny were interviewed by Rebecca Jarvis, the *ABC News* business correspondent, for the panel called "How Big Is Big? Navigating Revenue and Investment Return Expectations in the World of Venture Capital."[14]

It was a revolutionary idea. But to be successful they had to literally change consumer behavior. And it wasn't easy.

"Women had never rented clothes prior to Rent the Runway. Men had rented tuxedos for, like, one occasion per year, but women had never rented clothes," Jenn told us a few months after the event. To pull it off, they relied heavily on word of mouth. "We had to convince [women] that renting clothes was cool and smart and aspirational, so that if they ever rented, and someone complimented them, they would actually tell others that they had 'rented the runway'—that they wouldn't hide it," Jenn said. If customers had hidden the source of their clothes, Rent the Runway would not have been able to grow because its customer acquisition costs would have been astronomical, she told us when we asked about their early ah-ha moments.

Rent the Runway found itself on the cutting edge of a whole new category of business—the rental economy. Yet neither woman had any fashion or technology experience when they began Rent the Runway in 2009, while they were still living in the dorms at Harvard Business School. They would load their course schedules with Monday and Tuesday classes so they could drive down to Manhattan to pound the pavement the rest of the week, cold-calling and trying to get fashion designers to sign on to the service. The superstars would go on to raise money from venture capitalists before graduating from Harvard. And they would eventually raise $186 million in venture funding and attract more than six million customers by the summer of 2016. Jenn's point in telling the story of that first pitch presentation was that you have to think *big*.

"Women are more conservative. They are not going to go into a room of venture capitalists and say, 'I have the next billion dollar idea!' So we thought, *How can we inspire and encourage women to think big and to realize the full potential of how their ideas could change the world?*" Jenn told the crowd listening to the kickoff of an April 2016 weekend summit they hosted to motivate the next generation of women entrepreneurs.

With their success seven years later, the partners decided the way to pay it forward wasn't as simple as sharing their startup story. They wanted to pass on the advice and insights they wished someone had shared with them when they were starting out: how to figure out the right investors, how to find the right team to accelerate your business, and how to network to find the best talent to build your company. They decided on a program called Project Entrepreneur, sponsored by the Rent the Runway Foundation and UBS, the financial services company. We were there to observe the packed day in which their mentees got tips from Jenn and Jenny and a host of other successful entrepreneurs, who joined the pair to share personal experiences and guidance on hiring, customer acquisition, and even how to manage financial projections and tips for hiring engineers.

"Jenny and I didn't have other people to talk to in the early days of Rent the Runway . . . We did not have engineering backgrounds. A lot of entrepreneurs at the time did, so they had different problems than we had," Jenn told us when we asked about the importance of creating an all-women event. She and Jenny want to help build the community of female founders. "I think that part of what makes the journey fun is having these other people around—to learn from [them] and celebrate with them—and that makes entrepreneurship a lot more rewarding," she said.

The weekend at a swanky downtown Manhattan hotel culminated with coaching on pitch presentations and a competition of twelve companies for three prizes of $10,000 each and three spots at Rent the Runway headquarters to work on their businesses for five weeks. As we waited to hear the winners announced, we struck up a conversation with some of the enthusiastic women who had spent the weekend exchanging business cards and soaking up the success stories of people like Carley Roney, co-founder of the Knot, the online wedding planner, and Alexandra Wilkis Wilson, co-founder and CEO of Glamsquad, an on-demand beauty service, as well as co-founder of and strategic adviser for Gilt, the online shopping site. Aside from one awkward moment, when Bethenny

Frankel, guest speaker and founder of Skinnygirl, the low-cal everything brand, was asked about strategies that women of color should use for pitching investors, and her answer was to get a white male co-founder, the weekend seemed to truly inspire the attendees.[15]

For Manal Kahi, the co-founder of Eat Offbeat, a meal delivery service that capitalizes on the culinary talents of refugees living in New York City, meeting other female entrepreneurs was uplifting. She was even more energized because it was a women-only event.

"You have to see it to be it. It gives us the courage to keep going and that, yes, we can get there," she said. Suelin Chen, who holds a PhD from MIT in materials science and engineering and formerly ran the Lab@Harvard, a program in the university's School of Engineering to support students' startup ideas, won one of the opportunities to be mentored by Jenn and Jenny. She told us that thus far, the outright sexism she had experienced as a tech entrepreneur was worse than anything she ever experienced in the science lab or academia.

Her focus for the five weeks at Rent the Runway headquarters was to hone her fund-raising pitch for her company, Cake, a platform for end-of-life planning, in the hope of raising a first round of investment in the next few months.

"What I'm working on now, and what I really hope to get out of Project Entrepreneur, is to be so overprepared, just so that there can be no doubt of my seriousness, my commitment, my knowledge, my capabilities," Suelin said.

To us that sounded like Suelin may have been suffering from the same lack of confidence we had heard other women express. But Jenn pushed back hard when we asked her what she thought. In fact, she said confidence is not the issue at all. It's that women founders simply haven't been getting as much advice, help, and feedback as their male counterparts for the incredibly challenging task of convincing investors to back them.

Women are "just getting less feedback. They're hearing less important information about how they should change the information that is actually in their pitch, the data that's there, [and instead it's] the way they stand, their tone of voice. A lot of this is about increasing avenues for women to meet with more people, to have more relationships, to increase the size of their network," she said. She added that Suelin had actually been given bad advice that led her to oversimplify the explanation of her product instead of imbuing it with the sophistication it and she deserved. Jenn was determined to get Suelin's pitch back on track in the coming weeks.

Despite all her success, Jenn wants to keep evolving and growing. And like many other tech CEOs, she has her own coach. During a recent "360 evaluation" he told her that some of her investors and board members thought she was too passionate. They wanted her to be less enthusiastic in meetings or in the language she uses about new initiatives. Instead of conforming, she challenged the feedback.

"It's a more feminine quality to be very enthusiastic and very warm and passionate," Jenn said. "I would say, more often than not a female leader is going to do that. Number two, that's actually what makes me me. That's part of me as a leader, that I am going to lift someone up, and they're going to feel incredible by nature of working on this new initiative at Rent the Runway, or by nature of coming into the team. No, I'm not going to scale that quality down in myself."

Still, few women have risen to the rank of CEO, and Jenn said that is part of the problem she wants to tackle with Jenny and the female founders, Eventbrite's Julia Hartz and ClassPass's Payal Kadakia, who found success at the same time Jenn and Jenny did. Jenn wants to bring visibility and acceptance to a new model of corporate leadership.

"There's not a lot of people to learn from, both for me as the leader and as the CEO, but also for my investors. They don't have any other female CEOs in their portfolio that lead board meetings or that they've seen grow and scale a company. I'm their only example, and all of my investors sit on many, many, many boards, and have sat on many boards for twenty to thirty years, and I'm their only example. It's a problem for all of us, that there aren't more examples," Jenn said.

Through Project Entrepreneur Jenn and Jenny are betting that Suelin and the other two founders who topped the competition will become those next-generation role models. As Suelin wrapped up her time with the program and prepared to face investors, she worried about another potential hurdle in building her business, one the boot camp did not address: motherhood. When we spoke, she was four months pregnant and working with Jenn to polish her business plan and presentation. Yet she hadn't told anyone at the accelerator of her good news.

"This is presenting a new challenge for me, a new kind of time pressure, which is sad, because it's so happy and exciting, but it's also something I'm hiding professionally," she confided.

CHAPTER 5

BUILD NEW WAYS TO WORK
Work-Life Warriors

The mommy penalty is real.
—SHERYL SANDBERG

I have a brain and a uterus, and I use both.
—CONGRESSWOMAN PATRICIA SCHROEDER'S
reply to "How can you be a lawmaker
and a mother?"

There is no such thing as work-life balance.
Everything worth fighting for unbalances your life.
—ALAIN DE BOTTON

Julia Hartz was on the brink of new motherhood when she and her husband, Kevin, opened Eventbrite, the largest online ticketing company in the world. It was 2006, and the company operated out of an old shared warehouse in San Francisco's Portrero Hill; the place was furnished with odd used pieces, including a red velvet chair shaped like a high heel that was so dirty Julia refused to sit on it. The couple had not yet turned thirty, lived on ramen, and worked non-stop. And they had a baby before they hired their first employees. Julia told us that going through the crazy transition to parenthood while starting Eventbrite influenced a lot of their decisions about the company's culture.

"We had a perspective of, 'Hey, if I were coming to a company and I was going through what we just went through, how would I want to feel? How would I want to be supported?'" she said.

From the weekly "Hearts to Hartz" open dialogues, which encourage "Britelings" (as Eventbrite refers to its six hundred employees) to ask any question they might have of Julia and Kevin, to the company's "Take the Time You Need" policy, which offers employees unlimited vacation time and a work-from-home option whenever needed, the couple's goal from the outset has been to create an environment in which people come first. They also provide an impressive "wellness hallway" with fully equipped nursing rooms that can be converted for massage, acupuncture, and nutrition sessions.

"At Eventbrite we care about the whole you, not just the employee you," she explained over lunch at Cavalier, a British brasserie two blocks from her office. Cavalier, run by restauranteur Anna Weinberg, whom Julia calls "a fierce female founder," looks like a scene from a Ralph Lauren ad, with its deep red walls adorned with horse prints and a hunting scene mural.

Julia, dressed in a crisp white shirt and classic black slacks, fit right in. The server greeted her like an old friend and brought over a complimentary appetizer.

We had met her only once before, but this thirty-seven-year-old mother of two has a way of making you feel like a friend. The woman named one of *Fortune*'s "most powerful women entrepreneurs" dished on the ultimate hack for child care (her mother, who lives close by), how she's experimenting with a meditation app to get more centered, and that even though she races home by six for dinner, she's rarely on e-mail after nine at night because she's just exhausted by that point. She acknowledged feeling guilty and anxious—and often embarrassed—about the amount of time she spends traveling for work, recently to Nashville, where the company was opening a new customer service center. To add to the guilt, her older daughter was becoming more vocal about her mother's frequent absences.

"I combat that by being truthful with her that I get sad every time I have to leave, and that actually seems to help ease her sadness," Julia said. "I know my daughter was dealt a very, very good birth card, but sometimes I feel like I want to honor the fact that she also drew a lottery that she didn't get to choose, which is that there is this thing called Eventbrite in our lives and it sometimes takes precedence."

While she conceded that being open about her own challenges in managing her personal life and work might strike some people as soft, she said that same openness is at the core of Eventbrite's success and its impressive record for hiring and retaining women. According to the company, in the fall of 2016, 48 percent of Eventbrite's employees were women, and nearly 43 percent of the company's management positions were held by women, statistics that earned it a nod from *Fortune* in 2015 as one of the best workplaces for women. A few weeks after our lunch Julia took over from Kevin as CEO, and they informed employees in the fall that he would be taking temporary leave to deal with an undisclosed medical issue. From the beginning, through new babies and running a startup, she and Kevin have always shared the work-life load equally, she emphasized.

"Kevin and I have really benefited from being fifty-fifty partners," she said. "Dads today want to be involved. They want to have time off to parent and leave work early and have a life outside of work too. It's not just the women."

She said that Kevin is the go-to guy in their household in the morning. He brings their school-age girls downstairs and makes them breakfast, including green smoothies. Even though she's up religiously at 5:55 a.m. to work out with her Pilates instructor or to spin on her Peloton bike and hang out a bit with the kids, she typically has no time for a morning meal. When the girls hear her heels clicking down the stairs at 7:30, they know it's time get on the road.

Since the early days of Eventbrite, which in September of 2016 was processing more than eight million tickets per month in 187 countries, cultivating strong female leaders has been Julia's passion. We witnessed this firsthand at a recruiting event where she invited a panel of "badass" women to share their experiences with prospective hires. She said she pushes women to take on leadership roles while providing them with the support and accommodations they need when life happens.

"It's important for women role models to really show up and continue to develop their own careers and be active role models for other women," she explained. "There is nothing more important, in hiring a female engineer, than to have a female engineer in the interview."

But she also wants the women in leadership to show their human side and be candid about how hard it can be to lean in while also raising kids and taking care of family. Because Julia has made that belief clear to her employees, Melody Mai was comfortable telling her boss that she was starting to burn out, a result of her hourlong commute and caring for her three children, one of whom was an infant. She knew she needed to take a few more vacation days, and she also wanted more flexibility so she could fit workouts into her days.

"It's really made a difference to know that my need for balancing time is supported," said Melody, the company's director of program management. "Knowing that I had the support I needed from the leadership really freed my guilt and made me more productive and engaged at work."

Eventbrite's offices feel like a place that tries cater to its employees' needs and tastes. The nursing rooms offer free disposable supplies and are equipped with hospital-grade breast pumps that cut the pumping time down to ten minutes. The bike room is crammed with commuters' cycles. And employees are free to work from comfy bean bag chairs, hammocks, and standing and treadmill desks. The company, which *Fortune* named one of the top one hundred workplaces for millennials, actually solicited ideas from the staff ahead of the move about what they wanted from their new South of Market digs, which also feature a library and expansive views of San Francisco.

On the day we visited, the room getting the most action was the boost bar, or the maker station, as Julia calls it. It's a DIY juice bar that's stocked daily with colorful fresh fruits and veggies, coconut water, milk of every variety—cow, almond, rice, soy—and scores of protein powders and "boosts." A woman was blending kale, cucumber, pineapple, banana, and coconut water in one of the two commercial mixers as we swung through. Julia, a former ballet dancer who started her career in cable television developing edgy programming for MTV and FX, said she came up with the juice bar after calculating how much money the company was spending on an outside vendor that delivered fresh, cold-pressed juice to the office a few times a week. She has found that the juice bar also encourages collaboration.

"It's part of our sharing economy at Eventbrite," she said with a laugh. "Not in the traditional sense, but in that you can't just make one serving. People collaborate and share their drinks."

Like many of its Silicon Valley counterparts, Eventbrite is watching its workforce of twentysomething college grads quickly mature into thirtysomething parents who care more about perks like the fully equipped nursing rooms, paid parental leave, and flexibility to manage child care than they do about foosball and beer on Fridays. Eventbrite's culture has had to evolve over time—not just its policies but its support systems.

The company recently upped its paid family leave to sixteen weeks for mothers and twelve weeks for secondary caregivers. Her goal is to get female employees past the first eighteen months of new motherhood, when many women drop out of the workforce, and to encourage them to look ahead five years and consider where they want to be.

"As Britelings started to have babies, whether it was the employee or their partner, we got them involved," Julia said. "We asked, 'What is it like to either have your partner expecting a baby, adopting a baby, or being pregnant yourself?' We try to offer an end-to-end support system that really celebrates the notion of having a baby, salutes its heroicness, and also supports the person because we don't want to be doomsayers. But I'm never going to tell anybody that having a baby is easy."

And, of course, neither is parenthood. As we finished our lunches, we found Julia candidly discussing how the responsibility of family can weigh heavily, something she wants her growing company to acknowledge to its employees in its bid to create a sense of respect for the work-life balance.

"It has everything to do with career development, leadership development, how we show up every day. What kind of tone and vibe does Eventbrite have inside the walls? How do we walk the walk? When push comes to shove, are we putting people last or people first?"

■   ■   ■

Conquering the Live-to-Work Mind-set

Working marathon hours is part of Silicon Valley's culture. The intensity and fast pace of the startup world were what drew co-author Samantha Walravens to the industry in the early days of the dot-com boom. The problem, however, is that this "live-to-work" mind-set favors the young—and puts at a disadvantage ambitious women who want to have children or anyone who wants to have a life outside work.[1]

"We didn't have a nonwork life: Life was work and work was life," writes Katherine Losse in her 2012 tell-all, *The Boy Kings: Into the Heart of the Social Network,* a book about her experiences as Facebook employee number 51 and eventually Mark Zuckerberg's ghostwriter.

"We did this because we expected that we would be rewarded accordingly—any short-term losses, such as the option to date casually and devote energy to nonwork pastimes would be more than compensated by long-term gain in the form of stock options we hoped would one day be worth millions of dollars. Facebook, we understood implicitly, was looking for soldiers, not journeymen," she reflects in the memoir, making it clear why anyone, especially those with caregiving obligations, would find it hard to work in such an inflexible environment. Research shows that more than half of mid-career women in the booming technology industry drop out—more than twice the rate of men.[2]

"But it doesn't have to be this way," argues Facebook cofounder, Dustin Moskovitz, who addressed the consequences of the fast-paced work-all-night culture of tech companies in a *Medium* post in August 2015.

"The research is clear: beyond ~40–50 hours per week, the marginal returns from additional work decrease rapidly and quickly become negative," wrote Zuckerberg's college roommate and Facebook's first chief technology officer. Moskovitz's essay refers to recent studies showing people actually perform more efficiently when they work fewer hours and fewer days per week. In the summer of 2015 a *New York Times* exposé of the bruising inner workings at Amazon and its unhappy white-collar employees was what inspired Moskovitz, who by then had gone on to co-found the workflow platform Asana, to take aim at the industry's work habits.[3]

"It is with deep sadness that I observe the current culture of intensity in the tech industry," Moskovitz declared. "My intellectual conclusion is that these companies are both destroying the personal lives of their employees and getting nothing in return."[4]

Moskovitz's is just one of many voices calling for tech companies to reexamine their ideas about work-life balance. Not long after he published his wake-up call, his old partner, Zuckerberg, the quintessential hacker in a hoodie, posted photos of himself changing his newborn daughter's diapers during his very public two-month paternity leave.

In fact, three-quarters of millennials today say that work-life balance and job flexibility are key determinants of their career choices. "New parents, and especially millennials in particular, crave opportunities for flexibility in their family lives and work lives," according to a 2016 Ewing Marion Kauffman Foundation report on entrepreneurship and motherhood.[5] Couple this with the increasingly difficult search for qualified technical workers, and it's easy to understand why tech companies have a new focus on work-life balance, especially parental leave policy. Across every industry corporations and startups alike will need an army of highly skilled employees to meet the demands of the digital age. Some employers are beginning to rethink whether being in the office every day—or at all—is still a necessity.

Redefining Who Works in Tech

And at the grassroots level, thanks in part to increasing opportunities to learn new high-tech skills, there are signs that new ways to work are becoming possible, especially for women who live far from Silicon Valley. That's what led Sarah Greer, thirty-nine, to go back to work.

At dusk on a Sunday evening in northern Atlanta, the Greer household, a family of six, had just wrapped up five hours of homeschooling led by Sarah. She and the children had focused all day on multiplication problems and on a Harry Potter unit in which they compared the wizarding world to the real one. After Sarah zipped to the supermarket to grab a couple of staples, the girls, aged three, eight, and ten, and their fifteen-year-old brother helped with dinner. It was make-your-own pizza night, and they were hanging in the kitchen, spreading sauce and sprinkling cheese on bread, while their parents popped their creations into the broiler. When dinner was over, they brought their plates to the sink, and the eight-year-old rinsed the dishes as Sarah settled into her "second shift" of the day in front of her laptop. She was running CodeGreer, her website design business. And business was booming.

"I built a website for a doula and [another one for] a copy editor. Right now, I'm working on one for a gentleman who sells nutritional supplements. A fitness trainer is coming up. A theater that's starting needs one. Oh—and a political campaign," she told us one morning as her children took a break from studying to play in a local park. Working at night in her living room for $50 an hour, Sarah can make more than her husband, Brian, who works for an information security company from home.

"It's not the kind of money right now that's paying my bills, but I have to say that I'm making per hour more than double what my husband does," Sarah said and went on to tell us that their long-term plan is to go into business together after the kids are grown and flown.

Sarah does not have a computer science degree. She attended

Georgia State for a year, and until she was laid off more than a decade ago, she worked in sales for EarthLink, an early Internet service provider that was recently acquired. But she loves coding and initially taught herself some basic programming so she could build a website to show off her baby photos. When Brian lost his job in 2007, Sarah started looking for a part-time gig to bring in a little extra money. She was turned down everywhere—even at Target.

"Nobody would look at me. Nobody would hire me. I had been out of the workforce for only a few years, but it was, like, 'No, you haven't worked in three or four years.' I just couldn't believe it. It was just shocking to me that just because I stopped to have kids, or because I got laid off, I was no longer hirable. In our homeschooling group, there were a lot of moms who felt the same way," she said.

But she and her friends did not simply accept that the working world could do without them. One by one the enterprising women in her circle began to start their own small businesses from home.

"These women were not going to let it stop them," she said. "I wasn't going to let it stop me either."

As she was trying to figure out what she would do, she happened to hear a podcast in late 2013 about the technical jobs of the future and the coming labor shortage of computer programmers. The interviewer was speaking to the founder of a fledgling online coding school, Skillcrush, that is aimed at women. Sarah checked out its website and signed up for classes that evening. First, she took a refresher in HTML, and a few weeks later she advanced to JavaScript, the programming language used to create the layouts, color schemes, and functionality that make a website engage its audience. She worked on the assignments at night, sometimes until midnight, with a break to walk on the treadmill for forty-five minutes. After three months a golf instructor who was friend of a friend approached her about designing a site to promote his lessons for children, and her new business, CodeGreer, was born.

Skillcrush is the brainchild of Adda Birnir, thirty-one, who set out to reinvent the outdated nine-to-five workplace and provide a new model of flexible, remote work that gives a woman like Sarah Greer, a college dropout and mother of four, the opportunity to start a business while homeschooling her kids.

"You deserve to have a creative, exciting job that makes you WANT to get out of bed in the morning," the Skillcrush website declares next to a photo of a hipster mom sporting nerdy glasses, an ornate tattoo on her bicep, and a stylish baby on her lap as she gazes at her computer. Adda describes the Skillcrush vibe as "feminine and a little punk rock."

Adda, tall and blonde with a playful smile, looked more like the fresh-faced girl next door than the badass rebel we were expecting. We first ran into the Southern California native, who grew up surfing and playing water polo in Santa Barbara, at the Write/Speak/Code conference in New York City in the spring of 2015 (see chapter 4). Some of the female software developers who attended that conference were Skillcrush grads. Those techies were trying to reach the next level on their unorthodox paths in a field full of men—exactly the attitude Adda's classes try to instill in Skillcrush students. The daughter of two University of California professors told us she started her business in New York City in 2012 after getting laid off from her marketing job just a few years earlier. She recalled looking around the office at the people losing their jobs that day and realizing the only staffers who had been retained had technical skills. The photography and African American studies major had always been curious about computer programming but never pursued it. But by the time her two weeks of severance pay ran out, she had taught herself HTML by reading a book, and she immediately started hawking her skills to friends who needed help creating websites. Her first job paid $1,000—more money than she had realized was possible. As she took on more projects, she sought out free online tutorials and e-mailed a former colleague when questions came up.

"I think I sort of just stumbled my way through it. A lot of it was just out of pure necessity. I definitely got work before I knew how to do that work," she said. She eventually parlayed everything she learned into Skillcrush, including how she figured out how to navigate and get taken seriously in a man's world.

"It's a little transgressive for a woman to want to go into a male-dominated industry like tech," she said with a grin. That's exactly how she markets her three-month courses, which she calls blueprints—and still teaches some herself. The classes appeal to a student with a taste for rocking the boat, the Yale grad said. "They have to want a little bit to be, 'Yeah, I can do that.' I want them to be, like, 'Fuck yeah, I can code.'"

As this book went to press, Skillcrush was charging $399 for each blueprint. For an hour a day for twelve weeks, they are schooled in the basics of front-end web design, mobile web design, social media marketing, and software development, and they have homework. Throughout the course they get a daily assignment and can videochat with teaching assistants and link up with a community of students and the mentors who coach them on marketing themselves, putting together portfolios, and drumming up freelance business.

The program also seeks to demystify the culture of the tech world, Adda said, by sharing the shortcuts nobody tells you about—how to get students comfortable with essential communication tools like Slack messaging and GitHub—as well as by translating the notoriously confusing insider jargon of Silicon Valley. One of the most important messages that Skillcrush imparts to its grads is that they will always be learning new skills on the job, they have the confidence to do it, and many companies will even pay for their ongoing training. "They don't need to master everything to get started," Adda explained.

Skillcrush is just one of the small but growing array of avenues for women to learn in-demand computer programming skills that will prepare them for the growing number of technical jobs in the United States. The for-profit programs run the gamut from online classes that run for weeks or a few months to intensive, in-person coding boot camps such as Hackbright Academy and Fullstack, which can cost more than $15,000, require a full-time commitment, and promise to funnel students directly into jobs. Forty-three percent of students graduating from the immersive U.S. coding schools were female in the fall of 2016, according to Course Report, a company that rates the programs.[6] What's different about Skillcrush is not only its focus on women in a virtual classroom but its entrepreneurial bent. The company does not promise a job upon completion of the classes. It seeks to educate students about how they can start earning money right away.

"My goal is to help women, to give women skills that allow them to increase their earning potential, and basically [to] have a positive economic impact on their lives," Adda said. It isn't far from what her father, a math professor, had famously predicted she would do with her life when he told family and friends at her high school graduation party that he couldn't wait for Adda, who had always been a bleeding heart, to "use science to save the world."

"I remember everyone was, like, 'What is he talking about? Science? I was, like, '*Ugh*, Dad. You're so ridiculous. Pushing your math agenda on me. It's so obviously not what I want to do.' He totally has the last laugh now," she said.

When we asked her for an update in the spring of 2016, she

reported that the company was enrolling about four hundred students per month. More than seven thousand people had already taken classes, and the majority were women, including twentysomethings in entry-level or administrative jobs who wanted to expand their earning potential. The second biggest group is mothers, like Sarah Greer, who are looking for a second act or a chance to earn extra cash while they stay home with their children.

As we chatted with Adda in a corner of Civic Hall in Manhattan, a wide-open co-working space that is home to a variety of social-good startups and a place where "headphones are the new walls" is literally true, she told us the company was growing quickly and had just closed on a $1 million investment, its first outside funding. She has a staff of thirty, including an all-female technical team, and Adda is convinced that opportunities to work in technology should not be limited by pedigree, location, schedule, or employment by big tech corporations.

"At the end of the day, I don't think that Google is allowed to be a gatekeeper for whether or not women get to take advantage of the opportunities that tech can afford you," she stressed.

Meet the MotherCoders

Indeed, you don't have to get hired by Google or any of the Silicon Valley giants to work in a range of technology jobs these days. With the digital revolution disrupting every sector of the global economy, technology touches most vocations, and technical jobs are plentiful. Technical talent is not. The oft-cited statistic from Code.org is that the United States will have 1.4 million computing-related job openings by 2020; as of late 2016, more than 523,000 positions were unfilled.[7] Code.org reports that computing jobs are the number-one source of new employment in the United States.[8] MotherCoders, a San Francisco part-time for moms looking to change careers or return to work after years at home, seeks to open mothers' eyes to the possibilities.

It all started with a middle-of-the-night meltdown. It was fall 2013, and Tina Lee was stretched thin—nursing her newborn, caring for her toddler, and sneaking in weekend classes to relearn some coding. She had always worked in tech, but with her economics and politics degree from Mills College she gravitated to the business side, not the "building" side. Yet she was always intrigued by the idea of making things. By the time she had her first child, she had completed a master's in Stanford's Learning, Design and Technology program but still craved more practical tech skills. So she had set about relearning CSS, a programming language used to design and develop websites, while pregnant with her second child and working in the California Controller's Office. As she sat at home in tears between breast-feeding sessions that night, Tina realized she had been trying to do the impossible: taking classes despite sleepless nights and few options for babysitting. And that's how MotherCoders, her tech orientation program offering on-site child care, was born.

"[It's] for women who are, like, 'I know I want to do something but I don't know where to start,'" Tina told us one foggy morning in San Francisco's Richmond District two years after the infamous meltdown. "The analogy I use is it's like immigrating to a new country, and we're like the welcome desk that says, 'Let's give you some language classes, let's teach you some of the customs and history so you understand why these people are the way they are, give you some friends so you can feed off that.'" She said that MotherCoders gives students an overview of the industry. As a finalist in the 2015 Google Impact Bay Area Challenge, MotherCoders had received $100,000 from Google for its service to the Bay Area and its innovative approach. In spring 2016 she was looking ahead to upcoming sessions in two new neighborhoods, planning to expand the program.

Sarah Doczy was one of the first women to sign up when Tina started the first class. Sarah, who had a toddler at the time, had been trying to learn to code on her own through tutorials offered by Codeacademy.com. She wanted more, but as she searched for in-person workshops and seminars, she found that their hours often conflicted with her full-time job and her family responsibilities. When she found MotherCoders on Twitter and saw the courses were held on Saturdays *and* offered babysitting, she was all in. From the very first class she felt like she belonged.

"That was the first time during my coding journey that I never felt like I had to explain myself because, being a mom, you have all these other responsibilities. I can't just go home and code whenever I want or learn new skills," she told us by phone from Dayton, Ohio, where she had moved with her husband and daughter a year after we spoke with her and landed a web developer job with a local startup right away.

The initial MotherCoder classes, held on six Saturdays at a co-working space in San Francisco's Portrero Hill, featured coursework by Skillcrush. Tina expanded the program to nine weeks and added the language JavaScript in 2016. But as the program evolved, Tina decided the women, all of whom were college educated and many of whom had been out of the work-force for as long as ten to fifteen years, needed a more human touch and a greater emphasis on their potential. She started to bring in women who were working in tech, including mothers, to share their stories and their career paths. She put her Stan-ford training in design thinking to work by focusing the small seminars on problem solving rather than teaching only the rudiments of computer languages.

"You pick a problem that you feel passionate about, then you figure out how tech plays into that. You don't start with tech, you start with a problem. Then we try to connect the dots," she said of the orientation she gives students to fields ranging from data science to security to software development.

"We're teaching moms to participate at the product level: 'We identified this problem. This is the way we're going to solve it.' That's preparing them to engage in a way that's more than just 'I'm going to decide if the button should be red or blue and go here or there.' It's really like, 'I am solving a problem as a human and I'm going to use everything that I have to do that,'" she said.

Tina wants her students to feel empowered about the career possibilities ahead. Sarah was fortunate to step into a junior developer job with the beauty retailer Sephora as soon as she graduated, which led to her new full-fledged developer position in Dayton. But her story is the exception. Most of the MotherCoders will need more coursework or experience before they can move into a new career. And that's okay, said Tina, whose energy is infectious. The goal is for them to figure out what they like and how to get there. One of most important points she tries to impress upon her students is the flexibility that many of the new jobs can offer.

"What mainly drew me to it was, 'Hey, you don't have to work a nine-to-five job in this position," Sarah said. "You could have very flexible hours. You very often can work from home. You basically just need a computer and the Internet, and that's about it."

That was how thirty-year-old Erin Foust found herself working forty hours a week from home for the Yelp-like baby product review site weeSpring, the result of a stressful eight-month job search with her own new baby in tow. She and her husband, Tyler, a Marine Corps combat veteran, were scrimping to get by, living off savings and his GI Bill stipend in a cramped apartment in a suburb of Salem, Oregon, in the spring of 2015 while she interviewed for jobs and he went back to school. Erin, who grew up in the area, had been looking for work since recently graduating with a degree in digital communication and after taking some coding classes online. She finally found a position as a product manager and designer that allowed her to work from home around her son's schedule. She was matched with her Boulder-based employer by PowerToFly, a fast-growing marketplace that connects women with technical skills to businesses that may feature jobs that don't require employees to work on-site.

"If we have a doctor appointment we need to run our kids to, we can work at any time, to make up those hours—like, after my son goes to sleep, I'll just work during that time. It's really flexible, especially if you're the go-getter type," Erin told us. The product manager communicates with her colleagues on Slack throughout the day as she collaborates on coding e-mail newsletters, building the site's portal for product reviews, and designing materials. Erin, who drops two-year-old Liam at a neighborhood day care at eight each morning and picks him up each night at five, says telecommuting is not for everyone. She has to be extremely disciplined and organized to meet her deadlines, but she likes to work independently and doesn't crave the social outlet of an office.

Working Anywhere, Anytime

"The future of work for women is not in an expensive office space. It's in the cloud. It's around the virtual water cooler, not in a cubicle or tech 'campus.' It's women working from where they are most productive for their lives and careers," proclaims the slick marketing materials for PowerToFly, the company that found Erin her position. By the spring of 2016, a year and a half after it opened for business, the venture-backed global platform had vetted and enabled more than 80,000 women from 143 countries to connect with full-time and contract technical positions at 1,500 companies, including BuzzFeed, Hearst, Time Inc., Aetna, and Caterpillar.

So it makes sense that the first time we talked to the brains behind PowerToFly, we did so over Skype in the middle of a New York blizzard—all of us in distant locations. In fact, we didn't meet co-founders Milena Berry and Katharine Zaleski face to face until we finally got together a year later on a rare day that they were in a traditional office, the trendy digs of Lerer Hippeau Ventures, the SoHo venture capital firm that invests in startups early and one of PowerToFly's first backers. Milena, who was born in Bulgaria and speaks six languages, was accustomed to running operations from a distance. She had worked from home in a C-suite job without the suite while nursing her three children over six years. Her friends who were mothers thought she had the ultimate gig, running back-end operations for the international political organizing platform Avaaz.org from her home office with a nanny to help her manage.

"I was there nursing . . . and solving a server crisis in India or something. I think my experience was wonderful, being able to retain a CTO-level [job] while breast-feeding my three kids," she told us over Skype from her Manhattan apartment. She was busy overseeing remote computer programmers on six continents when in 2013, her mentor and idol Red Burns, the New York University computer scientist known as the "godmother of Silicon Alley," died at the age of eighty-eight. Milena, who is married to Paul Berry, the founder and CEO of RebelMouse (the first digital platform for publishing on social media), was so moved by Burns's death that Milena immediately started poring over Burns's writings on communication and cultural diversity, and it sparked a business idea.

She recalls thinking: "What if we could solve the problem that everybody's talking about, not having enough women in tech, by extrapolating my experience, of working six years with three kids, to women around the world? Yes, the model can work, because I've seen it work with Avaaz."

Milena's inspiration and global perspective evolved into a high-tech head-hunting business that matches technical women with long-distance jobs, freeing them from long commutes and inflexible or unreliable child care and opening up thousands of new opportunities to women around the world. Companies subscribe to the service, which also offers payroll management; job seekers use it for free. After a fateful coffee date in early 2014, Milena teamed up with Katharine, a former senior editor at the *Huffington Post* who worked with Milena's husband when he was its chief technology officer and Ken Lerer—the Lerer of Lerer Hippeau—was *HuffPo*'s chairman and co-founder.

Katharine, a thirtysomething who moved with ease in elite New York and Washington media circles, was a go-getter living the hipster lifestyle with her filmmaker husband and newborn. After leaving *HuffPo*, where she had been the sixth hire, she continued rocketing quickly through the ranks of digital journalism, including heading digital news at the Washington Post Company. Katharine eventually landed at *NowThis News* and was on maternity leave from her managing editor post when she got the call from Milena. Katharine, who had majored in history at Dartmouth, was known for her workhorse habits, boasting about twelve-hour days and being the last one to leave the office at night. But the birth of her daughter changed all that. When she met Milena that morning at a downtown bookstore cafe, it was the first time in weeks she had emerged from her apartment, and she was struggling with the impending end of her parental leave.

"I really wanted to go back to work. I was really bored. It was lonely. It's the darkest winter ever. Maybe it was darker because I was up at three o'clock every morning," she said of the particular pains of new motherhood.

"I've always been very career driven and made more money than my husband. I've always had a career that really pushed farther. I just felt like I had all these choices in the world, and then they were very quickly cut down to two choices: Am I going to go back to work full time or am I going to find a way to be able to nurse and be able to be around my kid?" Even as she was struggling with her own work-life dilemma, she wasn't entirely convinced of Milena's idea—that remote work could be an answer, she said. But eventually she came around, and in a few weeks she started developing the distinct editorial content and voice of PowerToFly.

"I just realized how crazy it was to have to leave every morning at 7:30 and then be home every night at 7:30. I was just never going to see [my daughter], and so I was confronted with this issue that millions and millions of mothers are confronted with every year. It very quickly became personal for me," Katharine explained.

A year later PowerToFly's president set off a firestorm when she published a now-infamous apology to working mothers on *Fortune.com* in which she admitted that until she became a mother herself, she had quietly undermined moms because she saw them as not committed to their careers. In the piece, which was published a few months after PowerToFly opened for business, Katharine confessed she would "schedule last-minute meetings at 4:30 p.m. all the time" and "secretly roll her eyes when a mother couldn't make it to last-minute drinks."

In that commentary she acknowledged that "for mothers in the workplace, it's death by a thousand cuts—and sometimes it's other women holding the knives." The raw admission, which went viral, elicited such strong reactions from supporters and naysayers alike that she appeared on the *Today* show to defend her motherhood epiphany while touting the new company.

Twenty-four-year-old Brittany Hadfield, seven months pregnant and stressed out, had the TV on that morning. The aspiring web designer was taking a full load of courses and working three jobs to pay for school. She knew that once she graduated from East Stroudsburg State in Pennsylvania and moved to Florida to be with her fiancé, making enough money to cover day care for her newborn would be next to impossible. And she wasn't so sure she wanted someone else to watch the baby, but she really was going to need a job.

Brittany's parents were pressuring her to figure out a plan when she saw Katharine talking up PowerToFly and created a free profile on its website on the spot. By commencement a couple of months later, Brittany had a thirty-hour-per-week contract with the startup weeSpring, the same review site for new parents that employs Erin Foust. Now Brit's typical day starts at 4:30 a.m. when she wakes to nurse little Owen, then puts him back to bed, grabs coffee and a shower, and is working on social media marketing and laying out the content for weeSpring's weekly newsletters before the sun comes up. She works around Owen's two naps until 5 p.m., when her new husband, Travis, returns from his job to take over the baby's care. She takes breaks from work when Owen needs to go for his checkups or sometimes they even head to the beach in Port Saint Lucie for a playdate, which is what they were doing the day we spoke by telephone. She stays on e-mail until it's time for bed, and she has taken on some freelance projects to supplement her work with weeSpring. Her husband isn't crazy about her e-mailing late at night, but it's a sacrifice they make so Brit can keep up with her work. "If it's six o'clock here and I have a client in California, it's only three o'clock there. Their workday is still going. I kind of have to be on for their workday," she said. But she knows this schedule won't last long, so she's already lined up the help of Owen's godmother and another stay-at-home mom in the neighborhood. Once Owen drops his morning and afternoon naps, she'll need them to take over while she works.

In fact, Milena says the point of PowerToFly is not to help mothers get around child-care needs. "There is a misconception out there that you can pull off a remote job with a lot of responsibilities and be taking care of your kids or work while they're napping," she said. "That's not what we're talking about, and that's not the platform that we're building. In fact, we are educating all of our talent that that's not fair to the employer."

But the company is open about serving a need for mothers of young children by affording them flexibility in managing their responsibilities. In contrast to the days when women in offices feared displaying their children's artwork or family photos on their desks, PowerToFly highlights and celebrates their stories on its website.

"The whole idea is that, you know, women are sort of being women. In a way, it feels like it shows more of their motivations. We're completely transparent about that: 'I need this job: I have three mouths to feed. Obviously I'm incredibly dedicated, and I'm also really good at time management because I have three mouths to feed,'" Katharine said.

Solutions for the Sandwich Generation

Caregiving is not limited to one's children, of course. No one knows that better than Kristen Koh Goldstein, who made a

heart-wrenching decision the day her father was dying. Ironically, the founder of HireAthena, a software platform that au-
tomates payroll, accounting, and other back-office support for
small companies and nonprofits with remote workforces, was
slated to speak about the future of work at an innovation
conference sponsored by the mayor of San Francisco. Her
dad, who she says was her best friend, had been living with
Kristen, her husband, Mark, and their three children throughout his battle with cancer. Now doctors told the family that his
organs were failing. Her brothers decided that she should have
the honor of holding their father's hand as he took his last
breaths. But her father had other ideas: he did not want Kristen to shirk her commitment to speak. He squeezed her hand
to let her know he wanted her to go to the conference. So in a
last-minute frenzy she sped from the University of California
San Francisco Medical Center to the event downtown and
raced back two hours later, praying as she rode in an Uber that
she would make it back in time. It was the longest ride of her
life, but she made it.

"I told him it went great. I told him about what I said, about
the fact that we're trying to reinvent the future of work for his
grandchildren, and he squeezed my hand twice, let me know
he was proud of me, then he passed away," she told us. The conversation had us all in tears.

The bitter conflict she faced that day typified the problem
Kristen had been trying to solve for herself when she set out
six years earlier to start a company she claimed could bring a
million mothers back into the labor force. She wanted to help
high-level professionals who didn't want to put their careers on
hold. It was a conundrum intimately familiar to the Harvard
MBA and former Goldman Sachs investment analyst. Spurred
by the deaths of several friends as a result of 9/11, she had decided to switch to the operational side of banking and eventually

went on to co-found a software company, Loyalty Lab, with her husband, a serial entrepreneur. During that period she worked as the company's CFO and gave birth to two children. She soon realized the nutty hours were wreaking havoc with her personal life, and finally she quit. She started to look for another position and came up short.

"I couldn't find a job where they thought it was normal for me to work from home or have a flexible work schedule because I happened to be supereducated, and the jobs that were available to me that would exercise my skill set and experience required lots of travel and twelve- to eighteen-hour days," she recalled. "I didn't want to be a captain of industry for just those ten scarce years where my children need me when they're young."

Choosing to leave the workforce left Kristen, who is now forty-six, depressed and questioning whether she would ever feel relevant again in the professional world. Along the way she started talking to other women with fancy graduate degrees and long résumés in her tony San Francisco suburb. They, too, craved career opportunities they could tackle during the school day, and Kristen believed technology could help them do it but she was so down on herself she felt stifled. The turning point came with a strong nudge from a longtime friend and neighbor, the venture capitalist Aileen Lee.

"Aileen told me it was not an option to wallow in self-doubt. She was firm," Kristen recalled of her friend's insistence that she still had much to offer the professional world. And she told us Aileen wasted no time introducing her to business connections, parlaying personal capital to make sure Kristen went back to work. In a heartfelt LinkedIn piece that ran in 2015, Kristen referred to Lee's help as an example of the "secret society" of Silicon Valley.

With her friend's encouragement, Kristen ultimately went

on to found BackOps, the first iteration of HireAthena, a cloud-based service for small businesses to manage and automate payroll, accounting, and human relations by tapping the expertise of work-at-home mothers. BackOps quickly spun off a second venture called Scalus, proprietary enterprise software Kristen developed to help her clients objectively assess the productivity of remote workers. When we first spoke with Kristen, who was born in South Korea and grew up on Guam, she was working full tilt, running both startups at the same time.

In the spring of 2016, a few months after her father died, she merged Scalus and BackOps into HireAthena, named for her daughter. The company has raised a total of $10 million in equity financing from some of the best and brightest venture investors in the Valley and by the fall of 2016 had begun to turn a profit. Tired yet exhilarated, she wished she had more time to spend with her girlfriends—to hike or share a glass of wine with members of the sisterhood, which includes Lee, venture capitalist Heidi Roizen, and Square's chief financial officer, Sarah Friar. As Kristen works long hours once again, her tight circle of peers and their work-life challenges continue to remind her that what she is doing matters.

"We are the sandwich generation," Kristen said. "We have parents we must take care of, we have babies to take care of. Hopefully we all make it long enough that we can take care of ourselves. This is the story of me and my friends."

Designing a Human Company

While Kristen was developing Scalus's technology in San Francisco, another entrepreneur on the opposite coast got her own chilling reminder of the fragility of life. On the night of the 2014 holiday office party CEO Sara Holoubek learned that one of her team members had suffered a late-stage miscarriage. No one in the office had ever faced such a devastating personal crisis, and she wasn't sure how to handle it. She was deeply saddened and in the back of her mind, she also wondered what was the "right" thing to do in terms of offering leave to her employee. The next day, after the shock wore off, the answer revealed itself, Sara said.

"Forget female friendly, forget family friendly, we just have to be a human company. It just hit me. We have to do the human thing, [and] the human thing is to tell her, 'Take whatever time you need. Don't worry about your check. It's still coming,'" Sara told us. That was when she decided that small and growing companies need help figuring out how to create a culture that values people, not simply their productivity.

Forget the sexy workspaces with free booze, bottomless candy bins, and pool tables that Silicon Valley tech startups typically use to lure young single bros to their workforces. Sara argues that the new generation of entrepreneurs, and the investors backing them, should reconsider the value proposition of the happiness, health, and well-being of their employees.

"When I look at the amount of money that is spent on really slick offices and keggers, I think, 'Wow, and that company's telling me they can't offer family leave, or they can't have a 401(k) matching program?' It literally makes me sick," she said.

In her *Human Company Playbook*, published in 2015, she shows how some high-growth companies like Pinterest, Birchbox, Etsy, and The Muse are starting to change their cultures by swapping the trendy perks that entice employees to work all the time and instead offer the real benefits that matter for the long haul, such as covering more health-care insurance costs and offering longer paid parental leave, better retirement plans, and equity stakes.

"I think tech is the perfect industry for this because these companies are new or early enough that they can evolve," Sara told us when we met on a spring afternoon in her sunny office around the corner from Manhattan's Flatiron Building. "Rather than asking women and families to fit into your company structure, we have to redefine company design and structure for women and families and fathers and people who just want to date or go to yoga. Whatever it is that you want to do, your company structure should allow for that."

Sara, who grew up on a small farm in rural Wisconsin between Madison and Milwaukee, said it didn't occur to her initially, but she realized as we probed that her childhood inspired her thinking. She grew up in what she calls a traditional Midwestern family where hard work and being neighborly were major threads in the fabric of the community. Her father was one of the early inventors of the iron-on patch, and his patents on the tape- and heat-transfer machines would be used by everyone from Harley-Davidson to government agencies. But while he worked long hours at his silk-screening business for forty years and then tended to the cattle, horses, and chickens, when he walked into the house at night he always made time for family. He and her mother, who ran her own licensed apparel company, both drove home the value of giving back and taking care of others.

At her strategic consulting firm, Luminary Labs, Sara strives for a similar culture—where people work hard but, she hopes, won't have regrets about the choices they've made in the work-life juggle. And that requires the people at the top to walk the walk, she said. If a job offers flexible work hours but *flexible* means no one, including the boss, is really ever off the clock, that's not human, as she put it.

"It's heartbreaking that we are raising an entire generation to believe that unless you sacrifice your life, you will not succeed. You have to model it," Sara told us.

In her own firm she tries hard not to send e-mail after hours. Sara, who has two children at home, will often work over the weekend and put correspondence in a draft folder to send on Monday morning instead of bothering her staff when they should be relaxing and tending to their own lives. If she leaves before five to pick up her kids, she expects that others on the team will too. And Luminary Labs offers eight sick days *and* enforces a "stay home, get better" policy that sends employees home to rest and recuperate at the first sign of a sniffle.

Her mantra is "We've got your back."

CHAPTER 6

CRUSH THE STEREOTYPES
Campus Crusaders

*A ship in port is safe, but that's not what ships are
built for. Sail out to sea and do new things.*
—U.S. NAVY REAR ADMIRAL GRACE HOPPER

The most effective way to do it is to do it.
—AMELIA EARHART

Kelsey Hrubes could feel the eyes of her classmates on her
platinum blonde tresses, dramatic eye shadow, and long, deeply
tanned legs as she descended the steps of the lecture hall for the
first day of Intro to JavaScript Programming. It was her first
time away from home, and in her too-short minidress, she was
trying to live out her freshman fantasy of being the hot sorority girl on the sprawling Iowa State University campus in Ames.
She was, admittedly, clueless about how her look would play in
the computer science department.

Some people in the mostly male class stared when she
walked in. Others tried to look away as a scene ripped straight
from *Legally Blonde* unfolded in front of them. A guy Kelsey recognized from her high school strolled over and asked her what
she later realized everyone else was probably thinking: "What
are you doing here?" She told him she was planning to major
in computer science.

"And he actually scoffed, like a TV character," she recalls.

That moment shook her confidence. But more than that, it made her angry. She dove zealously into her studies, went on to secure a coveted summer internship at Google in Mountain View, California, and started the first coding camp for high school girls in Iowa. What really helped, she said, is that she had taught herself HTML and the programming language CSS back in middle school, albeit for the purpose of impressing her friends by having the coolest MySpace profile.

With that background, "the logic of coding clicked right way," she said. "And the party girl image I longed for faded away with my tan."

When we met her in early January 2016, Kelsey, by then a college junior and still blonde but more understated in a dark gray knit dress and black tights, was presenting a programming project she had worked on tirelessly for five days with a half-dozen other female college students. This was the culmination of Code Camp, a sought-after weeklong apprenticeship at the sleek offices of Square, the publicly traded on-the-go credit card payment company founded and run by Jack Dorsey, co-founder of Twitter. Kelsey had spent the week with nineteen other young women handpicked from colleges and universities around the country, including Harvard, Vassar, and Mount Holyoke. Like most tech companies, Square needs to find more talent. And inviting promising female engineers to see what it's really like to work inside a growing company, with free sushi, made-to-order smoothies, and on-site yoga classes, is one way to do that.

Kelsey confided that because she was from a large state university, she was at first intimidated by the accomplishments of her cohort on paper, especially those from the Ivy League. But after a week she had learned that most of them had certain worries and struggles in common. The friendships they cemented after living and working together in San Francisco were invaluable. They confided in each other their concerns about what they had heard about the "masters of the universe" culture of Silicon Valley and their personal struggles with perfectionism. With Square mentors they role-played and practiced strategies for their upcoming job interviews and learned how to handle the intimidating whiteboard challenges (computer programming tests software engineer interviewees face during job interviews) that would call upon them to display their coding prowess. And they met real women kicking ass and succeeding in the industry, like Square CFO Sarah Friar.

"The best part of having gone to Code Camp is the network I have access to. Code Camp alum are at every major tech company, and [they are] creating the next generation of innovative startups. The quality of mentorship available to me is crazy," Kelsey said.

The young women clearly left Square feeling that they were part of something bigger than themselves. Forging crucial ties in a field with so few women is one reason two computer research scientists, Anita Borg and Telle Whitney, got together more than two decades ago to start the first annual gathering of female technologists. It would grow into the largest event of its kind in the world and become a key recruiting tool, especially since tech companies have come under pressure to diversify. Of course, we wanted to experience the Grace Hopper Celebration of Women in Computing for ourselves.

On a searing October afternoon in downtown Houston, the blinding sun was glinting off mirrored skyscrapers high above us and beating down on the wide asphalt boulevards as we made our way to the George R. Brown Convention Center. We were heading to the 2015 Hopper conference. Tickets for the event, named in memory of a pioneer many Americans have never heard of, sold out in a record eight days. U.S. Navy

Rear Admiral Grace Murray Hopper, known as the queen of code, was one of the creators of COBOL, the forerunner of today's modern computer programming languages, and the person credited with coining the term *debug*, which means fixing an error in a line of code. She is one of the most important figures in the history of modern computing, beginning in 1944 with her U.S. Navy assignment as a mathematical officer to maintain the Harvard Mark I, "a room-sized, relay-based calculator" that was the first programmable digital computer.[1] Megan Smith, chief technology officer of the United States since 2014, has referred to Hopper as " 'an Edison-level American' without Edison-level recognition."[2] But for this crowd, "Amazing Grace," who was laid to rest in Arlington National Cemetery in 1992, is a rock star.

As we entered the massive hall, which stretches eleven city blocks, we were immediately swept up in the girl power vibe. Everyone seemed to greet one another with the warmth and openness of long-lost friends. And then it hit us. Being here, surrounded by nearly twelve thousand female computer scientists and engineers, really was like being on another planet for these women—for once, they were the majority.

"I think it's hard to imagine being in a field where you feel like you're the only one a lot of the time. Then you go somewhere else and you're, like, 'Oh, my God, there are so many of us,'" gushed twenty-year-old Mopewa Ogundipe, a Carnegie Mellon University senior majoring in computer science and robotics, who arrived in Houston ready to interview at the epic career fair for six-figure entry-level jobs in the Valley. She already had one offer in hand and was in contention for another software developer position at a big company, but she wanted to see what else might be interesting, perhaps a product manager job. But like many of the college women we met there, Mopewa and her friend Niki Maheshwari, also a CS major, told us they weren't eager to start their own companies, at least not right away. They wanted job security and benefits upon graduation. And they were not enticed by the rollercoaster ride of all-night hackathons, Red Bull, and a last-man-standing mentality.

In its two-decade history this was the biggest Hopper yet, nearly doubling in attendance from the year before. The young, racially and ethnically mixed crowd was clad in backpacks, jeans, and t-shirts. Most attendees were younger than thirty-four, still in their first or second jobs or studying their hearts out in grueling academic programs. The college contingent was why we were there. We had heard many people blame the small numbers of women in tech on a paucity of women pursuing computer science and engineering degrees since the mid-1990s. It's true: although the numbers appear to be inching up, female students still make up a fraction of the recipients of degrees in computer science in the United States. Only 14.1 percent of CS degrees were conferred on women in the 2013–14 school year, down from the all-time high of 37 percent in 1985, as reported by the National Center for Education Statistics.[3] But as we looked around at the tribe of confident young women hugging each other hello, swapping strategies for acing the whiteboard portion of their job interviews, and trading inside info on internships, we realized we had hit the motherlode. The future innovators were in Houston, and they were ready to roar.

Next to the long buffet table set with fresh fruit kebabs, dainty plastic cups of granola, and bottles of water was a massive chalkboard that beckoned attendees to fill in the blank in the affirmation "I am most proud of _____." Scrawled in hot pink, electric blue, and bright green, their powerful responses told us a lot about this tenacious group:

> I am most proud of my perseverance and my family.
> I am most proud of fighting for what I deserve.

I am most proud of MY MEAN CODING SKILLS.

I am most proud of being a role model.

I am most proud of surviving.

The theme for the conference was "our time to lead," and the idea that "a rising tide lifts all boats" was woven throughout the hundreds of panels, workshops, and town halls on the three-day agenda. These women were told at every turn that they have a responsibility to each other. "Ask yourself for five minutes a day what you have done to empower somebody else," Cal Poly software engineer Carol Willing entreated hundreds of young programmers who had packed into a panel on sisterhood. "Raise up the women around you. Assume people want to help because they do."

As we strolled through the exhibit hall, we didn't know where to look first. The carnival of colorful, brightly lit booths featured such companies as Yelp, Macy's, Lockheed Martin, GoDaddy, Accenture, Fidelity, and Airbnb and showed off a range of enticing opportunities for this suddenly sought-after group. In one corner Capital One bank was raffling off Apple watches. Across the way SurveyMonkey beckoned candidates with a sign that said, THE MONKEY WANTS YOU. Square handed out purple t-shirts as its recruiters talked up Code Camp and encouraged students to apply.

"It's like a Disneyland of opportunities," bubbled Brianna Fugate, a nineteen-year-old Spelman College sophomore who was amazed to see recruiters from Disney's Pixar Studios and investment banks like Goldman Sachs when she first attended in 2014. "I didn't know that technology was so permeating in our lives that you can do CS anywhere," she said. "That's really what Grace Hopper taught me, that you can do CS anywhere. All these companies are looking for people like me."

As they chatted, eagerly introducing themselves, the women

seemed pumped to be making new friends, schmoozing with recruiters from tech giants and startups alike at the job fair, and being inspired by a lineup of luminaries that included You-Tube's Susan Wojcicki; Reshma Saujani, founder of Girls Who Code; and Hearsay Social's Clara Shih. Make no mistake: this was a pep rally. And its head cheerleader in 2015 was none other than their idol, Sheryl Sandberg, who delivered a fifty-minute fireside chat just six months after tragically losing her husband, Dave Goldberg.

With her Starbucks Grande in hand, the leader of the Lean In movement was the perfectly coiffed yet accessible exec in skinny black suede knee-high boots, caramel suede mini, and dark V-neck sweater. She took questions from the huge crowd and answered with the intimacy and realness of a big sister. She acknowledged she'd be better at her job if she knew how to code. She confided that she wasn't always proud of being smart when she was a teen and that being good at math wasn't cool at her large public high school in Miami. She told the crowd to battle feelings of insecurity by keeping a small notebook by the bedside, as she started doing after her husband died, and to write down three things each night they do well. "Not something I'm grateful for. Not something someone else did well. Not something I didn't do well. But three things I did well," she said of how she boosts her confidence these days. And Sandberg evoked loud whoops and applause as she begged the crowd to "stay in tech."

"These are the best jobs, and this is an incredible industry, both in terms of impact and in terms of flexibility. Stay in. Stay in for yourselves because they are better careers, and stay in for the women who follow you. And stay in for my eight-year-old daughter," she said as the hall exploded in cheers.

But "staying in," as we heard from the hundreds of women we interviewed, is easier said than done. With more than half of technical women dropping out at mid-career, the "leaky pipe-line" is real. And this group of young women, many of whom attended the conference on scholarships sponsored by their universities and other non-profits supporting women in tech, had a palpable hunger for practical strategies and guidance about how to stay in tech. On the first evening of the conference, we attended a standing-room only panel, "How to Become a Badass Woman in Tech," where veteran software engineers from Morgan Stanley, Uber, and Intel shared stories of how they had overcome some of the adversity of working in a man's world—how they found guys in the office to champion them, built partnerships with those male allies, and pushed themselves to speak up in meetings and volunteer for new projects.

"You will be outnumbered, and strongly outnumbered," said Rahima Mohammed, a lead engineer at Intel, who cautioned that hard work isn't enough and advised that they will need to work on their communication skills and style to get ahead. "You need to speak up, even if you have difficulty," she emphasized.

"A lot of students don't have leadership in mind [when they enter the field] because they think being a woman in tech will hold them back," noted Paulina Ramos, an Uber software engineer and member of the #LadyENG group at the company. "But being a woman in this industry, you *are* a leader." She and the others went on to detail leadership opportunities—both large and small—that young women can take on as mentors and volunteers both in the office and in their communities.

Cracking the Code

The message of the responsibility these women have to each other resonates with a cluster of enthusiastic students and recent grads of Harvey Mudd College in Claremont, California, seated next to us at the Houston conference. The close-knit liberal arts college of about eight hundred students is known for its rigorous science, math, and technology undergraduate programs—and is an incredible overnight success story. Today, more than half of Mudd's computer science grads are women, up from a historic average of 12 percent.[4] The school changed the ratio over five years and it continued to hold steady. Mudd was one of several colleges and universities we visited because they are beginning to convince more women that computing and engineering are for them—reversing the troubling downward trend.

The Mudd students came to Houston, they told us earnestly, because they want to change the world. And they were not exaggerating. This was the vision behind the college's commitment, since 2006, to pay the registration fee plus expenses for every first-year female student to attend Hopper, the first in a three-pronged approach to boost the number of women in CS. Women at Mudd who are thinking about majoring in CS are given research projects as the second prong during their freshman year so they can see the real-world application of their studies. And prong three was the revamping of CS5, the required introductory course for first-year students.

Samantha Echevarria, a senior at Harvey Mudd, told us she was planning to be a chemist when she arrived on the elm-and-eucalyptus-lined campus about thirty-five miles east of downtown Los Angeles. She never considered majoring in computer science, even though she loved solving problems and was known as the techie in her Ohio family—the kid her parents leaned on to fix the Internet connection when it was down. But the retooled class, and its engaging professor, Zach Dodds, reeled her in.

"You basically get a lot of exposure to the different possibilities of computer science. And I think everyone finds something that they're really curious or interested about, and that convinces them to take the next level," said the twenty-year-old who also loves poetry and is a member of the college's competitive Ultimate Frisbee team. She was here at Hopper to size up job prospects.

"I will go anywhere to anyone who will pay me," she told us. "I kind of just want to get out there, start making a difference, learn a lot."

The other thing that made the intro computer science class attractive to Samantha and other students was that it is geared to young people who don't know how to code or have had limited exposure to it. This was a major shift in the curriculum.

"I think a huge part of what discourages people with no experience from pursuing computer science in college is that they get into those classes, and they feel [left] behind from the second they sit in their seat," Dr. Christine Alvarado, one of the Harvey Mudd professors who created the new course, told researchers for a report to the American Association of University Women.[5] The Mudd faculty found that most of the female first-year students didn't have any coding experience. They didn't even understand what the study of computer science is or how it can be applied to many careers, so they never even considered it. This was a common situation for young women across the United States, according to the AAUW report.

So Alvarado and her colleagues created two different intro courses for CS and distinguished them with the school colors, gold and black. CS5, the more accessible class that Samantha took, is known as the gold track. The more advanced introductory course is known as the black track and covers more challenging applications of the same basic concepts.

"The intro course is key," said Ruthe Farmer, chief development officer for the Boulder-based National Center for Women &

Information Technology (NCWIT), as she laid out some of the key questions academics are tackling as they experiment with new ways to recruit and retain women in CS. "How are you presenting computing in that first course, and is that a gendered way of presenting it? Looking at what are the exam questions. Are the projects all about making first-person shooter games or solving problems that are not relevant to a larger group of people? Is it interesting to a wide swath of kids, and not just sort of the early-adopter types?"

In addition to revamping the intro course, Harvey Mudd made all its first semester classes pass/no credit, and the school has developed a network of "grutors," tutors who help grade assignments and can reach out to struggling students. Samantha enjoyed stepping into that role because it immersed her in a culture of collaboration that even includes "homework parties" in the dorms, which are mixed by gender and class year. Younger students often casually seek out her help.

"The overall idea is you frame what students are learning as creative problem solving. You also emphasize teamwork and collaboration, which we do as a whole at Harvey Mudd," college president Dr. Maria Klawe told us when we sat down with her in her office on a sunny afternoon in March 2016. "Creativity and problem solving, teamwork, and communication skills are all going to be things that women think of themselves as being good at, whereas if you are just emphasizing, 'Okay, you are going to be a great coder,' not so much. Or, 'You're going to be a great person in the machine shop,' not so much." This was the approach that helped her boost the overall female population at the college to 47 percent (in 2015) since becoming the college's president in 2006.

The laid-back California ambience—rows of skateboard racks and students lounging on the green in shorts—belies the seriousness of the students. It's a highly selective school known for attracting bright teens who excel in math and science. For many Mudd is where they get their first B.

"Everyone who comes to Mudd is super, super smart, and did super well in high school," Samantha, the senior we met in Houston, explained. "And they tell you during orientation, 'You will not be the best person here. You will struggle when you're here.' The average GPA after the first year is something like a 2.6."

Taking CS to the Masses

Mudd is collaborating with at least fifteen other academic institutions to prove that its success in attracting more women to computer science is not exclusive to its rarified population. In a similar effort, more than three thousand miles from the sunny Southern California enclave of Claremont, at the largest, most diverse public university system in the nation, a new crop of ambitious female students, most of whom had also never been exposed to computer science or met people in the field, were working on exactly the same assignments as the freshmen at Mudd. CS5 was in session at Macaulay Honors College of City University of New York (CUNY) in January 2016, led by the charismatic Professor Dodds, who spent a month in Manhattan teaching the class. With 275,000 students and campuses spread across New York City's five boroughs, CUNY is the polar opposite of the exclusive liberal arts college. The student body of this massive group of urban academic institutions traces its heritage to 205 different countries. More than a third of undergraduates here are first-generation Americans, and 42.2 percent are the first in their families to go to college.[6]

"They're sort of the un-millennials. They don't expect anything to be handed to them," said Dr. Ann Kirschner, former dean of Macaulay Honors College, which hosted the inaugural course for forty CUNY students through WiTNY (Women in Technology and Entrepreneurship in New York), a public-private partnership of the university; Cornell Tech (Cornell University's New York City–based Graduate School of Technology); founding partner Verizon; and half a dozen other corporate sponsors.

"They expect that they will have to work hard for everything. They tend to be humble and hungry," she said of the student body, when we spoke a couple of months after the class concluded.

Twenty-year-old Moné Skratt loved it. The native New Yorker was one of the few students in the CUNY course who had taken AP computer science in her public high school on Staten Island but said she didn't really have a full grasp of the concepts until she took Dodds's course. Moné, who sports a playful shock of short blonde curls and describes herself as both creative and inquisitive, is the daughter of two postal workers. She will be the first in her immediate family to obtain a college degree when she graduates. She said she was most interested in studying American Sign Language and wasn't sure she would continue in CS. But she found the class fascinating, and what she appreciated most as she learned the programming language Python, and worked on building a maze game with her friend Genevieve, was the way Dodds showed how the material they covered could be applied outside the classroom and to many fields. And he didn't make anyone feel they had been left behind.

"He was able to make the class really engaging and interesting by dressing up in costumes, acting out codes being run, making computer science–related jokes," she wrote to us not long after finishing the class. "He really understood that people came with different skill sets to the class and different objectives and he kept that in mind, offering his help and checking in with the tables constantly."

Dr. Judith Spitz, the Verizon executive-in-residence at Cornell Tech and one of the architects of WiTNY, said the opportunity to recruit women at CUNY could be a bonanza for cultivating new tech talent for companies like Verizon. She said the tech industry can no longer afford to draw only from exclusive programs like that at Mudd. And more than 60 percent of CUNY's students are women.

"If you are really trying to get the numbers, you can't rely only on the 'exceptions to the rule'—the one in a hundred young women who 'self-identify' and say 'Since I was nine, I've always loved playing with computers.' You've got to get the masses," she told us on a December afternoon in her temporary Cornell Tech office in Google's landmark building in Manhattan's booming Chelsea neighborhood.

Tech is "where the good jobs and money are. I don't care what your perspective is, it seems inherently unfair that women are sitting on the sidelines while the guys are making all this money and getting access to so many great career opportunities. In the spirit of go-where-the-puck is going, virtually every profession is becoming a tech profession. Women are sitting on the sidelines of that," said Judith, who served as chief information officer for Verizon and has been with the company for more than two decades. She's a petite woman, and her slight New York accent and anecdotes about her adult twin daughters endeared her to us immediately. You can tell she speaks from the heart, providing maternal wisdom mixed with the grit of an experienced executive who's been there, done that. In efforts to get New York City college women off the sidelines, Judith and WiTNY started a two-week summer workshop in 2016 for forty-two entering first-year women to introduce them to the world of designing and developing digital products. The program also offers scholarships and helps with internship placement. And along with the city, WiTNY is also working with college counselors in New York's public high schools to help educate them about career tracks and to try to dispel the stereotype of the nerdy guy that often keeps girls from even considering tech as an option. Judith said that even one of her daughters became disenchanted with computer science as a freshman at Colgate when she looked into the classroom and saw lots of "geeky guys" and said, "No way."

Changing the Hacker Culture on Campus

Recasting the image of who works in computing is a key part of attracting women to the field, and it's how another prestigious university, using an entirely different tactic, made striking progress starting in 1999.

From the moment you set foot inside the futuristic Gates Center for Computer Science on the Pittsburgh campus of Carnegie Mellon, you notice there are women. Lots of them. In the orange-and-green cafe we saw groups of friends—male and female—drinking coffee and eating salads as they huddled over laptops with Beats headphones and kicked back in the low-slung chairs. Purple hair, skirts, Doc Martens, and tattoos abounded, but so did easy smiles and laughs. In the ladies' room was a poster advertising a weekend-long hackathon to develop innovative ideas for combating gun violence and promoting gun safety. Upstairs, grad students, male and female, were hanging out and playing video games together on a large flat-screen TV in a comfy lounge. What has changed here, the faculty will tell you, is not the curriculum. It's the culture.

In the fall of 2016, women made up 49 percent of first-year students at Carnegie Mellon University's School of Computer Science, up from 12 percent in 1994.[7] And the graduation rate since 2011 has been nearly identical for men and women, according to professors Carol Frieze and Jeria Quesenberry: 89.5 percent of men and 88.9 percent of women graduate in six years.[8]

The numbers of women applying to the computer science program at CMU were already inching up in 1999, when Lenore Blum, a distinguished mathematician and professor of computer science, joined the faculty. She had been working on gender issues for her whole career, starting in the early 1970s on the heels of Title IX, when she founded the mathematics and computer science program at Mills College in Northern California. There she helped start Expanding Your Horizons (EYH), a pioneering organization that encourages middle school girls to consider careers in math and science. Although funding for science education initiatives dried up during the Reagan administration, EYH continues today and offers workshops for teens and tweens around the nation. Yet as Lenore showed us the faded black-and-white pamphlets and fliers from its debut more than four decades ago, she mused that, although times have changed, the underlying issues that keep girls from pursuing STEM persist. Much work remains to be done.

She invited us into her bright office on a spring Monday, as a new crop of doctoral students was interviewing for the next year's research jobs, to tell us about the history of CMU's culture shift. Lenore explained that the then dean of the School of Computer Science, Raj Reddy, had decided in the late 1990s, just before she arrived on campus, that it was time to bring a new kind of student into the program. Instead of automatically offering admission to students whose applications showed lots of programming acumen, good grades, high math test scores, and little else, the school started looking more closely at other factors, such as outside interests and extracurricular activities. The thinking was that the people who would become the leaders and innovators of tomorrow needed to have interests in the world beyond computing, a notion supported by a landmark 2002 study of CMU students by Jane Margolis, a social scientist, and Allan Fisher, the then–undergraduate dean for CS education. They found that previous experience with programming was not necessary for completing a bachelor's degree in CS.[9]

Once students with a wider range of personalities and interests entered Carnegie Mellon, the "familiar geek culture largely reflected in computing culture" started to lose its dominance on campus, according to Frieze and Quesenberry.[10]

Yet even as the makeup of classes was changing, Lenore and her then–doctoral student Frieze believed the women needed more support if they were going to succeed in CS. Women were still outnumbered, and they were not getting the same opportunities for homework help, internships, jobs, and research opportunities as the men.

"[If] you're a woman in those early years, you didn't have a roommate in the field, so you would not very often call up a guy in the middle of the night and say, 'Help. Let's work on homework together.' You didn't have that easy access. You didn't have the role models. Your teachers were probably all men. You didn't see anybody like yourself, [or have] anybody to talk with," Lenore recounted. "All those things—the professional things of mentors, role models, community, leadership possibilities, all of that, which was just built in for the guys— was not available for the women, so they weren't having the same experience. Take away those [experiences] from any of those successful men in the field, and they wouldn't have been this successful."

She and Frieze set out to create Women@SCS (Women at the School of Computer Science), a new professional organization that would provide a way for women to get to know each other, pass on insights and opportunities, and help each other get ahead. From public speaking to salary negotiation workshops to coed hack events, sixteen years later its work was evident all around us. Mopewa Ogundipe, the double major in CS and robotics whom we had met in Houston, said she had made some of her best friends and even found her apartment roommates through Women@SCS. Mopewa's family is originally from Nigeria and she attended a selective technology magnet high school in the suburbs of Washington, DC. The poised, outgoing young woman was stylishly dressed in polka-dot frocks or cropped jackets and t-shirts with trendy accessories every time we saw her—even in the robotics lab in the basement of Newell Simon Hall, where she showed us what she was building with two male classmates. It was a prototype for a hands-free, voice-activated handcart. The team seemed chummy to us. One of her teammates told us that there's a feeling among the men that having a woman partner is an asset because the women tend to be more organized and keep the teams on task. But at times, Mopewa confided, she had felt like she didn't quite fit in. Like the time a male partner in one of her first robotics classes asked straight out, "How did you get here? You don't look like the typical CS major." Venting to her girlfriends helped a lot.

"Having them is super helpful. I just know they're always there. It's not because we all come together and go, like, 'sisterhood' kind of thing," Mopewa said as we chatted in the cafe with her and two of her female classmates. "I think what brings the group together is us trying to give back to the community."

Community outreach is one way the women here bond. And that was why, as the sun set on an unseasonably mild March day, we were hanging out in the basement of the Hunt Library with Mopewa and a cluster of girls in braces and ponytails who had come to campus from around the city and surrounding suburbs. The sixth- and seventh-graders were talking animatedly with each other about homework and sports. We

had watched their parents quickly drop them off and saw
how the girls bounded into the computer lab lined with desk-
tops; the girls were excited to see their friends and mentors—a
dozen volunteers from Women@SCS, including Mopewa—
who would be teaching them that evening.

Ada Zhang, who was getting her PhD in robotics, came up
with the challenges, ranging from computer science to mechanical engineering to math problems, that the middle school girls
tackled each week. "I like that they get to meet other women in
computer science to show them that we are real and that we exist and we are kind of cool and that they can connect with
other girls," Ada said of the weekly Tech Nights offered for
eight sessions each semester.

"People think that the world of computer science is filled
with these nerdy men, and that's not true. It is very sad that
there is this weird social stigma that prevents people from ever
walking in the door," she continued. "Mostly we want to allow
the girls to explore STEM fields in this safe environment where
they can just be themselves and go crazy."

That night they would be learning the Python programming language. After five minutes to socialize, eighteen girls
were seated in front of computer monitors and ready to work.
A computer science teaching assistant with a nice smile welcomed them and introduced the seven women, also TAs in the
Intro to Programming class, who would guide them through
the commands to run a game that features a big fish chasing
after little fish. The girls immediately quieted down and focused on the directions. Then Mopewa and the other mentors
spread out through the room and partnered with the girls.
They worked for about an hour on their task—getting the big
fish to eat the little fish.

Thirteen-year-old Caroline Kenney proudly told us that she
had already decided she wants to go to CMU, thanks to this

program, and that she already knew what she wants to be when she grows up—a computer scientist or roboticist for Google.

"We need more women. For all of history, girls have been told they are not as good as boys, but if we can get ahead with programming and STEM, we can show the world what we can do," she declared.

As the class came to a close, Caroline and her friends were rewarded for their hard work with more time to hang out and chat with each other and with the college and grad students—and attack a big platter stacked with Oreos iced with the pi sign and 3.14. One of the mothers supplied the snacks. It's Pi Day—March 14—and in the spirit of total nerdiness, the girls literally ate it up. At 8:30 on a school night the parents who had returned to pick their daughters up clearly were eager to get home, but these girls were in no rush. The CMU students looked energized too. They loved showing the girls that computing is cool. It meant a lot to them to be role models, validating all the hard work they were putting into their studies.

Women@SCS creates other opportunities for female students to get to know each other and boost their confidence, including matching first-year women with big sisters. Thanks to social media, many of those relationships transcend the years they are in school together. Kirn Hans, a curly-haired junior from New Delhi, India, said her big sister met with her at least once or twice every couple of weeks during her first year, helping her cope with roommate troubles and worries about keeping up with schoolwork. Kirn said she continues to rely on her mentor, who had graduated and now works at Facebook.

"I'll message her and be, like, 'Big sister, help! Work is really hard.' And she's, like, 'Don't worry, I have a lot of friends who are taking this class and it is hard, it's not just you,'" said Kirn, who had worked hard to overcome her perfectionist instincts. Among the college students we met across the country on campuses large and small, the consensus was that computer science is just plain tough—regardless of whether you are female or male. The problem, say researchers, is that young women often feel like outsiders from the outset and internalize failure much more readily than their male counterparts, especially when the women are in male-dominated arenas.

"If your perception is you don't feel like you belong in the field, any sign, like getting a bad grade, might feel like a signal to quit," said Catherine Hill, co-author of the report for the American Association of University Women. Understanding that everyone else is struggling and that failure is part of the learning process is key to retaining students in these truly demanding programs. That search for collegiality was what led Grace Gee, then a sophomore at Harvard University, to kickstart a new way for college women around the country to connect with each other online.

A Generation of STEMinists Unites

While growing up in Port Lavaca, Texas, a tiny town on the Gulf Coast, Grace Gee, who laughs easily and has a wide, open smile, felt like she was a million miles from Harvard, where she would eventually earn her bachelor's degree in applied mathematics, computer science, and statistics. She has loved math for as long as she can remember. Grace recalls learning graph theory in middle school and how she and her younger brother, John, debated it one humid afternoon as they bounced on the trampoline in their family's backyard as they waited for their parents to come home from work. Their rural high school, Calhoun High, resides in Calhoun County where more than a quarter of children live below the poverty line and in 2013, the county had the highest teen pregnancy rate in Texas.[11] Resources for advanced students were scarce although she managed to take

12 AP exams (scoring 5's on all). But their teachers found ways to accommodate Grace and John's insatiable aptitude and talent for math by allowing them to use the computer lab to take online classes, even an undergraduate-level linear math course through MIT. And there was a math team. Their parents would shuttle Grace and John a hundred miles to math competitions in Houston nearly every weekend. Grace's life was centered on math and small-town life until she received a prestigious award from NCWIT and was invited into Aspirations in Computing, its burgeoning Facebook community of high school girls. It opened up a whole new world.

In the private Facebook forum the girls, some as young as fourteen, collaborate on coding projects, discuss their hopes and dreams for college, share tips for applying for scholarships and internships, and post openly about what it feels like to be one of a handful of women in a class or at a conference. A recent conversation about "what NOT to say to a woman at a tech conference" stirred up hundreds of rapid-fire responses from young women confiding their own experiences, such as being asked if she was "with a boyfriend" or being told she was "too pretty to code."

"I sometimes refer to these girls as our little feminist army," said Ruthe Farmer, who, in addition to heading development for NWCIT, was appointed by the White House in 2016 as a senior policy adviser on tech inclusion. "These girls, they are informed. They are talking about every issue, every day, and they bring things to each other and ask for help and talk things through."

Grace told us the frank discussions with her virtual support network prepared her for the grueling process of college applications and interviews. In 2011, she arrived on Harvard's iconic Ivy League campus along the Charles River and immediately felt out of place. And it wasn't easy to meet other female students to work on computer science projects. She continued to rely on her online friends because she felt she had no one in Cambridge she could go to with questions and concerns or seek as a role model, especially after she hit her functional programming class during her second semester and thought she might have to drop the course because she felt so lost. She ultimately met a few other women in the class and got through it. She returned to school sophomore year to find new women in tech groups forming on campus, such as Developers for Development and Harvard Women in Computer Science. That was when she had her lightbulb moment. She wondered about women on other college campuses who didn't have the same access to a group of like-minded students and who had not been invited into the online group while they were in high school. Why not ask NCWIT to open it up to every woman studying computer science?

That was the fall of her second year at Harvard, and even after she went home to Texas for Christmas break, she couldn't get it out of her head. Grace, who is naturally entrepreneurial—today she is running her own health insurance startup, Honey-Insured—said that late one night she finally messaged Ruthe on Facebook with a lengthy proposal. Ruthe, a longtime advocate for girls in STEM and the woman behind the Girl Scouts' initiatives in robotics and computing, responded right away—even though it was 1 a.m. NCWIT signed off almost immediately. Within a year Hewlett Packard had provided a $1 million grant to get the program going. In 2014 the NCWIT collegiate network, also called Aspirations in Computing, was born. It's now the largest group of its kind, affiliated with 450 colleges and universities, with more than five thousand members, and, according to its organizers, growing 30 percent year over year.[12]

Eighteen-year-old Teresa Ibarra, a freshman at Harvey

Mudd, told us the Facebook group kept her going during her first year of college. In addition to checking in with her mother, a reliable cheerleader, Teresa turns to Aspirations in Computing when she gets a low grade or struggles with assignments or feels lonely. Teresa, a ballet dancer who had already competed in hackathons in high school, was still struggling with insecurities both as a woman and a person of color. But she said she has been deeply inspired by the range of women who provide her with advice and encouragement, essential in a field where failure is considered learning. The iterative nature of technology, and coding specifically, can be challenging for girls accustomed to making perfect grades, as they tend to berate themselves the moment they make a mistake.

"Anytime a girl is, like, 'I totally just failed one of my classes,' you get fifteen girls who are, like, 'Hey. It's totally okay and you're totally awesome,' and, like, 'It's, like, all going to work out.' You get this huge outpouring of support from other women, which is great," Teresa told us.

In the fall of 2015, with funding from Google and in partnership with the women's arm of the Association for Computing Machinery (ACM-W), Aspirations in Computing awarded grants of $3,000 to $15,000 to women to start new in-person tech groups on more campuses and to help them expand their activities, Ruthe said. The latter could be anything from running a campus hackathon to setting up a startup incubator for students to sponsoring scholarships for women to attend the annual Grace Hopper Celebration of Women in Computing, so they can meet other technical women, especially those already in the world of work.

That exposure to real women in the tech industry is what was missing for Ayna Agarwal when she was a first-year student at Stanford University in 2010. Like so many college women we met, she first learned about computer science when she got to college. When Ayna was growing up in New Jersey, she had always excelled at math and science. Because she loves animals and even started an animal rescue non-profit as a kid, she and her family assumed she might become a veterinarian someday. But her curiosity about tech was piqued when she took an Intro to Computer Science class and enjoyed the unexpected collaboration among the students on their problem sets. She was pleasantly surprised when she started to learn how programming might lead her to a career in which she could help people. Many college women we interviewed told us that seemed to be a crucial connection—the idea that computer science could be an avenue for a career with maximum social impact. It was something they had not understood until they met real people working in the field and learned about their jobs. But encountering those role models wasn't so easy at the time, even for a student at Stanford, ground zero for the innovation culture. The only women Ayna and her friends saw who were kicking butt in the industry were the stars—Sheryl Sandberg, Marissa Mayer, Meg Whitman, Susan Wojcicki. Ayna said she and her friends craved relatable role models.

"I didn't think I could look to Marissa Mayer and say I will be her in fifteen years. That's so hard as a college girl, to say that's the path I want to follow. While it's really inspirational, you just need something a little more realistic," Ayna told us as she relayed the story of how she and her college roommate, Ellora Israni, started a women-in-tech day they called she++ ("she plus plus"—a play on the programming language C++). It began as an on-campus conference in April 2012 to bring together 250 tech women of different ages and stages of their careers. Google, Facebook, Dropbox, and Pinterest were just some of the companies represented at the event to help "dismantle the untrue stereotype that computer science is not a career for women." But while the conference was well received,

Ayna and Ellora wanted to do something with more lasting impact. They produced a documentary film in 2013 that highlights the ways computer science intersects with many other fields, including music, politics, and film. And they showcased women in tech who were thriving despite the dismal reports about the persistent gender gap and the sexism. Then they added the #include Fellowship Program, a summit for introducing high school girls to computer science. The impact on campus was direct.

"We can say at least that every single computer science professor that we've talked to, including the head of the department, has said that she++ has had a massive impact on the number of female computer scientists who not only take computer sciences earlier but who persist through the major," said Ayna, who now is a product manager working on criminal justice data analysis at the intriguingly secretive company Palantir Technologies. Indeed, a spokesman for Stanford University told us that she++, along with a host of other department initiatives, has led to more young women graduating with CS degrees since 2012.[13]

Early in 2016, we ventured to Palo Alto to sit in on a she++ meeting. We had met some of these impressive young women at Grace Hopper in Houston, where the group hosted a "Mojitos and Making" party under the stars at Batanga, a fun Latin restaurant. As they chatted over the salsa music in the warm evening air, they tinkered with tiny electrical circuits meant to embellish pretty greeting cards on the tables. Sitting next to us were college junior Reynis Vazquez-Guzman, co-director of the organization, and senior Lucy Wang, who told us that being involved in she++ had enriched their years at Stanford.

"Not only have I made friends who have inspired me but I have also grown so much from being part of a non-profit. I've learned skills outside my major," Lucy says.

A few months later, Lucy and Reynis welcomed us into a meeting room on campus, where a dozen she++ members sat around a table in Stanford's Old Union Building brainstorming how to get more publicity for the non-profit. They also were knee-deep in planning their signature event, the summit, set for a weekend in early April. They would fly in thirty high school students from around the country for an all-expenses-paid introduction to CS, campus life, and meetings with successful women who work for some of the biggest tech companies. Applicants did not need technical experience, an important strategy for recruiting girls who may never have considered a career in tech. Reynis said that hanging out with the wide-eyed girls and giving them sisterly advice about college life is one of her favorite parts of the event.

A few months later we attended the culmination of the program, a glamorous gala at the Computer History Museum in Mountain View that hosts the largest collection of computing artifacts on the planet. The gala marked the end of two full days of demos and meetings with female go-getters at Oculus VR, ThoughtSpot, VMware, Google Cardboard, Facebook, and GoDaddy. As we approached the entrance to the party, the check-in line looked more like what you would see behind the velvet rope at a trendy new dance club in LA—beautiful young women with long hair, short sequined dresses, and sky-high heels, laughing and hugging each other and looking happy to be around their people. There was nothing nerdy about these women. They were animated, dressed to the nines, and excited to share their love of computing.

The group's head of public relations, Madelyne Xiao, then a sophomore, whose passion is digital humanities (she was studying the applications of technology to linguistics, literature, and design), greeted us in a festive red dress. She bubbled with excitement as she told us the organization expected five hundred people to attend, a record turnout for its five-year history. Most of the she++ leadership team was there, busy with a raffle, check-ins, and making sure everything was flowing according to plans. And Ayna, poised and gracious as ever, had flown in from Manhattan, where she'd been working on a project for Palantir for six months, to lead a fireside chat with surprise guest Trae Vassallo. Trae, the 1994 Stanford mechanical engineering grad and former Kleiner Perkins partner, had recently released her "Elephant in the Valley" survey documenting sexism in Silicon Valley.

Trae's remarks were well received. Ayna got her to talk about her personal story and give career advice. But the most raucous cheers were for the two-minute speech by freshman Nishtha Bhatia about the community she had found through she++ and her newfound activism. Nishtha, who two years before had been one of those high school girls in the room, spoke about how much she++ had opened her eyes to the possibilities of working in technology—and how its members had welcomed her into the sisterhood. Nishtha stood at the podium in a black cocktail dress with a sparkly flared skirt and smiled as she confessed that during her childhood she had never known any women who worked with computers and had just assumed tech was a job for dads. When she was sixteen, she attended the she++ summit as a high school junior and learned otherwise. The experience disrupted all her previous assumptions and showed her that there was room in the industry for someone like her. She++ energized her passion for technology and awakened a new sense of purpose so powerful that it demanded its own postmodern label.

"Today I am a STEMinist," she declared as the applause rose. "And I always will be."

CHAPTER 7

IGNITE THE NEXT GENERATION
Pipeline Promoters

The first problem for all of us, men and women,
is not to learn, but to unlearn.

—GLORIA STEINEM

When you stroll through the biggest toy exhibition in the world with the founder of a company that went from Kickstarter to Toys "R" Us in six months, her star power is hard to ignore. Everyone seemed to want to chat up Debbie Sterling, the CEO of GoldieBlox and the young inventor whose mission is to inspire little girls, like our daughters, to see themselves as tomorrow's engineers and innovators—the next generation of women in tech. This was Debbie's fourth year of triumphantly showcasing her award-winning GoldieBlox action figures and play sets for international retailers and the media at the 2016 Toy Fair inside New York's enormous Jacob Javits Center—and two years since the GoldieBlox Super Bowl commercial had made history with its unapologetic call for girls to think beyond pink, rise up, and build the future. We had been lucky enough to start following her long before all the fanfare; otherwise, she would have been hard to reach.

This Toy Fair felt like a whole different world from its 2012 iteration, when Debbie had arrived from California in a blizzard, only to learn that none of her supplies had made it and the flight of her lone sales person had been canceled. In a panic she had phoned her mentor Terry Langston, co-founder of Pictionary, for advice. He asked simply, "What would Goldie do?" She took a deep breath. "Well. Goldie would probably, like, run to the hardware store and whip together a booth and just make it happen," she replied. And that's what the twenty-eight-year-old did. Goldie, of course, is the sneaker-clad, overall-wearing, tool belt–toting heroine of the GoldieBlox franchise who, with her intrepid best friend, Ruby Rails, solves all kinds of problems with their squad of buddies in BloxTown.

"It's crazy to think that before GoldieBlox there was literally no female engineer character," Debbie said. "And I can just list off all of the boy builder, boy engineer, boy genius characters, which goes on and on."

In fact, getting a spot in the "tech toys" section of the Toy Fair was a struggle back then, although at the time that category was kind of a wasteland anyway, she said. Organizers didn't know what to do with GoldieBlox; they'd never seen anything like it. Debbie fought for it, persuading the Toy Industry Association (TIA) that GoldieBlox would one day incorporate technology in its products and that she was confident it represented the future of play. Much has changed in a few short years. She marveled as we walked past rows and rows of today's hottest toys—robots, drones, coding games, and circuit kits.

When we paused for a moment as she quickly took it all in, she said, "Every booth is STEM. A lot of it's centered around girls. It's amazing. I guess it makes me feel I'm happy to see it. I think I knew that there was such a huge gap that when I started GoldieBlox. It was so obvious it needed to happen, and it seemed like such a no-brainer. Now it's crazy. This is cool. It's great that we've helped. I think we've helped validate the market. Now that gives people permission to be, like, 'Oh, okay. It's the smart thing to do.'"

Designers and marketing reps rushed over to say hello as she looked over their new products and campaigns. They asked what she was planning to do next and filled her in on their own Kickstarter efforts. She noted that crowdfunding has opened up many doors for people to raise money and test their ideas. In many ways her own campaign set the bar. Dressed understatedly in a black-and-white print dress, black flats, and little makeup, she was gracious, asking the women behind IAmElemental, a line of female action heroes, how things were going and warmly invited them to stop by the GoldieBlox booth. Several other female inventors who are hoping to follow in her footsteps stopped Debbie to say hello and perhaps soak up some of her advice. One was working on RaceYa, a line of gender-neutral race car kits, and others were the female founders of Blink Blink, sewing kits featuring conductive thread and LED lights to make circuits. It was the geek girl network in full effect.

The National Retail Federation had just named Debbie to its 2016 list of Disruptors, "true originals who rock the boat with ideas so crazy, they just might work," part of the organization's annual list of People Shaping Retail's Future. One of the federation's board members, Debbie's affable mentor Mitchell Modell (CEO of Modell's, the regional sporting goods chain), swung by the massive fuschia-and-turquoise Blox Shop, a small store lined with shelves of Ruby and Goldie action figures and a large TV playing an endless loop of cartoons featuring Goldie and her friends. He heaped praise on the young woman he calls his third daughter before taking Debbie aside for a quick confab. With GoldieBlox toys on the shelves of six thousand stores and in the hands of more than one million girls; a movie-making app that has been downloaded one million times; a children's book series published by Random House; and even a GoldieBlox float in the Macy's Thanksgiving Day Parade three years in a row, Debbie seemed to be right on schedule with her plans for the next phase of GoldieBlox: to grow the company into a global brand on the order of Dora the Explorer and Bob the Builder.[1]

"You could have GoldieBlox clothes, GoldieBlox arts and crafts, GoldieBlox video games," she said, ticking off her list of licensing ideas as we walked with her head of product development. One of her longtime goals is to see GoldieBlox become an animated TV show. The company has released two shorts on YouTube that give a taste of what a cartoon might look like. But she has been careful with the brand since the beginning, even rebuffing early interest from Disney and other Hollywood studios that approached her in the early days. She didn't want to lose creative control. When we got a chance to peek behind the scenes of Goldie's real-life workshop, the company headquarters in Oakland, California, two months earlier, she had explained, "For me, GoldieBlox is a social mission at its core, and so making a deal with an entertainment company to just give them the rights to make a GoldieBlox cartoon felt wrong to me because I don't know what they're going to do with it. Currently, as of today, it sells pretty well, but [back then] I couldn't take that risk. I just said, 'Okay. Let's wait. Yes, it would be a cartoon one day and all these other things, but I need to have control of how it ends up.'"

Debbie acknowledges that she has always envisioned Goldie as a role model, and she developed the spunky character to be the best version of herself, someone who isn't afraid of failure or taking risks, a girl who embraces the challenge of figuring things out when they don't go as planned. She always was open with us about the ups and downs of her efforts. The pivotal YouTube *Princess Machine* video that her husband, Beau, produced features three kindergarteners who are constructing a magnificent Rube Goldberg set to a feminist remix of the Beastie Boys' song "Girls." It got huge media attention but also landed Debbie in a dispute with the band over copyright infringement that she settled for an undisclosed amount. Early on, the company shipped toys that had fit issues and offered new ones, along with a personal note to any customer who had ever purchased the products.[2] And while GoldieBlox received all kinds of kudos for its inspiring Super Bowl commercial, some of the first reviews of the toys themselves were not great. Some parents thought the product did not live up to the hype. They complained that GoldieBlox and the Spinning Machine was too simple for the five- to nine-year-olds at whom it was aimed.

"It was cranks, spools, and some things that spin, all tied together with a somewhat confusing narrative that wasn't terribly compelling. Nor was the building process that engaging. My daughter gave it a half hour a couple times, then she was done," wrote one parent, Amanda Clayman, in a 2013 Tumblr entry, "I Hate to Be the Feminist Grinch Here."[3]

Debbie and her team regrouped. They reassessed their audience, made some changes to the manufacturing process, and worked hard to figure out how to make it better. Debbie said being relentless is just part of who she is.

Thinking outside the box also comes naturally to her. She has always loved art and making projects out of whatever she could find around the house. She aspired to be an artist like her grandmother, one of the first female cartoonists and a creator of Mr. Magoo. When Debbie was growing up in a small Rhode Island town, she would fashion elaborate Halloween costumes of cardboard and tin foil, and she would build castles out of sugar packets with her father. But she said she had no idea that what she was doing was engineering. In fact, when the straight-A student was applying to college and was thinking about Stanford, her high school math teacher advised her to consider majoring in engineering. Debbie thought the woman was crazy.

"I was embarrassed that I didn't even know what engineering even was. I thought it was like an old man who fixes train engines, and I just assumed it was for boys only, and I always thought of myself as such a creative person," she told us a few months after her successful Kickstarter campaign in 2012.

With the voice of her math teacher in her head, Debbie went on to Stanford and signed up for Mechanical Engineering 101. It was not at all what she thought it would be. She was building machines and suddenly saw clearly the intersection of math, problem solving, art, and design. Engineering combined many things she enjoyed. She decided to major in mechanical engineering and product design—and found herself sticking out as one of the few women in her courses. It was difficult, and she often thought about quitting. She later realized that some of her struggles in class stemmed from her underdeveloped spatial skills—the ability to visualize three-dimensional objects and their relationship to other things in space. This became clear the day one of her teachers humiliated her in front of her classmates. It was the final exam for Perspectival Drawing, a course she had initially been excited to take because she loved to draw. The teacher told everyone to tape their projects to the walls of the classroom so they could examine each other's work. Debbie was horrified when he walked over to her drawing, pointed to it, and asked everyone in the mostly male class to raise their hands if they thought she deserved to pass.

"I walked out crying. I thought I wanted to quit," she told us. But a guy in the class came to Debbie's defense and later told her she shouldn't give up, that she could work at it and train herself to get better at understanding spatial relationships—a skill she would later learn is often developed in early child-hood by playing with Legos and Erector Sets—toys marketed mostly to boys. The incident only emboldened her to finish the program.

The humbling memory of being called out in class didn't hold her back, but it stayed with her as she looked for work in San Francisco. She started in branding and design, which she found unfulfilling. She looked for inspiration in India, where she had moved for seven months to work with a non-profit. She was craving a path with greater purpose. And to that end, when she got home from her travels, she and a group of entre-preneurial friends in the Bay Area started to meet for what they called "idea brunches" to brainstorm about all the stuff they *really* wanted to do with their lives.

"Each person would have five minutes to get up and say how they are going to change the world. And my friend Christy started complaining about growing up with three older brothers and playing with their hand-me-down Legos. She didn't like that they were considered her *brothers'* toys and not hers," Debbie told us of the moment she discovered her mis-sion. She was dazzled by the idea of making an engineering toy that girls could call their own. Before they'd even finished their coffee, Debbie confided to Christy, a Stanford engineering classmate, that she thought she might want to spend her life building the kinds of toys they'd wanted as kids.

Right away, she and Christy started hammering away on the project at night and on weekends, for nine months. They called the first version Grapple. By December 2011 Debbie had quit her job and was all in. She wanted a year to give it a real shot. She was drawing her inspiration from visits to toy stores that separated toys by pink and blue aisles, and she was glean-ing important insights from schools and more than forty fami-lies in the Bay Area who allowed her to observe their young daughters at play. She immediately noticed the girls' affection for reading and storytelling.

By the spring of 2012 Christy had decided not to give up her day job, so Debbie went on to build the company solo, although the two remain good friends, she said. By then Debbie was convinced that a construction toy for girls had to have an engaging storyline attached to it. She pored over research about gendered play and concluded that if she wanted girls to build something, she needed a character to pull them in and a narrative for them to follow. She was already experimenting with characters who had to build simple machines in order to solve problems. She wrote and illustrated the first storybook herself—"GoldieBlox and the Spinning Machine"—and started putting it in front of girls. She first tried to integrate an engineering activity into the physical book itself: a ribbon that girls would have to loop around spindles to make what's known as a belt drive machine. But the prototype had one big problem—kids couldn't turn the page without undoing the ribbon.

"That was just one of many, many, many, many ah-has that happened through the course of play-testing that first prototype," she said.

On the day we visited Debbie in her office, a rainy afternoon two months before the Toy Fair, we saw the latest ah-has in progress. In the playful office, where lavender and green paper lanterns dangle overhead and a fuchsia banner affirms LIVE LIFE BY YOUR OWN CODE, two of her twenty-five team members were testing a new cardboard prototype of what they hoped would be their hero product for the year. The young women thoughtfully consulted a photo of what the new dollhouse should look like after a child builds it. They experimented with the rods and washers to see how quickly a six-year-old might be able to fit together the parts to make a bed for Goldie that converts into a trap door. All the play sets are meant to be modular, so that children can use their imagination to build what they want. That requires the designers to put themselves inside the mind of a child.

We later learned that the team had hoped to put this product, called the Invention Mansion, on the market the previous Christmas. It turned out to be a learning experience. Debbie told us the "dollhouse on steroids" ended up being way more ambitious and costly than they had realized at first. They really needed eighteen months to do it right but had given themselves less than half that time. So they pulled it from production and scrambled to come out with a series of minikits for the holiday season instead. We were in New York when the 350-piece "un-dollhouse" was finally unveiled at the Toy Fair, where it won early kudos as a "hot holiday toy for 2016" from *Good Housekeeping*. That was just one of the hiccups that Debbie tries to take in stride as she and her team map out the goals for the year.

"From the outside I think it [being an entrepreneur] looks so glamorous and so amazing, but the honest truth is that every single day it's mostly really hard. Every now and then, taking a step back and being able to really celebrate and appreciate what's happened, it is something that's rare for me. It's something that I need to try and do more [of] to really enjoy it, and take a breath and appreciate what's going on," she reflected before running off to another marketing meeting on the day we visited her office.

Six months later, in the summer of 2016, with the Invention Mansion on the market, the new book deal inked, a YouTube series called *Toy Hackers* about to debut, and her dreams of an animated TV series starting to come to fruition, Debbie, then thirty-three, told us that coding was the next frontier for GoldieBlox. Goldie's storylines have included mechanical engineering concepts, but a new app that features Goldie and Ruby starting a cupcake business, and a rocket-powered skateboard that runs amok, was designed to entice girls as young as four to learn to code. It turns out that Ruby, Goldie's cool best friend, has a superpower—and it's computer programming.

"She's a coder and she's African American and she's into fashion, like, 'Whoa! If someone can be stylish and code? Yes!' To make that completely normal and for kids to grow up with that, I think, is huge," Debbie said as she considered the impact.

It *is* huge—especially for our three daughters, who happened to fit right into the GoldieBlox audience when we first started researching this book in 2011. Role models are absolutely key to inspiring digital natives—kids who have been using computers and the Internet since they were little—to see themselves as tomorrow's women in tech. As GoldieBlox continues to try to expand its reach beyond the preschool set to older girls and tweens, its success as a game-changing brand and in raising seed money on Kickstarter has encouraged a raft of entrepreneurs to jump into the market with new engineering-focused toys for girls or a gender-neutral market. These include DIY kits and even smart jewelry to stimulate interest in STEM. Engaging middle school girls has become an especially popular goal. The 2012 report for the Girl Scouts of America is influencing a mix of toy makers, educators, and entrepreneurs.[4] It underscores that preteen girls, especially girls of color and girls from disadvantaged backgrounds, are often influenced by stereotypes that portray boys as better at math and science than girls—even though standardized test scores show girls their age outperform boys in those areas.[5] Middle school is considered the danger zone, when girls veer away from STEM. With growing daughters of our own now moving into their preteen years, we wanted to meet two women who were starting to tackle this notoriously fickle demographic with their girly take on tech.

Making Tech Cool for Tweens

When Sara Chipps and Brooke Moreland first introduced their big idea to inspire preteens to learn to code, they got an earful from their target audience. The business partners assumed the middle schoolers would fall in love with smart friendship bracelets that they could program to change colors to match their outfits. Instead, the girls rolled their eyes.

"They were, like, 'That sounds really stupid. We wouldn't ever do that,'" Sara, thirty-four, recalled of the long process she and Brooke undertook in 2014 to design something the girls would actually covet. At the time Girls Who Code, which targets teen girls with coding lessons, had already been up and running for three years, and Code.org had started its national initiative, Hour of Code, to demystify computing for young people. The idea of coding as cool was starting to catch on, so the two inventors decided to keep working on a truly fresh toy to appeal to tween girls.

They spent months listening to Girl Scout troops, girls in classrooms, and girls in after-school programs around New York City. The lightbulb moment came one afternoon when they were shooting a video with a bunch of fifth-graders for a fund-raising campaign. Brooke and Sara noticed the ten-year-olds were talking to each other about classmates in a sort of secret code—using long, elaborate acronyms to describe kids in different groups. Sara and Brooke were fascinated, and the girls finally drew a complex diagram on a whiteboard to illustrate the social strata of their entire school.

"They just let us into their world and even showed us their group text thread and explained what everything meant," Brooke said. That was when the two inventors decided their product, Jewelbots, needed to focus on relationships and to build on the ways girls (and boys) were already interacting with each other through messaging and social media.

"We just talked to them and just heard the same things: friendship, friends, connecting with my friends, hanging out, [those were] the things that were important to them," said Sara, who wears a subtle hoop in her nose. "We're building a product that's not for ourselves and, if anything taught us anything about the whole diversity movement, it's, like, when you're building something for someone else, you need to listen."

Eight iterations later the bracelets now focus on friendship. Kids can make them light up when a friend wearing her (or his) charm bracelet is nearby. They can create secret messages and Morse-like codes with buzzing and blinking through an app that teaches basic coding, and if they connect to a computer, they can learn and apply more sophisticated commands. Like Debbie Sterling, the founders of Jewelbots turned to Kickstarter to raise their first cash. Sara and Brooke raised more than $166,000 in 2015 to produce a prototype and continued to involve kids in the process by asking them to vote on the charms they might like to see on the bracelets. The first editions will feature a teal flower or a green robot on gender-neutral gray, neon yellow, or melon-colored fabric bands. The hope is that by engaging kids and their friends, the tweens will naturally want to keep playing with the bracelets and create more advanced features. Sara and Brooke said the physicality of the toy brings the programming alive for kids.

"Programming is boring, and it's really hard to make it interesting, and when you actually have something that you can see how you're affecting it, that makes it much more interesting," explained Sara, who taught herself to code at twelve and later studied computer science at Penn State. She was home-schooled as a kid in New Jersey. Her parents brought home their first computer and dial-up modem when she was ten or eleven, and that planted the seed for a career as a technologist. But the impetus was purely social, as she chatted online with other kids on a local message board and eventually started playing role-playing video games with them. When she hit high school and took her first CS class, she was hooked.

"I took a C++ class, and that was just the first thing that I was, like, 'This makes so much sense. I really love this. I always want to do this, whatever it is, that's what I always wanted to do,'" she said, smiling as she summoned the memory of discovering her passion.

When we visited Jewelbots's offices, we almost walked right past the nondescript metal door that leads inside the historic Witty Brothers building, an old clothing factory on Manhattan's Lower East Side with an ancient elevator operated by a man who speaks only Chinese. The building's storefront level is home to the yellow-and-red sign of the Sunrise Chinese restaurant and lives in the shadow of huge public housing towers. Across the street is a New York City public high school where students who speak eighteen different languages attend classes to learn English. This is a neighborhood where immigrants chasing the American Dream have settled for generations, which somehow felt significant to us.

As soon as we entered the sunny office of Jewelbots, we noticed on the window seat next to the partners' facing desks a white pillow with an iconic image of Sheryl Sandberg and this question in bold: w.w.s.d.? (What Would Sheryl Do?) Once again, the network of geek girls loomed large as we learned that Sara and Brooke got to know each other through New York's flourishing tech scene. Both were early members of the underground networking group known as the TheLi.st and had wanted to work together for a while. When they first started raising money on Kickstarter, TheLi.st rallied to get the word out. Listers offered to let their daughters participate in Jewelbots focus groups as Brooke and Sara tested early prototypes of the bracelets. And angel investor Joanne Wilson, a longtime Lister herself, would go on to back the company and become a trusted adviser as its founders graduated from the prestigious startup boot camp Techstars New York.

Sara, who dresses in bohemian prints and often changes her hair color, is a longtime software developer and was already on the leading edge of the movement to make coding more accessible to women through her then-role as CTO of Manhattan's Flatiron School, a tech school. She started Girl Develop It, the national non-profit that helps women to become software developers. She was used to being an outsider in the male-dominated software engineering world. Sara remembers going to her first big developer conference and feeling like she had a pit in her stomach when she was invited to grab a drink with a group of middle-aged men, one of whom droned on and on about his sexual exploits with prostitutes. The other men just looked at their feet and shuffled awkwardly. She didn't want to be rude, so she let the jerk finish his story, but she didn't let that uncomfortable moment keep her away from other tech events. She said she eventually found some incredibly supportive male mentors and colleagues. But that incident, and a few others she declined to share with us, inspired her activism on behalf of women in tech.

Brooke, whose dirty blonde hair is shoulder length, came from a completely different background. She dropped out of her first computer science class at the University of Texas at Austin. Like many of the young women we met, she entered a typical introductory CS class with enthusiasm, only to grow frustrated with the way it was taught. The professor seemed to be speaking a foreign language. She left a few weeks into the semester and didn't look back until she came up with an idea for a fashion tech startup. After working as an editor in reality TV and on documentaries, the Texas native eventually taught herself basic coding at night and on weekends and started her business in 2009. It was called Fashism, and it grew into a popular mobile app that let users snap selfies in the dressing room and solicit their friends' opinions about the clothes the users were trying on.

"I kind of saw myself in these girls," Brooke said. "I wish I had this product when I was younger. I wish I didn't have to wait till I was already in the workforce to learn what programming is or how it's beneficial to help me grow a business. I wish all that was on my radar at a younger age. That's how I see it and why I'm passionate about it, because I want it for my younger self." Now, with Jewelbots on the brink of delivering its first five thousand bracelets, they felt confident that preteens are the right fit for their product. Sara noted that these are the years when girls start to lose interest in math and science and worry more about their clothes and boys. Sara and Brooke believe that ten, eleven, and twelve are prime ages at which girls can be inspired to consider a future in tech. They don't yet have the cynicism or self-consciousness of high schoolers, and they still say whatever pops into their heads. In other words, Brooke said, the youngsters are "old enough and smart enough cognitively to be able to get these concepts but still kind of fearless and not overly concerned with their image yet. I think it's the perfect sweet spot."

While toys can provide girls like our daughters with lots of new and exciting ways to play and experiment with engineering and computing, closing the gender gap in tech is beyond the power of the $25 billion North American toy market.[6] How schools will rise to the challenge of teaching computer science to the next generation is a big piece of the puzzle, according to tech industry leaders, policy makers, and advocates. In our daughters' public elementary schools in suburban New York and outside San Francisco, coding is not yet part of the regular curriculum. We have cobbled together a range of after-school clubs, camps, and classes that expose our kids to computer programming. And it was one of the reasons we started researching this book. We found it baffling and frustrating that our communities and schools weren't offering more. As we are writing, only one in four U.S. schools offers computer science education, according to Code.org. This is an important statistic because girls are ten times more likely to choose a computer science major in college if they took AP computer science in high school.[7] But there are encouraging signs of change. In January 2016 the White House announced the president's plan to seek $4 billion in his budget to expand computer science education across the country.[8] Some major urban school districts were already moving in that direction. In June 2015 the San Francisco Unified School District announced it would expand computer science offerings for all students, from prekindergarteners through twelfth-graders. That September, New York City announced its Computer Science for All initiative, promising $81 million over ten years to expand CS education to all students.[9] And in February 2016 Chicago Public Schools instituted computer science requirements for the class of 2020. The message is that CS is as important as reading, writing, and math for succeeding in twenty-first-century jobs—the ones New York is eager to fill as its tech startup scene continues to rival Silicon Valley's.[10]

"If we were still living in an agricultural society, we'd be teaching kids farming techniques. Now we really have to face the reality that no matter what jobs that our school kids end up with, they're going to need computer skills to do that job," said Minerva Tantoco, former New York City chief technology officer, and a force behind the city's effort to offer computer science to the one million students in its public school system, the largest in the country. "The fact that [CS is] available to all, that further chips away at the divide between people who don't have computers at home or who don't want to geek out on the weekends with their friends or don't play video games. It's school."

Turning Consumers into Creators

Not far from the offices of Jewelbots, and at about a month after Sara and Brooke were closing out their Kickstarter campaign in October 2015, fourth- and fifth-graders were learning how to code with a new tool that was just starting to enter New York City classrooms. Vidcode draws kids in with an activity they know and love—taking selfies and shooting videos on their smartphones. Girl Scouts traveled to Manhattan from the Bronx, Brooklyn, and Staten Island to spend a morning with their troops and others to play with Vidcode. While intently working in pairs, the ten- and eleven-year-olds attending Tech Jam mastered the building blocks of programming by creating funny videos of themselves and sharing them with their friends. Unlike typical editing software such as iMovie, whose user clicks a mouse to execute commands, Vidcode takes children behind the scenes and introduces them to the language that tells the computer what to do. When they want to add music or text or special effects with Instagram-like filters, they have to construct a block of programming. Tomika Rodriguez, who runs the Girl Scouts of Greater New York, said it was amazing to see the girls make the connection. By the end of the morning the girls were creators using technology, not merely consumers of technology.

"Learning to code via video is a perfect marriage of learning a hard skill and then enjoying it in a way that you normally enjoy it in your life," Tomika told us. "I remember seeing their faces and how assured they felt at the end, a new way of thinking."

That result was exactly what Alexandra Diracles had envisioned when she came up with the idea for Vidcode in 2013. The artsy professional photographer, whose friends call her Allie, was in grad school at New York University and was taking her first computer science course. Until then she'd never been exposed to programming and didn't have the slightest interest but took the course to stay current in her field. She suffered from the same misconceptions about computing that have turned many women away—that it would be boring, not collaborative, and definitely not creative. Even though she worked in the arts, her industry was quickly changing from analog to digital, and she wanted to keep up. But she was blown away by how creative it was. By her second year of grad school, she was obsessed with making art using code and kept wishing she had learned about it much earlier in her life.

And then it hit her. The creativity she had found by using digital editing tools in class might also be a powerful way to entice girls to learn computer science. Allie knew young girls were already creating tons of content on YouTube, Instagram, and Snapchat. Thanks to YouTube celebrities like Michelle Phan and the explosion of visual sharing apps like Pinterest, teen girls were far outpacing boys in their use of social media to express themselves.[11] If girls were already sold on the idea of using tech to express themselves, why not lift the hood and show them how it actually works? Allie's thesis project became teaching coding to teens through "selfie documentaries."

Then Allie heard about a startup hackathon at which software developers and entrepreneurs could get together to brainstorm educational approaches to tech, and the tall, dark-haired Midwesterner decided it might offer a good opportunity for research. It was serendipity. She met her co-founder, Melissa Halfon, a mathematician who had been working on a trading desk and also was dying to get involved with efforts to get girls interested in science, math, and tech. They combined their ideas and teamed up with Leandra Tejedor, a UX, or user experience, software developer. All three were passionate about building a software platform that would target teen girls. They worked on it non-stop all weekend and took top prize at the hackathon. Not long after, they started a $30,000 Kickstarter campaign to fund the building of Vidcode. Along the way they looked hard at research coming out of Girls Who Code and other groups that were studying the gender gap in tech. And they continued to talk to teens and tweens. Just as the Jewelbots founders discovered with younger girls, Allie, Melissa, and Leandra found older girls craved something social.

"They told us they wanted to pursue [learning to code] with friends, be creative, and be social and also rigorous," said Allie, who grew up in downtown Minneapolis, where she proudly started the first feminist club at her inner-city high school. She'd always been drawn to social justice as much as to the arts—so it's no surprise that she's now heading her own mission-based company.

By then it was 2014, and coding as a necessary skill of the future was emerging as a pressing topic among parents and educators. Academics and school officials identified the shortage of teachers qualified to teach computer science in public schools as one of the biggest impediments to expanding the curriculum for more students and schools. And the market for innovative educational solutions was quickly opening up, and with good reason. Educators, including Diane Levitt, senior director of K-12 education at Cornell Tech, told us software like Vidcode is an important stopgap for computer science instruction in public schools while school districts work to get more teachers trained.

"It is a tool that teachers can assign and that students can learn from without teachers having to be computer scientists," she explained. "Teachers can recognize the product—it's a video, not just lines of code—but also find out from the dashboard just what students have learned about code."

In 2015 Vidcode got a huge boost of confidence when Allie, Melissa, and Leandra secured an investment from Intel and started partnering with the Girl Scouts; an after-school program called Level Up Village; and local public schools in New York City. And in typical geek girl fashion, Debbie Sterling hosted the team at her workshop in Oakland and made some key introductions for Allie and her crew.

In three years Vidcode has grown to the point that Allie, Melissa, and Leandra are building out a seven-year program for sixth- through twelfth-graders. Vidcode is in ten thousand schools around the country, from McMinnville, Tennessee, to Riverdale, New Jersey, to Oakland, California, as of this writing. When President Obama rolled out what would become his ambitious computer science initiative during his final State of the Union address, he called for states to develop plans for teacher training in computer science. Although funding for the proposal was given little chance of congressional approval as of this writing, the National Science Foundation committed $120 million over five years for teacher and curriculum development across the country.[12] Allie hopes Vidcode software will one day allow teachers to seamlessly integrate computer science in lessons in humanities classes like history, social studies, English, and visual arts. And her goal to reach more girls was quickly becoming closer to realization in the summer of 2016, when the team was accepted for training at the well-known startup accelerator Y Combinator and received the program's $120,000 investment. Allie, Melissa, and Leandra moved to Mountain View for four months to continue to build their customer base of school districts and get closer to their goal of teaching twenty million girls to code by 2018.

"We want to see girls telling their parents about [coding].

We want girls telling their friends about it. We want the experience that they have on Vidcode to incite those conversations," Allie said.

The Rocket Scientist Who Makes Sewable Circuits

The self-expression and creativity that Allie tapped into through filmmaking is also what engineer Nicole Messier believes can provide girls with a powerful gateway to tech. Instead of computers and coding, Nicole's tools are tactile: fabric, a needle, and thread. Twenty-eight-year-old Nicole co-founded Blink Blink, a company that sells crafting kits with an engineering twist.

If you have ever seen video of the magical dress designed by Zac Posen that debuted during the 2015 New York Fashion Week, you've seen the possibilities of what can happen when fashion and technology collide. It was adorned with patterns of tiny blinking pink, green, and blue LED lights, thanks to the circuitry built by the imaginative technologist Madison Maxey.[13] The dress is still featured on Google's Made w/ Code website, a destination built to inspire girls to learn about tech. And like the famous dress, Blink Blink incorporates electrical engineering in sewing projects, marketing scarves, tote bags, and other items that crafters can embellish by hand with colorful LED light-up patterns.

When we first connected with Nicole and her twenty-nine-year-old partner, Alex Tosti, they were gearing up for their first-ever Toy Fair to show off their futuristic crafting kits for kids aged eight to twelve. Nicole and Alex, who met as classmates at the Parsons School of Design, were heading to Toy Fair fresh from raising $30,000 on Kickstarter. Nicole, an aerospace engineer, had never even heard of sewable circuits, or e-textiles, until she went back to school to get her master of fine arts degree. Like many of the geek girls we met, Nicole had experienced the gender gap in tech as one of the few women in her college engineering classes. The daughter of an Air Force air traffic controller, she had always loved math and science as a kid growing up on a New Jersey military base. And it just so happened that all her AP math and science teachers in high school were women. She dreamed of becoming an astronaut one day and decided to major in aerospace engineering at George Washington University. But she then she realized how few women were in her program.

"It just felt like a boys' club. I don't think the guys or my male professors were trying to make it a boys' club, but it just felt like a boys' club," she said. "Then you did have moments when there were inappropriate things that happened, and then the person that you were supposed to report it to was also a man."

After two years she felt isolated and burned out. She was already filling out transfer applications when she learned that the national women's engineering sorority, Alpha Omega Epsilon, had a chapter on campus. It was a lifeline. Now she found study groups and started to meet some really good friends. And she found older sorority sisters were more than happy to listen and give advice when uncomfortable things happened. Inspired by the sisterhood, she, too, wanted to make it easier for the next generation. And she carried that passion into her first job as a technology consultant for Deloitte and later to grad school. When she started classes at Parsons School of Design in New York in 2014, she was searching for a way to get involved in the efforts to engage girls in STEM.

"All the women in our program gravitated towards making these amazing fashion and wearable tech projects, but there was tons of engineering that had gone into them," Nicole recalled as she told us about discovering "soft robotics," the one sector of high tech where women actually dominate. "Then my friends and I were just sitting around, and we were, like, 'Why didn't we have this when we were kids?' I've studied engineering and I've never seen these materials."

She started investigating the use of e-textiles in education and stumbled on research from the MIT Media Lab's High-Low Tech Group that was led by designer, engineer, and artist Leah Buechley from 2009 to 2014. Buechley experimented with simple household crafting materials like fabric and paper and combined them with traditional electronic components. She found that putting those things together by hand gave girls and boys a way to learn to build circuits that was much more engaging than traditional methods. Girls in particular really enjoyed the design aspect.[14]

"What we're finding is that the sort of new nexus of technology and crafts starts to open the doors to more equitable participation," explained Kylie Peppler, an Indiana University professor who wrote several papers with Buechley. Peppler has continued to build on the initial MIT research to see how it can be applied in schools and to boys as well. "I think one of the important points is that it's not just about inviting girls, it's really about creating better tools for learning," she emphasized.

This area of research continues to influence the growing maker movement in the United States that started to become popular at about the same time as coding. *Makers* is the popular term for the free-wheeling, eclectic cohort of DIY hobbyists who range from tinkerers to robotics enthusiasts to cooks to musicians to crafters focused on innovation and tech. Makers have started "makerspaces," also called fablabs, in schools and public libraries for pursuing their collaborations and ideas, and they have formed clubs, held local festivals, and written publications. This is an important development for engaging girls in engineering and computing. In 2015 Intel and the Girls Scouts of America released a report, "MakeHers," which declared that "girls who make, design, and create things with electronic tools develop stronger interest and skills in computer science and engineering."[15]

This is what Nicole saw happening as she led fifty workshops for more than a thousand girls around New York, New Jersey, and New Orleans while she worked on her thesis. She found that the do-it-yourself aspect of making wearable tech built the girls' confidence. They could experiment, make mistakes, try again. They could see the parts working together, which can seem abstract on a computer. Most important, they weren't intimidated by the components.

"The conductive thread just looks like thread. The copper tape looks like a sticker. They can quickly, in ten minutes, build a circuit and receive positive feedback," she excitedly explained. "Even though there's no coding, they still are learning about parallel circuits and circuit theory and logic, so they're building the same skills they need for coding. They're just doing it in a tactile manner but also embedding [it] in a project that they want to make."

Now, eighteen months after Nicole and Alex graduated and started the business, seven specialty retail shops are carrying the kits, and they are sold at fab.com. In a sweet twist of fate for Blink Blink's CEO, who once aspired to be an astronaut, the company has collaborated with the National Aeronautics and Space Administration on some educational programs for kids. With a thousand kits sold, Alex and Nicole feel they have a foothold in the market and planned to soon start pitching some of the feminist financiers known for supporting women-led startups.

"It's great to produce something and then see it go out into the world, and then to have a social mission behind it and hopefully make change at the same time," Nicole said.

Girls Make Games

While Blink Blink's founders prepared to present their business plan to investors, across the country in San Jose, California, an enterprising young woman was working hard to create a sisterhood among girls who play video games by teaching them how to make them. In the domestic $23.5 billion video game industry, only 12 percent of developers are women, according to the Entertainment Software Association.[16] Laila Shabir, the founder of Girls Make Games, wants to empower girls with the skills to play a much larger role in the market. The CEO of the educational gaming studio started with just twenty girls in the Bay Area in 2014 after trying to recruit female game developers to work on a project and not finding any.

The young girls she attracts to her Girls Make Games summer camps around the world love online role-playing games in which they take on the fantasy lives of characters and interact with other players. Just like the games Sara Chipps played as a girl and that ultimately led her to take her first CS class and later start Jewelbots. But girls' obsession with games, a pastime that is still overwhelmingly male, can make some feel at odds with their peers at school because they don't feel like they fit in.

"Confidence starts at a very early age, and that's why I really like the group that we tackle, which is between nine and fourteen. We actually see girls come in with shattered self-esteem, go through our program, and within three weeks start to see a difference," Laila said. "That, to me, is incredible, that you can actually add something to their life that they didn't have before. They now have a sense of belonging."

However, Laila herself has always been an outlier. Long before she started Girls Make Games, she was a rebellious girl in her small town of Al Ain in the United Arab Emirates. Her parents raised Laila and her sister to be independent thinkers, but their relatives and neighbors had strictly traditional views of the role of women and their education in UAE society. A defining moment occurred when she was twelve years old. During the regional badminton finals at her school, she decided to take off the headscarf she was required to wear. It was windy, and she couldn't see because the scarf kept blowing into her eyes. After she won the championship, her school invited all her classmates to an assembly. But instead of praising Laila, the principal shamed her in front of the entire school for daring to take off her scarf—an affront to Islam, he said.

"He opened with, 'I wish I could be proud of my student, but I can't. She chose to disown her own religion and culture,'" she said, shuddering as she recounted the story for us.

She confided she hadn't thought about that day for a long time because it was so traumatic. But in many ways she feels her experience of being labeled and shunned for just being her twelve-year-old self is what a lot of girls in the United States experience because of the deeply embedded stereotypes of how a girl should behave, in contrast to the expectations for boys. She could relate to the pressure on many levels.

"I see a lot of parallels in my upbringing and the way the girls are growing up here. I think a lot of obstacles we faced were physical. Here it is more subconscious, the biases and the way things are perceived. The social pressures are more subtle," she said.

Laila, a straight-A student, ultimately left the school that shamed her and completed her studies at home through her high school years. When she applied to universities in the UAE, she was rejected by all, even though she had earned high marks on her exams. Once again, she stood out because she had not attended local schools. But she was determined to go to college.

Against the wishes of their extended family, who thought she should be married off, her parents gave Laila their blessing to move to Cambridge, Massachusetts, where she enrolled at MIT, planning to major in economics, then pursue a PhD and career as an economist. But love intervened. She met her husband, a brilliant, nationally ranked mathematician who played the video game *Halo* semi-professionally. Laila had only played video games on an old Atari console as a young girl, but she quickly became obsessed and started thinking about creating a video game to teach SAT vocabulary. She and her husband started an educational gaming company and developed a game called *Penguemic*. Then Laila started going to gaming conventions like PAX in Boston to recruit some developers for the project. She said that experience was totally alienating, as if she'd shown up at the wrong party.

"I went to MIT. I was in finance. I was at a think tank. I was doing all these different things, and I never felt like I was in a boys' world until I entered video gaming. It is truly, truly a boys' world," Laila said. "That's really mind-boggling because women are great storytellers, and they love video games growing up. They make up over 50 percent of consumers at this point. Why is it so far lagging behind? It's the culture. The gaming culture is very, very—I don't know if there's a term for it, but it's such a bro culture,"

She ultimately hired seven men to build the game, and four of them moved into a hacker house with Laila and her husband to save money. When they moved the company, Learn District, to the Bay Area in 2014, she decided she wanted to start an educational program for girls and gaming.

And this is where the story of Laila and Girls Make Games takes a star turn.

Another young woman who had grown up an outsider—a self-proclaimed geek girl who loved video games even though most of the girls she knew weren't into playing *Resident Evil 3: Nemesis* and *Metal Gear Solid*—and had become an international celebrity. Thirty-year-old AJ Mendez Brooks, aka AJ Lee, found a fantasy world that felt safe for role-playing games. As a teen she turned to games to survive homelessness and poverty in New Jersey. She reveled in the chance to become someone else on screen as she lost herself in the storylines and characters. She could "be" whomever she wanted to be while playing the game and revel in the fantasy of being a super hero.

She eventually became one of the most popular female wrestlers in the world and the three-time diva champion of World Wrestling Entertainment. In the ring and on TV, AJ, who sports a tattoo and shiny black hair, played up her tomboyish persona and love for comic book heroes and video games, in stark contrast to her glamorous opponents, who donned sequins, heavy makeup, and cleavage-baring costumes. She loved challenging stereotypes of being female. While growing up, she never felt like she fit in. "I felt different, I felt weird, I liked video games, I liked comic books, I liked wrestling. No one else did, and I felt weird because of that," she said, explaining why she wants to be a role model for young girls. So when she heard about Girls Make Games, she had to get involved. She loved the idea of girls becoming empowered through making their own video games. She reached out to Laila on Twitter one day in 2015 and asked how she could participate. Needless to say, having a celebrity spokesperson, a real-life superhero with a huge following, was an incredible coup for the small company.

"She reached out to us saying that she loved video games herself and she's always been trying to, I guess, shake up what a nerd girl or what a cool girl looks like, and she's really into that kind of thing. She loved Girls Make Games for that," Laila, who also is thirty, told us. And when we connected with AJ, now retired from wrestling after ten years and taking her first coding classes, she told us she was more than ready to pay her success forward.

"I just want to be a champion for different values and different messages. I don't just want to be a superhero in short-shorts. You know?" said AJ, whose home office is decorated with hundreds of comic book action figures.

AJ now sponsors an annual scholarship for girls to attend the Girls Make Games camp, which is offered in twenty cities to twelve hundred girls from Denver to Durham. For three weeks the girls, aged nine to fourteen, study game design, meet women in gaming who mentor them, learn about two-dimensional art and animation, and build their own role-playing games in teams. Five winning teams from the local camps receive an all-expense paid trip to Silicon Valley to present their games at Demo Day. AJ is slated to help judge the winners in 2017. At stake is a cash prize and a chance to have their game published.

For both Laila and AJ, Girls Make Games fulfills their own desire to help girls feel confident in who they are and to feel empowered by having the skills for creating something they love.

"They now have a sense of belonging. They now have a sense of community," Laila said. "They have a sense of 'it's okay to be the way I am. I don't have to be like everyone at my school. I don't have to be like my sister. I don't have to be like what I see on TV. It's me, and there are other girls like me, because I saw them at camp.'"

The theme of sisterhood runs throughout the landscape of women in tech. There is something powerful about not feeling alone, about connecting to something bigger than yourself. This crucial network is inspiring women to forge new paths in what is still a male-dominated world. Social media and women's dominance of those channels is a key force in that endeavor.

"I think what's different about the girls who are coming up now [is that] you cannot avoid those feminist messages that come to you constantly through your social feeds. It is raising a new generation of feminists who will not be denied," Susan Lyne, president and founder of BBG Ventures, the AOL fund that backs women-led tech startups, told us prophetically in the months leading into Election Day.

And as we write in the aftermath of President Trump's inauguration, those impassioned voices have only grown stronger and more urgent, evidenced by the millions of women who mobilized online and took to the streets in a massive display of solidarity.

The Next Generation of Geek Girls

Seventeen-year-old Aruna Prasad is one of those young change makers who has been influenced by all the empowering discussions around women and technology. She's an admirer of both Sheryl Sandberg and Grace Hopper, two women who represent the intersection of business and innovation. Aruna, a senior at the Spence School in New York City, is a coder, a grassroots activist, and a budding entrepreneur in her own right. She's the earnest young woman behind Nerdina, a YouTube channel and an interschool club, and she is the creator of tech experiment kits aimed at girls. One of her primary goals is to connect girls who aspire to work in technology. On her website she defines Nerdinas as "female nerds that have the potential to be leading technocrats." She candidly writes that being a Nerdina can be lonely and blending in can be tough. That's why she started Nerdina when she was twelve. Now it's in four elite New York City private schools, including three all girls' schools, plus three New Jersey public schools, and most recently, Nerdina expanded to a school in Kingston, Jamaica.

"In middle school I got really interested in programming, and it became my goal to be somebody who was a leader and an innovator, and I wanted to, when I grew up, be an influential person in the field of technology," the dark-haired teen told us as we sat in her bedroom amid stuffed animals and photos of a friend's Sweet Sixteen and family trips to India.

She was craving a way to learn more and wanted to connect with other girls who care about technology. The soft-spoken girl who loves country music and black licorice wanted girls to be able to learn together about the latest innovations and also to discuss people and inventions they admire. As more girls began to join the club, she realized something practical was missing from their discussions.

"I realized that if I wanted to be a creator and innovator, I needed to first look at the technology around me and understand what other people had invented. And that was me exploring the fundamentals of technology: the inner workings of a computer, circuits, or networking concepts. So, yeah, I'm using the Internet every day, but how do I connect to the Internet?" Aruna said. This led her to create a series of video tutorials in which she answers such questions as "How are e-mails sent?" And that led to her idea for the Nerdina educational kits. These are boxes of wires, batteries, LEDs, and other components with directions for electrical engineering experiments. She showed us one activity that could teach girls how a watch keeps time. Aruna assembled the first fifty kits on her own and has already given some of them to teachers at several schools whom she met when she talked up Nerdina at a STEM conference at Columbia University in 2015. Her dream is to partner with Girls Who Code. She met its founder, Reshma Saujani, when Saujani spoke to a group of Nerdinas in the spring of 2016.

From the time Aruna was tiny, her parents said, she asked

lots of questions. One of their favorite stories is about the time the cable guy came to their apartment to hook up their Internet connection, and five-year-old Aruna kept insisting he was using the wrong cable. Turned out, she was right. Her father, Jay, works in technology and her mother, Prabha, in finance, and they always encouraged Aruna to pursue her interest in how things work. She especially loves math and music. It was her passion for music, playing and composing on her violin and piano that originally turned her on to coding. She said she wanted to get inside the world of digital music and understand how to build devices like her iPhone, which gave her so much joy when she listened to it.

"Technology is a puzzle, and there's more than just one piece. It's not just hardware or coding. There are so many pieces, and the more of those pieces you can understand—hardware, coding, software, networking—really the more prepared we will be when we enter the tech world. And that's kind of how I'm thinking of developing the pipeline itself," Aruna said, explaining her grand plan to unite young girls around tech.

Encouraging more girls to enter the pipeline is, of course, not a panacea. It's one facet of what needs to happen for the entire innovation economy to capitalize on women's ideas and capabilities. Girls also need to be encouraged to be entrepreneurs and investors. That is why AOL's innovative #BUILTBYGIRLS summer internship for high school juniors and seniors splits their time between opportunities to apply their coding skills to product development and a crash course in venture capital that gives them an inside look at how BBG Ventures invests in female tech founders.

Girls need more role models on all fronts, which was why we took on this project—to fill what Chelsea Clinton called the "visibility gap" (when she spoke at the Grace Hopper Conference in 2015) with the stories of enterprising, innovating women who are emerging as a new generation of leaders across the tech ecosystem—geek girls rising. It is true that much work remains to change the cultures of tech companies, which have a tendency to regard young single men as the most valuable workers rather than more mature, diverse employees with outside interests and responsibilities. In the summer of 2016 the slow pace of change at the tech giants was still frustrating—the numbers of women and people of color had barely nudged up despite all the fervent discussion during the previous two years.[17] There still aren't many female decision makers in venture capital, and the numbers of women-led companies that are getting funded remains small. And yet, as we consider all the geek girls we met during our five years of research, women who are banding together to take on this unwieldy, complicated problem in schools, on college campuses, in boardrooms, in investment groups, and in their own companies, we have hope.

"I think we have made an enormous amount of progress. Women are starting companies left and right," Debbie Sterling said. "We are now starting to see more women pursuing STEM degrees and more people talking about women serving on boards. There is definitely a movement taking place, but I will say there is still a lot of work to do. There is a lot of talk. We need more action."

At the very heart of it are the values that kept Debbie going when she was first cranking out ideas in her apartment. In trying to come up with a toy and a pop culture icon, she helped fuel a new conversation about girls, women, and our potential as change makers. As Hillary Clinton declared in early 2017, she still believes "the future is female,"[18] and as four thousand women had already signed up to run for office in the next election cycle, the momentum to "persist" in breaking the glass ceiling is palpable.[19] And geek girls, the sisterhood of women in tech, won't stop pushing ahead and raising the bar until they are equally

ACKNOWLEDGMENTS

Many people have supported and guided us throughout this project. First, we would like to thank our wonderful editor at St. Martin's Press, Emily Carleton, for believing in this book and bringing it to life with the aid of her conscientious editorial assistant, Annabella Hochschild. This book would not have been possible without the dedication and unwavering support of our literary agent, Lisa Leshne of the Leshne Agency. Thank you, Lisa, for your guidance, friendship, and willing ear as we navigated the book-writing process. Kudos and thanks to the talented Nadine Gilden of Curious Light for designing geekgirlrising.com and advising on all things digital.

Fact checker Kevin McDonnell played an integral part in polishing the manuscript and making sure all our reporting was accurate and up to date. Researcher Katie Toth helped get us to the finish line with her tireless work on the first and last chapters, chasing down facts and figures about computer science education and doing some follow-up interviews for us. Julianne Wotasik helped us stay on top of release forms and organizing our sources. We would also like to thank researcher Anna Gress, who helped us organize the hundreds of interview transcripts and assisted with research for chapter 1. We especially would like to acknowledge Adam Quinton, Rachel Sheinbein, Shaherose Charania, Susan Lyne, Lisa Sun, Sukhinder Singh Cassidy, Erin Newkirk, Jenny Lefcourt, Natalia Oberti Noguera, Karen Catlin, and Neeraj Khemlani for informally advising on the project and making key introductions to sources.

We could not have completed this work without the enduring support of our families. Special thanks to Neeraj Khemlani, Heather's husband and best friend, for poring over drafts of the chapters at various stages and helping us shape some of the best narratives with his masterful talent for storytelling. Thank you to Vicki and Howard Cabot, Heather's parents, for reading early versions of the book and offering feedback and a healthy dose of cheering from the sidelines. Completing Team Geek Girl Rising were Alessandra DeCicco and Ruth Patino, who helped keep the Cabot Khemlani household going when Heather was on the road or holed up in the writing cave. To Ian and Sam, Heather's twins, thank you for your infectious smiles and unwavering encouragement. Your love for tech sparked this project. Keep asking questions!

We also want to express our gratitude to the Walravens clan—Matthew, Zach, Coco, and Gigi—for always making Sam smile and for being so understanding on those weekend mornings when she was writing this book instead of playing games. Keep coding, creating, and following your dreams! Sam gives special thanks to Jim and Grace Parent, and Philippe and Nicole Walravens for the countless times they cared for their grandchildren during our hectic schedules. Finally, to Sam's caring, loving, and supportive husband, Patrick: her deepest gratitude. She duly noted and much appreciated his encouragement when times got rough. Thank you for believing in her and the book even when she was experiencing self-doubt and for reminding her that, as they say at Facebook, "Done is better than perfect."

And to all the women and men who are working, in the words of Rachel Sklar, to "change the ratio" and increase visibility and opportunity for women and underrepresented minorities in technology: thank you for taking action to make the world a more inclusive place.

For more resources and more information supporting geek girls on the rise, please check out geekgirlrising.com.

SOURCES

Debbie Sterling, Founder and CEO, GoldieBlox

Jocelyn Goldfein, Angel investor

Michael Freedman, Stanford University School of Engineering

Sarah Kunst, Founder and CEO, ProDay

Tracy Chou, Co-Founder, Project Include

Shelley Zalis, Founder, The Girls' Lounge, and CEO, The Female Quotient (TFQ) Ventures

Talia Bender, Director of Connections, The Girls' Lounge/TFQ

Rachel Sklar, Co-Founder, TheLi.st

Cindy Gallop, Founder and CEO, MakeLoveNotPorn

Jeanne Pinder, Founder and CEO, ClearHealthCosts.com

Casey Fiesler, Author, "Barbie, Remixed!" CU Boulder

Natalie Villalobos, Head of Global Programs, Women Techmakers

Kathy Pham, Product Lead, Founding Team Member, United States Digital Service

Vanessa Hurst, Co-Founder, Girl Develop It

Shaherose Charania, Co-Founder, Women 2.0

Angie Chang, Co-Founder, Women 2.0, Co-Founder, Hackbright

Trae Vassallo, Co-Author, Elephant in the Valley survey and venture capitalist

Keval Desai, Partner, InterWest Partners

Sukhinder Singh Cassidy, Founder, Boardlist and Co-Founder, Joyus

Fran Hauser, Venture capitalist

Deborah Jackson, Co-Founder, Plum Alley Investments

Michelle Phan, Founder, ipsy

Bing Chen, Co-Founder and Chief Creative Officer, Victorious

Flannery Underwood, Production Manager, Ipsy

Jkissa, YouTube beauty blogger

Cassey Ho, Founder, Blogilates

Dr. Candida Brush, Babson College

Shadi Mehraein, Co-Founder, Rivet Ventures

Kay Koplovitz, Co-Founder and Managing Partner, Springboard Growth Capital

Amy Rosen Wildstein, Co-Founder and Managing Partner, Springboard Fund

Rachel Sheinbein, Angel investor and Co-Founder, Makeda Capital

Charles Bonello, Co-Founder and Managing Director, Grand Central Tech

Matthew Harrigan, Co-Founder, Grand Central Tech

Kathryn Minshew, Co-Founder and CEO, The Muse

Adam Quinton, Angel investor and Founder, Lucas Point Ventures

Yunha Kim, Co-Founder, Locket and Simple Habit

Dr. Thomas R. Eisenmann, Harvard Business School

Bea Arthur, Founder and CEO, In Your Corner

Sheila Marcelo, Founder and CEO, Care.com

Nancy Bushkin, VP Communications, Care.com

Maren Kate Donovan, Founder and CEO, Zirtual

Maci Peterson, Founder, On Second Thought

Andrea Barrica, Venture Partner/ Entrepreneur-in-Residence, 500 Startups

Sarah Leary, Co-Founder and VP Marketing and Operations, NextDoor, Inc.

Clara Shih, Founder and CEO, Hearsay Social

Mariam Naficy, Founder and CEO, Minted.com

Danielle Applestone, Founder and CEO, The Other Machine

Jacqueline Ros, Founder and CEO, Revolar

Michelle Zatlyn, Co-Founder and CEO, Cloudflare

Abigail Edgecliffe-Johnson, Founder, RaceYa

Amy Willard Cross, Founder, BuyUp Index

Madison Maxey, Founder, Loomia

Stacey Ferreira, Founder and CEO, Forrge

Joanne Wilson, Angel Investor and Founder, The Gotham Gal

Susan Wilson, Founder, DriveThru Branding

Caren Maio, Co-Founder, and CEO, Nestio

Erin Newkirk, CMO, BrightHealth

Annie Dean, Founder and CEO, Werk

Tatiana Birgisson, Founder and CEO, MATI

Jessica Lawrence Quinn, CEO, New York Tech Alliance

Jeanne Brooks, Lead Producer of Emojicon

Jessica Banks, Founder and CEO RockPaperRobot

Jenny Lefcourt, General Partner, Freestyle Capital

Rebecca Kaden, General Partner, Maveron

Kara Nortman, General Partner, Upfront Ventures

Jenny Fielding, Managing Partner, Techstars

Theresia Gouw, Co-founder Aspect, Ventures

Jennifer Fonstad, Co-founder, Aspect Ventures and Co-founder Broadway Angels

J. Kelly Hoey, Angel Investor and Author

Alicia Syrett, Founder and CEO Pantegrion Capital

Dr. Alicia Robb, Senior Fellow, Ewing Marion Kauffman Foundation

Kristina Montague, Managing Partner, The JumpFund

Shelley Prevost, Managing Partner, The JumpFund and Founder and CEO, Torch

Cathy Boettner, Limited Partner, The JumpFund

JoAnn Yates, Limited Partner, The JumpFund

Mary Kilbride, Limited Partner, The JumpFund

Molly Hussey, Limited Partner, The JumpFund

Andrea Crouch, Limited Partner, The JumpFund

M. J. Levine, Limited Partner, The JumpFund

Ashlee Patten, Limited Partner, The JumpFund

Lucy Beard, Co-Founder and CEO, Feetz

Jewel Burks, Co-Founder and CEO, Partpic

Casey Casterline, Co-Founder, E-Divv

Shanna Tellerman, Founder and CEO, Modsy

Meaghan Rose, Founder and CEO, RocksBox

Joanna McFarland, Co-Founder, HopSkipDrive

David Belitz, Managing Partner, Chattanooga Renaissance Fund

Loretta McCarthy, Managing Director, Golden Seeds

Natalia Oberti Noguera, Founder and CEO, Pipeline Angels

Stephanie Lampkin, Founder and CEO, Blendoor

Marianne Hudson, Executive Director, Angel Capital Association

Arlan Hamilton, Founder, Backstage Capital

Susan Lyne, Founder and President, BBG Ventures

Nisha Dua, Managing Partner, BBG Ventures, and Founder, #BUILTBYGIRLS

Alexandra Friedman, Co-Founder and CEO, Lola

Geri Stengel, Founder, Ventureneer

Dr. Jeffrey Sohl, Center for Venture Research, Peter T. Paul College of Business and Economics, University of New Hampshire

Alison Wagonfeld, Vice President of Marketing, Google, and CMO, Google Cloud

Swati Mylavarapu, Partner, Kleiner Perkins Caufield & Byers

Dona Sarkar, Principal Product Person, Microsoft HoloLens

Melody McCloskey, Co-Founder and CEO, StyleSeat

Dr. Maria Klawe, President Harvey Mudd College

Irene Ryabya, Co-Founder, Monarq

Diana Murakhovskaya, Co-Founder, Monarq

Miriam Bekkouche, Founder, The Brain Spa

Christine Pha, Software Developer

Christine Moy, SheHacks Winner

Tracy Huynh, SheHacks Mentor

Rebecca Miller-Webster, Founder and CEO, Write/Speak/Code

Rachel Ober, Co-Founder and Chief

Technology Officer, Write/Speak/Code

Sofie Fader, Software Developer, Co-Founder, Harlem App Collective

William Falcon, Co-Founder, Harlem App Collective

Poornima Vijayshankar, Founder, Femgineer

Karen Catlin, Partner, Femgineer

Geeta Vinnakota, Senior Software Engineer, Kaplan Test Prep

Ari Horie, Founder and CEO, Women Startup Lab

Kerri Couillard, Founder and CMO, Babierge

Fran Maier, CEO, Babierge

Jill Richmond, CMO, Kraver

Aparna Pujar, Founder and CEO, NetFavrs

Sharon Vosmek, CEO, Astia

Allyson Kapin, Founder, Women Who Tech and Women's Startup Challenge

Craig Newmark, Founder, Craigslist

Sue Heilbronner, Co-Founder, MergeLane

Janis Collins, Co-Founder, The Refinery

Barbara Clarke, Founder and CEO, The Impact Seat

Abbey Kumar, Founder and CEO, Learnique

Kathryn Finney, Founder, digitalundivided and the BIG Acclerator

Jennifer Hyman, Co-Founder and CEO, Rent the Runway

Manal Kahi, Founder and CEO, EatOffbeat

Suelin Chen, Founder and CEO, Cake

Molly McGhee, Attendee, Project Entrepreneur

Marie Matousek, Founder, Dishing Out

Fon Powell, Founder, Sodium Analyte Level Test (S.A.L.T.) LLC

Julia Hartz, Co-Founder and CEO, Eventbrite

Melody Mai, Director of Program Management, Eventbrite

Terra Carmichael, Vice President,

Global Communications,
  Eventbrite
Sarah Greer, Founder, CodeGreer
Adda Birnir, Founder and CEO,
  Skillcrush
Tina Lee, Founder, MotherCoders
Sarah Doczy, Software Developer
Milena Berry, Co-Founder and CEO,
  PowerToFly
Katharine Zaleski, Co-Founder and
  President, PowerToFly
Erin Foust, Software Developer
Brittany Hadfield, Web Designer
Ally Downey, Co-Founder and CEO,
  weeSpring
Kristen Koh Goldstein, Founder and
  CEO, HireAthena
Sara Holoubek, Founder and CEO,
  Luminary Labs
Romy Newman, Co-Founder,
  FairyGodBoss
Georgene Huang, Co-Founder,
  FairyGodBoss
Dayna Sessa, Founder and CEO,
  Datonomy
Diana Rothschild, Founder, NextKids
Jean Miller Truelson, Co-Founder,
  Dogpatch Technology
Palmer Truelson, Co-Founder,
  Dogpatch Technology
Katie Bethell, Founder and Executive
  Director, PL+US
Kieran Snyder, Co-Founder and CEO,
  Textio
Melissa Sandgren, PL+US Board
  Member
Elizabeth Warren, Better Life Lab,
  New America
Dr. Sue Black, Founder, TechMums
  (UK)
Kelsey Hrubes, Iowa State University
  '17
Gloria Kimbwala, Diversity
  and Women in Tech Advocate,
  Square
Vanessa Slavich, Program Manager,
  Inclusion and Innovation, Kapor
  Center for Social Impact; former
  Head of Diversity, Square
Diversity and Inclusion Team, Square
Kathryn Hodge, Vassar College '17

Camille Ramseur, Florida Institute of
  Technology, '15
Hashma Shadid, Mt. Holyoke
  College '16
Kaya Thomas, Dartmouth University,
  '17
Brianna Fugate, Spelman College '18
Telle Whitney, CEO, Anita Borg
  Institute for Women and
  Technology
Mopewa Ogundipe, Carnegie Mellon
  University, '16
Kunle Ogudipe, Mopewa's mother
Niki Maheshwari, Carnegie Mellon
  University '16
Alexandra Johnson, Carnegie Mellon
  University '15
Teresa Ibarra, Harvey Mudd College
  '18
Tina Ibarra, Teresa's mother
Samantha Echevarria, Harvey Mudd
  College '18
Dr. Colleen Lewis, Harvey Mudd
  College
Dr. Beth Trushkowsky, Harvey
  Mudd College
Dr. Julia Hirschberg, Columbia
  University
Noura Farra, Columbia University
Samara Trilling, Columbia University
  '15
Jennifer Kane and Bernie Trilling,
  Samara's parents
Hyongee Joo, Columbia University,
  '16
Rachel Lowe, Barnard University
  '16
Chaiwen Chou, Columbia University
  '16
Iris Zhang, Columbia University MS
  '16
Mei-Vern Then, Columbia University,
  '16
Danielle Tomsen, Columbia
  University doctoral student
Dr. Judith Spitz, Cornell Tech
  Executive-in-Residence
Ann Kirschner, former Dean, CUNY
  Macaulay Honors College, CUNY
  Special Advisor to the Chancellor,
  Strategic Partnerships

Moné Skratt Henry, Macaulay
Honors College '20
Dr. Lenore Blum, Carnegie Mellon
University
Dr. Carol Frieze, Carnegie Mellon
University
Caroline Kenney, Carnegie Mellon
University Tech Nights participant
Ada Zhang, Carnegie Mellon
University doctoral student
Amy Quispe, Coalition for Queens
Kirn Hans, Carnegie Mellon
University '17
Anastassia Kornilova, Carnegie
Mellon University '16
Kimberly Lister, Carnegie Mellon
University, '16
Grace Gee, Harvard University '15
Dr. Catherine Hill, Vice President of
Research, American Association
of University Women
Ruthe Farmer, former Chief Strategy
and Growth Officer, NCWIT and
White House Senior Advisor for
Tech Inclusion, Office of Science
and Technology Policy
Brian Kernighan, Princeton Univer-
sity
Madelyne Xiao, VP Communications,
she++, Stanford University '18
Lucy Wang, Stanford University '16
Reynis Vasquez-Guzman, Stanford
University '17
Ayna Agarwal, Co-Founder, she++
Alexandra Steinberg, Syracuse
University '16
Katie Siegel, MIT '16
Samantha Swartz, Worcester
Polytechnic Institute '16
Tali Marcus, Wellesley College '16
Dr. Ayanna Howard, Geogia Tech
University
Dr. Belle Wei, San Jose State
University
Mitchell Modell, CEO, Modell's
Sara Chipps, Co-Founder and CEO,
Jewelbots
Brooke Moreland, Co-Founder and
COO, Jewelbots
Tomika Rodriguez, Director, Girls
Scouts of Greater New York

Alexandra Diracles, Co-Founder and
CEO, Vidcode
Melissa Halfon, Co-Founder,
Vidcode
Leandra Tejedor, Co-Founder,
Vidcode
Minerva Tantoco, Chief Technology
Officer and Senior Advisor, City
of New York
Nicole Messier, Co-Founder, Blink
Blink
Dr. Kylie Peppler, Indiana University
Dr. Diane Levitt, Cornell Tech
Laila Shabir, Founder and CEO, Girls
Make Games
Zoe Penston, Winner of Girls Make
Games Competition '16
AJ Mendez Brooks, former WWE
Wrestler
Aruna Prasad, Founder, Nerdina
Prahba Ram and Jai Prasad, Aruna's
parents
Jocelyn Leavitt, Co-Founder and
CEO, Hopscotch
Robin Hauser Reyolds, Director,
CODE
Amy McCooe, Co-Founder and CEO,
Level Up Village
John Keefe, Co-Founder, Girls Who
Mine
Jodi Jefferson, Co-Founder, Girls
Who Mine
Kaia Keefe, Girls Who Mine
participant
Jessie Arora, Embark Labs
Everett Harper, Co-Founder,
Truss
Dr. Vivek Wadhwa, Carnegie Mellon
University
Rebecca Lammers, Co-Founder and
CEO, Laika Network
Elizabeth Linder, Founder and CEO,
The Conversational Century;
former Government Specialist,
Facebook
Joelle Emerson, CEO, Paradigm
Ursula Meade, Founder and CEO,
InHerSight
Alison Derbenwick Miller, Vice
President, Oracle Academy at
Oracle

Elena Silenok, Founder, Clothia, and CEO, Sputnik Mobile

Leanne Pittsford, Founder and CEO, Lesbians Who Tech

Crystal Silva, Art Director, Big Fish Games

Coraline Ada Ehmke, Software Developer

Pamela Vickers, Software Developer

Doreen Bloch, Founder and CEO, Poshly

Asmau Ahmed, Founder and CEO, ColorModules

Ellie Cachette, Mobile Designer, Cachette Group

Jenn Shaw, Founder, NYTechWomen and Bella Minds

Rebecca Harris, Co-Founder, Purple

NOTES

Chapter 1: Join the Revolution

1. Nielsen, "Super Bowl Draws 111.5 Million Viewers," February 3, 2014, http://www.nielsen.com/us/en/insights/news/2014/super-bowl-xlviii-draws-111-5-million-viewers-25-3-million-tweets.html, accessed March 2016.
2. Heather Somerville, "GoldieBlox Super Bowl Commercial Uses Parody of Rock Song . . . Again," *Silicon Beat*, February 3, 2014, http://www.siliconbeat.com/2014/02/03/goldieblox-super-bowl-commercial-uses-parody-of-rock-song-again/, accessed March 2016.
3. Courtney Martin and John Cary, "Shouldn't the Breast Pump Be as Elegant as an iPhone and as Quiet as a Prius by Now?," *The New York Times*, March 16, 2014, http://parenting.blogs.nytimes.com/2014/03/16/shouldnt-the-breast-pump-be-as-elegant-as-an-iphone-and-as-quiet-as-a-prius-by-now/?_r=0, accessed June 2016.
4. Jodi Kantor, "A Brand New World in Which Men Ruled," *The New York Times*, December 23, 2014, http://www.nytimes.com/interactive/2014/12/23/us/gender-gaps-stanford-94.html, accessed June 2016.
5. "Degrees in Computer and Information Sciences Conferred by Degree-Granting Institutions, by Level of Degree and Sex of Student: 1970–71 through 2010–11," table 349, *Digest of Education Statistics*, National Center for Education Statistics, http://nces.ed.gov/programs/digest/d12/tables/dt12_349.asp, accessed September 2016.
6. Steve Henn, "When Women Stopped Coding," *Morning Edition*, NPR, October 21, 2014, http://www.npr.org/sections/money/2014/10/21/357629765/when-women-stopped-coding, accessed June 2015.
7. Alex Konrad, "What Diane Greene's Legacy at VMware Tells Us About Her Plans for Google Cloud," *Forbes*, http://www.forbes.com/sites/alexkonrad/2015/11/30/what-diane-greene-lessons-at-vmware-tells-us-about-google-cloud/#59923f4f4ae6, accessed June 2016.
8. Jessi Hempel, "A Women's History of Silicon Valley," *Backchannel*, June 30, 2016, https://backchannel.com/a-womens-history-of-silicon-valley-feea9279d88a#.sg1avqz79, accessed June 2016. Newsweek Special Edition, March 20, 2016, "The Founding Fathers of Silicon Valley"
9. Walter Isaacson, *The Innovators: How a Group of Hackers, Geniuses and*

Geeks Created the Digital Revolution (New York: Simon and Schuster, 2014), 415.

10. Andrew Kohut, Carol Bowman, and Margaret Petrella, summary of "Technology in the American Household: Americans Going Online: Explosive Growth, Uncertain Destinations," *Pew Research Center*, October 16, 1995, http://www.people-press.org/1995/10/16/americans-going-online -explosive-growth-uncertain-destinations/#introduction-and-summary, accessed March 2016.

11. Monica Anderson, "Technology Device Ownership 2015," *Pew Research Center*, October 29, 2015, http://www.pewinternet.org/2015/10/29/technology -device-ownership-2015/, accessed March 2016.

12. Cliff Kuang, "The 6 Pillars of Steve Jobs's Design Philosophy," *Fast Company*, November 7, 2011, http://www.fastcodesign.com/1665375/the-6 -pillars-of-steve-jobss-design-philosophy, accessed July 2016.

13. Deborah Fallows, "How Men and Women Use the Internet," *Pew Center for Internet and American Life*, December 28, 2005, http://www.pewinternet.org /2005/12/28/how-women-and-men-use-the-internet/, accessed March 2016; Monica Anderson, "Men Catch Up with Women on Overall Social Media Use," *Pew Research Center*, August 28, 2015, http://www.pewresearch.org /fact-tank/2015/08/28/men-catch-up-with-women-on-overall-social -media-use/, accessed March 2016.

14. Christianne Corbett and Catherine Hill, *Solving the Equation: The Variables for Women's Success in Engineering and Computing* (Washington, DC: American Association of University Women, March 2015), 8.

15. Catherine Ashcraft, Brad McLain, and Elizabeth Eger, *Women in Tech: The Facts* (Boulder, CO: National Center for Women and Information Technology, 2016), https://www.ncwit.org/sites/default/files/resources/ncwit _women-in-it_2016-full-report_final-web06012016.pdf, accessed September 2016; S. A. Hewlett et al., *The Athena Factor: Reversing the Brain Drain in Science, Engineering, and Technology* (New York: Center for Work-life Policy, 2008), http://www.talentinnovation.org/publication.cfm?publication =1100.

16. Jennifer L. Glass, Sharon Sassler, Yael Levitte, and Katherine M. Michelmore, "What's So Special About STEM? A Comparison of Women's Retention in STEM and Professional Occupations," *Social Forces* 92, no. 2 (December 2013), p. 743, 754 http://sf.oxfordjournals.org/content/early /2013/08/21/sf.sot092.abstract, accessed September 2016; Jennifer Hunt, "Why Do Women Leave Science and Engineering?" NBER Working Paper No. 15853, National Bureau of Economic Research, Cambridge, MA, March 2010, http://www.nber.org/papers/w15853, accessed September 2016.

17. Julia Beckhusen, "Occupations in Information Technology," *American Community Survey Reports*, ACS-35, U.S. Census Bureau, Washington, DC, August 2016, p. 9, https://www.census.gov/content/dam/Census/library /publications/2016/acs/acs-35.pdf, accessed August 2016.

18. Kara Swisher, "The Men and (No) Women Facebook of Facebook Management," *All Things D*, August 16, 2007, http://allthingsd.com/20070816 /the-men-and-no-women-facebook-of-facebook-management/, accessed July 2016.

19. Tracy Chou, "Where Are the Numbers?," *Medium*, October 11, 2013,

https://medium.com/@triketora/where-are-the-numbers-cb997a57252#
.x4eehpd8n, accessed March 2015.

20. Jeremy C. Owens, "Apple, Google, HP and Other Tech Giants Again Re-
fuse to Release Workplace Diversity Data," *San Jose Mercury News*,
March 18, 2013, http://www.mercurynews.com/2013/03/18/apple-google
-hp-and-other-tech-giants-again-refuse-to-release-workplace-diversity
-data/. The FOIA generally applies only to government agencies, but *CNN
Money* notes that "every U.S. company with more than 100 employees is
required to fork over an annual report to the government, called the
EEO-1, that categorizes U.S. workers by their race and sex." See Julianne
Pepitone, "Black, Female, and a Silicon Valley 'Trade Secret,'" *CNN Money*,
March 18, 2003, http://money.cnn.com/2013/03/17/technology/diversity
-silicon-valley/, accessed October 13, 2016.

21. Nancy Lee, "Focusing on Diversity," *Google Official Blog*, June 30, 2016,
https://googleblog.blogspot.com/2016/06/focusing-on-diversity30.html,
accessed June 30, 2016.

22. Michal Lev-Ram, "The powerful woman behind Intel's new $300 million
diversity initiative," *Fortune*, January 12, 2015, http://fortune.com/2015/01
/12/intel-diversity/. The article includes a clip from January 2015 describing the new program.

23. Hope King, "Tech Diversity Round Up," *CNN Money*, June 19, 2015, http://
money.cnn.com/2015/06/19/technology/tech-diversity-roundup/, accessed
June 2016.

24. Nathan Heller, "How Pinterest Engineer Tracy Chou Is Breaking the Silicon Ceiling," *Vogue*, November 21, 2014, http://www.vogue.com/4537369
/pinterest-tracy-chou-silicon-valley/.

25. According to Zalis, in a telephone interview by Heather Cabot, November 8, 2016.

26. Ann Friedman, "Shine Theory, How to Stop Female Competition," The
Cut, *New York*, May 13, 2013, http://nymag.com/thecut/2013/05/shine
-theory-how-to-stop-female-competition.html.

27. Office of the Press Secretary, White House, transcript of remarks by President Barack Obama at the White House Science Fair, May 2014, https://
www.whitehouse.gov/the-press-office/2014/05/27/remarks-president
-white-house-science-fair, accessed June 2016.

28. Josh Harkinson, "Welcome Back to Silicon Valley's Biggest Sausage Fest,"
Mother Jones, September 9, 2014, http://www.motherjones.com/politics/2014
/09/women-gender-gap-tech-crunch-disrupt-tcdisrupt and the policy:
https://techcrunch.com/events/disrupt-ny-2014/anti-harassment-policy/.

29. Mark Tran, "Apple Facebook to Offer Egg Freezing for Employees,"
Guardian, October 15, 2014, https://www.theguardian.com/technology
/2014/oct/15/apple-facebook-offer-freeze-eggs-female-employees.

30. "Barbie, Remixed: I (Really!) Can Be a Computer Engineer," *Casey Fiesler*
(blog), https://caseyfiesler.com/2014/11/18/barbie-remixed-i-really-can
-be-a-computer-engineer/; Robert McMillan, "Feminist Hacker Barbie is
Just What Little Girls Need," *Wired*, November 21, 2014, https://www
.wired.com/2014/11/feminist-hacker-barbie-just-little-girls-need/; Feminist Hacker Barbie, created by Kathleen Tuite: https://computer-engineer
-barbie.herokuapp.com/.

31. Candida G. Brush, Patricia G. Greene, Lakshmi Balachandra, and Amy E.

Davis, "Diana Report: Women Entrepreneurs 2014: Bridging the Gender Gap in Venture Capital," Arthur Blank Center for Entrepreneurship, Babson College, Wellesley, MA, September 2014, http://www.babson.edu/Academics /centers/blank-center/global-research/diana/Documents/diana-project -executive-summary-2014.pdf, accessed March 2015; Dr. Candida Brush, email interview by coauthor Heather Cabot, June 2016.

32. Megan Guess, "At Trial of Top VC Firm, Allegations Fly of Gender Bias, Messy Breakups," *ArsTechnica*, February 25, 2015, http://arstechnica.com /tech-policy/2015/02/in-trial-against-top-vc-firm-allegations-fly-of -gender-bias-messy-breakups/; Deborah Gage, "Former Kleiner Partner Trae Vassallo Testifies of Unwanted Advances," *Wall Street Journal*, February 25, 2014, http://blogs.wsj.com/digits/2015/02/25/former-kleiner -partner-testifies-of-unwanted-advances/.

33. Trae Vassallo et al., "Elephant in the Valley," survey by Women in Tech, 2016, http://www.elephantinthevalley.com/, accessed January 2016.

34. Nina Burleigh, "What Silicon Valley Really Thinks of Women," *Newsweek*, January 28, 2015, http://www.newsweek.com/2015/02/06/what-silicon -valley-thinks-women-302821.html.

35. Sukhinder Singh Cassidy, "Tech Women Choose Possibility," *Recode*, May 15, 2013, http://www.recode.net/2015/5/13/11562596/tech-women -choose-possibility, accessed May 15, 2013. An exit is when private investors reap a return on their investment in an early stage company following its merger, acquisition or IPO.

36. Michael Goodwin, "How New York City's Women Entrepreneurs Raised $3 Billion in Ten Years," *The Huffington Post*, January 24, 2014, http://www .huffingtonpost.com/michaelgoodwin/how-new-york-citys-women-_b _6213334.html, accessed September 2016.

Chapter 2: Kickstart Your Dream

1. ipsy valuation, September 14, 2015, CrunchBase, https://www.crunchbase .com/funding-round/f02fe780eb990c14c0422346f2de224b.

2. Michelle Phan, "Follow Me to Work at ipsy," YouTube video posted November 13, 2012, 5:07, https://www.youtube.com/watch?v=AuFOL JxutAM.

3. Megan Angelo, "Why I Believe Michelle Phan Is the Next Oprah," *Glamour.com*, March 31, 2015, http://www.glamour.com/story/michelle-phan -online-network.

4. Michelle Phan, *Makeup: Your Life Guide to Beauty, Style, and Success— Online and Off* (New York: Harmony, 2014), 10.

5. Michelle Phan, "Barbie Transformation Tutorial," YouTube video posted October 7, 2009, 8:39, https://www.youtube.com/watch?v=J4-GRH2nDvw.

6. Bill Carter, "Friends' Finale Audience is the Fourth Biggest Ever," May 8, 2004, http://www.nytimes.com/2004/05/08/arts/friends-finale-s -audience-is-the-fourth-biggest-ever.html?_r=0, accessed November 6, 2016.

7. Julie Naughton, "L'Oréal, Michelle Phan Part Ways: Em Michelle Phan Heads to ipsy.com," *WWD*, October 9, 2015, http://wwd.com/beauty -industry-news/beauty/loreal-usa-michelle-phan-part-ways-em-michelle -phan-heads-to-ipsy-com-10259153/.

8. Alicia Robb, Susan Coleman, Dane Stangler, "Sources of Economic Hope: Women's Entrepreneurship," Ewing Marion Kaufmann Foundation,

November 2014, p.11, http://www.kauffman.org/~/media/kauffman_org/research%20reports%20and%20covers/2014/11/sources_of_economic_hope_womens_entrepreneurship.pdf.

9. Candida G. Brush, Patricia G. Greene, Lakshmi Balachandra, and Amy E. Davis, "Diana Report: Women Entrepreneurs 2014: Bridging the Gender Gap in Venture Capital," Arthur Blank Center for Entrepreneurship, Babson College, Wellesley, MA, September 2014, http://www.babson.edu/Academics/centers/blank-center/global-research/diana/Documents/diana-project-executive-summary-2014.pdf, accessed March 2015.

10. Candida Brush, email interview by co-author Heather Cabot, June 21, 2016.

11. Peter Dizikes, "Women, Less-Attractive Men Lag in the Effort to Find Financial Backing for Startups," MIT News Office, March 17, 2014. The study is Alison Wood Brooks, Laura Huang, Sarah Wood Kearney, and Fiona Murray, "Investors Prefer Entrepreneurial Ventures Pitched by Attractive Men," *Proceedings of the National Academy of Sciences* 11, no. 12 (March 25, 2014): 4427–4431.

12. National Venture Capital Association, *Building a More Inclusive Entrepreneurial Ecosystem*, July 2016, http://nvca.org/ecosystem/diversity/. Venrock's Richard Kerby found 11 percent of VC's are women, 67 percent men. NCVA clarifies this is partner level and does not include junior associates.

13. Sukhinder Singh Cassidy, "Tech Women Choose Possibility," *Recode*, May 13, 2015, http://www.recode.net/2015/5/13/11562596/tech-women-choose-possibility, accessed May 13, 2015.

14. Sam Altman, "The New Deal," *Y Combinator* (blog), http://blog.ycombinator.com/the-new-deal.

15. Issie Lapowsky, "What Tech's Ugly Gender Problem Really Looks Like," *Wired*, July 28, 2014, http://www.wired.com/2014/07/gender-gap/, accessed July 28, 2014.

16. Cromwell Schubarth, "VC Theresia Gouw: Backing Diversity Is More Than Funding Female Founders," *Silicon Valley Business Journal*, March 18, 2015, http://www.bizjournals.com/sanjose/blog/techflash/2015/05/vc-theresia-gouw-backing-diversity-is-more-than.html, accessed January 2016.

17. Gené Teare and Ned Desmond, "Female Founders on an Upward Trend, According to CrunchBase," *TechCrunch.com*, May 26, 2015 https://techcrunch.com/2015/05/26/female-founders-on-an-upward-trend-according-to-crunchbase/, accessed May 26, 2015.

18. National Women's Business Council, *10 Million Strong: The Tipping Point for Women's Entrepreneurship*, 2015 annual report (Washington, DC: NWBC, n.d.), 7. https://www.nwbc.gov/sites/default/files/NWBC_2015Annual-Reportedited.pdf, accessed December 2015.

19. Yunha Kim, "What I Learned in My First Year as a Female Startup CEO," *Medium*, April 10, 2014, https://medium.com/women-in-tech/what-i-learned-in-my-first-year-as-a-female-startup-ceo-19ce929c9679#.rhcmcn34p, accessed April 2016.

20. Ingrid Lunden, "Mobile Shopping App Wish Buys Android Lockscreen App Maker Locket," *TechCrunch*, July 14, 2015, https://techcrunch.com/2015/07/14/mobile-shopping-app-wish-buys-android-lockscreen-app-maker-locket, accessed June 20, 2016.

21. James Surowiecki, "Epic Fails of the Startup World," *The New Yorker*, May 19, 2014, http://www.newyorker.com/magazine/2014/05/19/epic -fails-of-the-startup-world, accessed July 2016; Kristin Pryor, "Here Are the Startup Failure Rates by Industry," *Tech.co*, January 12, 2016, http:// tech.co/startup-failure-rates-industry-2016-01; David S. Rose, "The Startup Failure Rate Among Angel-Funded Companies," *Gust* (blog), August 17, 2015, http://blog.gust.com/the-startup-failure-rate-among-angel -funded-companies/; Erin Griffith, "Why Startups Fail, According to Their Founders," *Fortune*, September 25, 2014, http://fortune.com/2014/09 /25/why-startups-fail-according-to-their-founders/.

22. Deborah Gage, "The Venture Capital Secret: 3 Out of 4 Startups Fail," *The Wall Street Journal*, September 20, 2012, http://www.wsj.com/articles/SB100 00872396390443720204578004980476429190, accessed June 2016. Shikhar Ghosh's research indicates that as many as 75 percent of venture-backed companies never return cash to investors, with 30 to 40 percent of those liquidating assets, resulting in a total loss for their investors. His findings are based on research that encompassed more than two thousand venture-backed companies that raised at least $1 million from 2004 to 2010.

23. "Wait for It," lyrics and music by Lin-Manuel Miranda, 2015, http:// genius.com/Lin-manuel-miranda-wait-for-it-lyrics.

24. Susan Young, "Sheila Lirio Marcelo, JD 1998, MBA 1999," *Harvard Business School*, https://www.alumni.hbs.edu/stories/Pages/story-bulletin.aspx ?num=3985, accessed June 2016.

25. Michael B. Farrell, "Care.com's IPO Raises about $91M," *Boston Globe*, January 24, 2014, https://www.bostonglobe.com/business/2014/01/24/care -com-raises-million-ipo/N5navjOBBhUWRM1y0p0IBL/story.html.

26. Ezequiel Minaya, "Care.Com Receives $46.4 Million Investment From Google Capital," *Wall Street Journal*, June 26, 2016, http://www.wsj.com /articles/care-com-receives-46-4-million-investment-from-google-capital -1467235513; "Google Capital Invests in Care.com—Transaction Marks First Investment in Public Company by Google Capital," company press release, Care.com, June 29, 2016, http://investors.care.com/investors /Press-Releases/Press-Release-Details/2016/Google-Capital-Invests-in -Carecom—Transaction-Marks-First-Investment-in-Public-Company-by -Google-Capital-/default.aspx.

27. "Caring Across Generations, Care.com and New America Launch the "Who Cares" Coalition to Redefine the Social and Economic Value of Care and Caregiving," company press release, Care.com, June 14, 2016, http:// investors.care.com/investors/Press-Releases/Press-Release-Details/2016 /Caring-Across-Generations-Carecom-and-New-America-Launch-the -Who-Cares-Coalition-to-Redefine-the-Social-and-Economic-Value-of -Care-and-Caregiving/default.aspx.

Chapter 3: Fuel the Fire

1. "The Top Twenty Venture Capitalists Worldwide," *The New York Times*, March 13, 2016, http://www.nytimes.com/interactive/2016/03/13 technology /venture-capital-investor-top-20.html, accessed March 13, 2016 *The Top 100 Venture Capitalists*, CB Insights, March 13, 2016, https://www.cbinsights .com/blog/top-venture-capital-partners/.

2. National Venture Capital Association, *2016 National Venture Capital Association Yearbook* (New York: Thomson-Reuters, 2016), http://nvca.org

/pressreleases/2016-nvca-yearbook-captures-busy-year-for-venture
-capital-activity/, accessed May 2016.

3. Kathryn Finney and Marlo Rencher, *The Real Unicorns of Tech: Black Women Founders: The #ProjectDiane Report* February 2016, p. 7, http://www.projectdiane.com/projectdiane-report/y6msc43xwnucb0o3dc9ny ykezgi3xu.

4. Candida G. Brush, Patricia G. Greene, Lakshmi Balachandra, and Amy E. Davis, "Diana Report: Women Entrepreneurs 2014: Bridging the Gender Gap in Venture Capital," Arthur Blank Center for Entrepreneurship, Babson College, Wellesley, MA, September 2014, http://www.babson.edu /Academics/centers/blank-center/global-research/diana/Documents /diana-project-executive-summary-2014.pdf, accessed March 2015.

5. Gené Teare and Ned Desmond, "The First Comprehensive Study on Women in Venture Capital," *TechCrunch.com*, April 19, 2016, https://techcrunch.com /2016/04/19/the-first-comprehensive-study-on-women-in-venture-capital/, accessed April 19, 2016.

6. Dr. Candida Brush, e-mail interview by Heather Cabot, June 21, 2016.

7. Kay Koplovitz, interview by Heather Cabot, November 7, 2016.

8. Trae Vassallo et al., "Elephant in the Valley," survey by Women in Tech, 2016, http://www.elephantinthevalley.com/, accessed January 2016.

9. "Thin Air Innovation Festival to Debut in Park City, Utah—April 6–8, 2016," Marketwired, January 28, 2016, http://finance.yahoo.com/news /thin-air-innovation-festival-debut-184930452.html.

10. Ben Severman, "Northwestern Mutual Buys Online Planner LearnVest," *Bloomberg*, March 25, 2015, http://www.bloomberg.com/news/articles /2015-03-25/northwestern-mutual-buys-online-planner-learnvest.

11. Dean W. Arnold, *Old Money, New South: The Spirit of Chattanooga* (Chattanooga, TN: Chattanooga Historical Foundation, 2006), 7, 15.

12. Center for Venture Research, University of New Hampshire, https://paulcollege.unh.edu/research/center-venture-research/cvr-analysis -reports; Jeffrey Sohl, telephone interview by Heather Cabot, May 27, 2016.

13. Commodity and Security Exchanges, General Rules and Regulations, Securities Act of 1933, 17 C.F.R. § 230.501 (1933), http://www.ecfr.gov/cgi-bin /retrieveECFR?gp=&SID=8edfd12967d69c024485029d968ee737&r =SECTION&n=17y3.0.1.1.12.0.46.176.

14. Arlan Hamilton, "Dear White Venture Capitalists: if you are reading this, it's (Almost!) too late," *Medium*, June 13, 2015, https://medium.com/female -founders/dear-white-venture-capitalists-if-you-re-not-actively-searching -for-and-seeding-qualified-4f382f6fd4a7#.xby22sjc1, accessed May 2016.

15. Jason del Ray, "Hudson's Bay Confirms $250 Million Acquisition of Gilt Groupe," *Recode*, January 7, 2016, http://www.recode.net/2016/1/7/11588582 /hudsons-bay-confirms-250-million-acquisition-of-gilt-groupe.

16. Christine Magee, "Female Founders Fare Much Better," *TechCrunch.com*, January 30, 2015, https://techcrunch.com/2015/01/30/female-founders -fare-much-better-in-2014/, accessed January 30, 2015.

17. API definition: http://www.webopedia.com/TERM/A/API.html.

18. Alex Friedman, "Susan Lyne on Mentorship, Getting Funded and the Future of Female Entrepreneurs," *The Broadcast*, April 28, 2016, https://www.mylola.com/blog/susan-lyne-mentorship/, accessed May 2016; Alex Friedman and Jordana Kier, e-mail interview by Heather Cabot, June 20, 2016.

Chapter 4: Dream It, Do It, Own It

1. Dona Sarkar, "Arrive as Strangers; Leave as Friends," blog, May 31, 2016, http://donasarkarbooks.com/; Sean Ong, "My Experience at the #Holohacks Seattle HoloLens Hackathon," *Sean's Blog*, May 24, 2016, http://www.mrseanong.com/video-blog/my-experience-at-the-holohacks-seattle-hololens-hackathon?utm_content=bufferd1c73&utm_medium=social&utm_source=twitter.com&utm_campaign=buffer.

2. Vanessa Ho, "Meet the Windows Veteran Taking the Torch for the Windows Insider Program," Microsoft Story Labs, n.d., http://news.microsoft.com/stories/people/dona-sarkar.html.

3. Katty Kay and Claire Shipman, *The Confidence Code* (New York: HarperCollins, 2014), 88.

4. Vikas Bajaj, "Q & A with Carol Dweck," *The New York Times*, December 12, 2013, http://www.nytimes.com/2013/12/12/opinion/q-a-with-carol-s-dweck.html?_r=0; Christianne Corbett and Catherine Hill, *Solving the Equation: The Variables for Women's Success in Engineering and Computing* (Washington, DC: American Association of University Women, March 2015), 89.

5. Christianne Corbett and Catherine Hill, *Solving the Equation: The Variables for Women's Success in Engineering and Computing* (Washington, D.C.: AAUW, March 2015), 89.

6. Susan Price, "StyleSeat Raises $25 Million in Series B," *Fortune*, July 13, 2015, http://fortune.com/2015/07/13/styleseat-series-b/; "StyleSeat Acquires BeautyBooked To Expand Beauty and Wellness Platform," *PR Newswire*, January 19, 2016, http://www.prnewswire.com/news-releases/styleseat-acquires-beautybooked-to-expand-beauty-and-wellness-platform-300206017.html.

7. L. V. Anderson, "The Imposter Syndrome Is Real and It Does Affect Women More Than Men," *Slate*, April 12, 2016, http://www.slate.com/articles/business/the_ladder/2016/04/is_impostor_syndrome_real_and_does_it_affect_women_more_than_men.html.

8. Dana R. Carney, Amy J. C. Cuddy, and Andy J. Yap, "Power Posing: Brief Nonverbal Displays Affect Neuroendocrine Levels and Risk Tolerance," *Psychological Science* XX, no. X (2010): 1–6, DOI: 10.1177/0956797610383437, http://www.people.hbs.edu/acuddy/in%20press,%20carney,%20cuddy,%20&%20yap,%20psych%20science.pdf.

9. Optimal Solutions Group, "Resource Inventory for Growth-Aspiring Women Entrepreneurs: Findings and Future Directions," report for National Business Women's Council, Washington, DC, March 2016, p. 3, https://www.nwbc.gov/sites/default/files/NWBC%20Final%20Report%20032516.pdf, accessed June 2016.

10. Women Who Tech press release for 2016 competition from Allyson Kapin.

11. Kathryn Finney and Marlo Rencher, *The Real Unicorns of Tech: Black Women Founders: The #ProjectDiane Report*, February 2016, http://www.projectdiane.com/projectdiane-report/y6msc43xwnucb0o3dc9nyykezgi3xu, accessed February 2016.

12. "Irrational Exuberance," Investopedia.com, n.d., http://www.investopedia.com/terms/i/irrationalexuberance.asp?layout=infini&v=5E&orig=1&adtest=5E.

13. Kay Koplovitz, telephone interviews by Heather Cabot, June 3, 2016, and November 7, 2016.

14. "How Big Is Big? Navigating Revenue and Investment Return Expectations in the World of Venture Capital," Project Entrepreneur, New York, New York, April 9, 2016.

15. Valentina Zarya, "'Real Housewife' Bethenny Frankel Is Under Fire for Her Comments," *Fortune*, April 15, 2016, http://fortune.com/2016/04/15/bethenny-frankel-black-women/.

Chapter 5: Build New Ways to Work

1. Caroline Simard et al., *Climbing the Technical Ladder: Obstacles and Solutions for Mid-Level Women in Technology* (Stanford, CA: Michelle R. Clayman Institute for Gender Research and Anita Borg Institute for Women and Technology, Stanford University, n.d.), http://gender.stanford.edu/sites/default/files/Climbing_the_Technical_Ladder.pdf.

2. Katherine Losse, *The Boy Kings: A Journey into the Heart of the Social Network* (New York: Free Press, 2012), 74; Catherine Ashcraft, Brad McLain, and Elizabeth Eger, *Women in Tech: The Facts* (Boulder, CO: National Center for Women and Information Technology, 2016), https://www.ncwit.org/sites/default/files/resources/ncwit_women-in-it_2016-full-report_final-web06012016.pdf, accessed September 2016; S. A. Hewlett et al., *The Athena Factor: Reversing the Brain Drain in Science, Engineering, and Technology* (New York: Center for Work-life Policy, 2008), http://www.talentinnovation.org/publication.cfm?publication=1100.

3. Dustin Moskovitz, "Work Hard, Live Well," *Medium*, August 19, 2015, https://medium.com/building-asana/work-hard-live-well-ead679cb506d#.f851ilev3; Jodi Kantor and David Streitfeld, "Inside Amazon: Wrestling Big Ideas in a Bruising Workplace," *The New York Times*, August 15, 2015, http://www.nytimes.com/2015/08/16/technology/inside-amazon-wrestling-big-ideas-in-a-bruising-workplace.html?_r=0, accessed August 15, 2015.

4. Moskovitz, "Work Hard, Live Well."

5. *Labor After Labor*: Why Barriers for Working Mothers Are Barriers for the Economy," Ewing Marion Kaufmann Foundation, May 3, 2016, http://www.kauffman.org/~/media/kauffman_org/research%20reports%20and%20covers/2016/labor_after_labor_may3b.pdf.

6. Imogen Crispe, "Episode 6: September News Roundup," *Course Report*, October 3, 2016, https://www.coursereport.com/blog/episode-6-september-bootcamp-news-roundup, accessed November 9, 2016.

7. Code.org predicts the United States will have 1.4 million unfilled computing-related jobs by 2020, based on a Microsoft report, "A National Talent Strategy," n.d., https://news.microsoft.com/download/presskits/citizenship/MSNTS.pdf.

8. Gad Levanon et al., *Help Wanted: What Looming Labor Shortages Mean for Your Business*, report TCB-1601 (New York: Conference Board, April 2016), https://www.conference-board.org/publications/publicationdetail.cfm?publicationid=7191. See also "Summary of Source Data for Code.org Infographics and Stats," n.d., https://docs.google.com/document/d/1gySkItxiJn_vwb8HIIKNXqen184mRtzDX12cux0ZgZk/pub.

Chapter 6: Crush the Stereotypes

1. "This Day in History: August 7," Computer History Museum, http://www.computerhistory.org/tdih/August/7/; "Timeline of Computer History: Harvard Mark 1 Is Completed," Computer History Museum, http://www

.computerhistory.org/timeline/1944/; Allison McCann, "The Queen of Code,"*FiveThirtyEight*, January 28, 2015, http://fivethirtyeight.com/features /the-queen-of-code/.

2. Megan Smith remarks at CES 2016 as confirmed to coauthor Cabot in email interview with Kristin D. Lee, Communications Director and Senior Policy Advisor-The White House, Office of Science and Technology Policy, October 25, 2016.

3. Stuart Zweben and Betsy Bizot, "2015 Taulbee Survey: Continued Booming Undergraduate CS Enrollment; Doctoral Degree Production Dips Slightly," *Computer Research News* 28, no. 5 (May 2016): 21, http://cra.org /wp-content/uploads/2016/05/2015-Taulbee-Survey.pdf; National Center for Education Statistics, "Degrees in Computer and Information Sciences Conferred by Degree-Granting Institutions, by Level of Degree and Sex of Student: 1970–71 through 2010–11," table 349, *Digest of Education Statistics*, http://nces.ed.gov/programs/digest/d12/tables/dt12_349.asp, accessed September 2016.

4. Oliver Staley, "Harvey Mudd College Took on Gender Bias, and Now More Than Half Its Computer Science Majors Are Women," *Quartz*, August 22, 2016, http://qz.com/730290/harvey-mudd-college-took-on-gender -bias-and-now-more-than-half-its-computer-science-majors-are-women/.

5. Christianne Corbett and Catherine Hill, *Solving the Equation: The Variables for Women's Success in Engineering and Computing* (Washington, DC: American Association of University Women, March 2015), 78.

6. Office of Institutional Research and Assessment, City University of New York, "A Profile of Undergraduates at CUNY Senior and Community Colleges: Fall 2015," May 4, 2016, http://www.cuny.edu/about /administration/offices/ira/ir/data-book/current/student/ug_student _profile_f15.pdf.

7. Byron Spice, "Women Are Almost Half of Carnegie Mellon's Incoming Computer Science Undergraduates," press release, Carnegie Mellon University, September 11, 2016, https://www.csd.cs.cmu.edu/news/women -are-almost-half-carnegie-mellons-incoming-computer-science -undergraduates.

8. Carol Frieze and Jeria Quesenberry, *Kicking Butt in Computer Science: Women in Computing at Carnegie Mellon University* (Indianapolis, IND: Dog Ear, 2015), 28–29, http://women-in-computing.com/book.php.

9. The Margolis and Fisher study is detailed in Frieze and Quesenberry, *Kicking Butt in Computer Science: Women in Computing at Carnegie Mellon University*. See also Jane Margolis and Allan Fisher, *Unlocking the Clubhouse: Women in Computing* (Cambridge, MA: MIT Press, 2002).

10. Frieze and Quesenberry, *Kicking Butt in Computer Science:Women in Computing at Carnegie Mellon University*, 32.

11. Census data 2014—Calhoun demographics, Calhoun County Profile, compiled by The County Information Program, Texas Association of Counties, http://www.txcip.org/tac/census/profile.php?FIPS=48057, accessed November 9, 2016; Brian Hill, "Calhoun County Leading Teen Pregnancy," WJHG .com, October 7, 2014, http://www.wjhg.com/home/headlines/Calhoun -County-Leading-Teen-Pregnancy-278454561.html.

12. Ruthe Farmer, telephone interview by Heather Cabot, November 9, 2015.

13. Michael Freedman, Chief Communications Officer and Director Alumni Relations Stanford School of Engineering, says that in 2012 the number of

female CS grads was twenty-seven. By 2015, there were forty-three. Email interview with Heather Cabot, November 9, 2016.

Chapter 7: Ignite the Next Generation

1. Debbie Sterling, interview by Heather Cabot; company stats from Goldie-Blox materials handed out at the Toy Fair to retailers and confirmed by Sterling in follow-up interview, November 10, 2016.

2. Jon Blistein, "Beastie Boys Settle Lawsuit Over 'Girls' Toy Commercial," *RollingStone*, March 18, 2014, http://www.rollingstone.com/music/news /beastie-boys-settle-lawsuit-over-girls-toy-commercial-20140318; Jason Newman, "GoldieBlox Apologizes to Beasties: 'We Have Learned a Valuable Lesson,'" *RollingStone*, March 19, 2014, http://www.rollingstone.com /music/news/goldieblox-apologizes-to-beasties-we-have-learned-a -valuable-lesson-20140319; Catherine Clifford, "GoldieBlox CEO: How I Went From Kickstarter to the Macy's Day Parade in Two Years," *Entrepreneur*, December 3, 2014, https://www.entrepreneur.com/video/240370.

3. Kelly Faircloth, "GoldieBlox Means Well but Doesn't Live Up to the Hype," *Jezebel*, February 11, 2014, http://jezebel.com/goldiebloxs-marketing -campaign-is-better-than-the-prod-1516721344; Amanda Clayman, "I Hate to Be Feminist Grinch Here," *I Have Thoughts and Opinions* (blog), November 25, 2013, http://mandaclay.tumblr.com/post/68076398530/i-hate-to-be -the-feminist-grinch-here.

4. Kamla Modi, Judy Schoenberg, and Kimberlee Salmond, *Generation STEM: What Girls Say about Science, Technology, Engineering, and Math* (New York: Girl Scout Research Institute, 2012), http://www.girlscouts .org/content/dam/girlscouts-gsusa/forms-and-documents/about-girl -scouts/research/generation_stem_full_report.pdf.

5. Emma Brown, "Girls Outscore Boys on Inaugural National Test of Technology, Engineering Skills," *The Washington Post*, May 17, 2016, https:// www.washingtonpost.com/news/education/wp/2016/05/17/girls-outscore -boys-on-inaugural-national-test-of-technology-engineering-skills/.

6. NPD Group, "Annual Sales Data: U.S. Domestic Markets," Toy Industry Association, May 2016, http://www.toyassociation.org/TIA/Industry _Facts/salesdata/IndustryFacts/Sales_Data/Sales_Data.aspx?hkey =6381a73a-ce46-4caf-8bc1-72b99567df1e#.V5Ide5MrLow.

7. Rick Morgan and John Klaric, "An Analysis of Five-Year Academic Careers," The College Board, 2007, p. 9, http://research.collegeboard.org /sites/default/files/publications/2012/7/researchreport-2007-4-ap -students-college-analysis-five-year-academic-careers.pdf.

8. Davy Alba, "Obama Pledges $4 Billion to Computer Science in US Schools," *Wired*, January 30, 2016, http://www.wired.com/2016/01/obama -pledges-4-billion-to-computer-science-in-us-schools/.

9. "Board Approves Plans to Expand Computer Science Curriculum to All Grades," San Francisco Unified School District press release, June 10, 2015, http://www.sfusd.edu/en/news/current-news/2015-news-archive /06/board-approves-plans-to-expand-computer-science-curriculum-to -all-grades.html; Kate Taylor and Claire Cain Miller, "De Blasio to Announce 10-Year Deadline to Offer Computer Science to All Students," *The New York Times*, September 15, 2015, http://www.nytimes.com/2015/09/16 /nyregion/de-blasio-to-announce-10-year-deadline-to-offer-computer -science-to-all-students.html.

10. "New CPS Computer Science Graduation Requirement to Prepare Students for Jobs of the Future," Chicago Public Schools press release, February 24, 2016, http://cps.edu/News/Press_releases/Pages/PR2_02_24_2016.aspx; Amanda Lenhart, "Teens, Social Media and Technology Overview 2015," *Pew Research Center*, April 9, 2015, http://www.pewinternet.org/2015/04 /09/teens-social-media-technology-2015/.

11. "President Obama Announces Computer Science for All Initiative," White House press release, January 30, 2016, https://www.whitehouse.gov /sites/whitehouse.gov/files/images/FACT%20SHEET%2BPresident%20 Obama%20Announces%20Computer%20Science%20For%20All%20Initiative_0.pdf.

12. GovTrack.us, an independent organization, reported on September 21, 2016, that PredictGov, a marriage of law and tech that tracks pending federal legislation, had given the House bill only a 1 percent chance of passage. See https://www.govtrack.us/congress/bills/114/hr6095. On the National Science Foundation's commitment, see Endeavor Insight, *The Power of Entrepreneur Networks: How New York City Became the Role Model for Other Urban Tech Hubs* (New York: Endeavor Insight, 2014), 2, http://www .nyctechmap.com/nycTechReport.pdf.

13. Angela Natividad, "Zac Posen Debuts an LED Dress Made by (and for) Female Coders,"*Adweek*, September 10, 2015, http://www.adweek.com /adfreak/zac-posen-debuts-led-dress-made-and-female-coders-166801.

14. "Leah Buechley," Exploratorium, 2015, http://tinkering.exploratorium .edu/leah-buechley.

15. Jon Irwin, "Coding for Girls—Tools to Get Girls More Easily into Tech," *IQ*, January 26, 2015, https://iq.intel.com/inside-programming-tool-designed -get-girls-coding/.

16. Entertainment Software Association, "Essential Facts About the Computer and Video Game Industry," 2016, http://essentialfacts.theesa.com /Essential-Facts-2016.pdf.

17. Maxine Williams, "Facebook Diversity Update: Positive Hiring Trends Show Progress," *Facebook newsroom*, July 14, 2016, http://newsroom.fb.com /news/2016/07/facebook-diversity-update-positive-hiring-trends-show -progress/.

18. Daniel Kreps, "Hillary Clinton in New Video Statement: 'The Future Is Female,'" *Rolling Stone*, February 6, 2017, http://www.rollingstone.com /politics/news/hillary-clinton-in-video-statement-the-future-is-female -w465381.

19. Heidi M. Przybyla, "EMILY's List Begins 'Most Aggressive' Female Recruitment Effort," *USA Today*, February 6, 2017, http://www.usatoday.com/story /news/politics/2017/02/06/emilys-list-begins-most-aggressive-female -recruitment-effort/97463724/.

20. Claire Cain Miller, "Ad Takes Off Online: Less Doll, More Awl," Bits Blog, *New York Times*, November 20, 2013, http://bits.blogs.nytimes.com /2013/11/20/a-viral-video-encourages-girls-to-become-engineers/?_r=0, accessed July 2016.

INDEX